Jay Naidoo

Tracking down
Historical Myths

Eight South African Cases

AD. DONKER/PUBLISHER

AD. DONKER (PTY) LTD
A subsidiary of Donker Holding (Pty) Ltd
111 Central Street
Houghton
Johannesburg
2198

First published 1989

ISBN 0 86852 159 0

Typeset by M.M. Fourie, Johannesburg
Printed and bound by Creda Press (Pty) Ltd, Cape Town

paper books

Titles available in this series:

Lionel Abrahams
The Celibacy of Felix Greenspan

David Adey
Under the Southern Cross

Phyllis Altman
The Law of the Vultures

Jane Austen
Northanger Abbey

Ken Barris
Small Change

Michael Chapman and Tony Voss
Accents

Michael Chapman
and Achmat Dangor
Voices from Within

Michael Chapman
**The Paperbook of
South African English Poetry**

John Cleland
Fanny Hill

Joseph Conrad
**Heart of Darkness
and Typhoon**

John Conyngham
The Arrowing of the Cane

Stephen Gray
Market Plays

Janet Hodgson
Princess Emma

Steve Jacobs
Diary of an Exile

Steve Jacobs
Under the Lion

Dan Jacobson
The Price of Diamonds

Henry James
Washington Square

Henno Martin
The Sheltering Desert

Sarah Gertrude Millin
God's Stepchildren

Bloke Modisane
Blame me on History

Sisa Ndaba
One Day in June

Digby Ricci
Reef of Time

Sheila Roberts
Jacks in Corners

Olive Schreiner
The Story of an African Farm

Olive Schreiner
The Woman's Rose

Martin Trump
Armed Vision

Russell Vandenbroucke
Truths the hand can touch

Peter Wilhelm
Some Place in Africa

Peter Wilhelm
The Healing Process

CONTENTS

Acknowledgements 7

Introduction 9

1 Was the 'Van Riebeeck Principle' a Plea for Peace or a Plea for plunder? 18

2 Was the 50th Ordinance a Charter of Khoi Liberties? 35

3 Was Dr John Philip an Advocate of 'Segregation'? 49

4 Was Hintsa killed or executed? 65

5 Was the Retief Dingane Treaty a Fake? 82

6 Was Retief really an Innocent Victim? 106

7 Was the Makapan Cave Siege a Massacre and a Trekker Victory? 120

8 Was Gandhi's South African Struggle inspired by Race, Class or Nation? 133

Abbreviations 151

Notes 152

Bibliography 187

Index 200

For

Steve, Dulcie and Winnie

ACKNOWLEDGEMENTS

This book is based on a D Phil thesis for Cambridge University. I would like to thank Frank Finland, Jack Staine and Christopher Madeley, who read and commented on parts of the original manuscript, and Dr Veegee Naidoo, who spent a great deal of time collating and checking all my quotations, references and sources. My thesis benefitted in particular from the insights of Taffence Redford (who supervised) and Sheila Smith and Steven Sykes (who examined). Dennis York, a constant source of encouragement since the final stages of the theses, eliminated many of the more immoderate turns of phrase. I, of course, am responsible for the remaining immoderate ones.

A variety of scholarships and grants helped fund the research for my thesis. Thanks are due to the Beck, Gate, Burn, Prentiss and Locke Trusts. The book assumed its present form in the course of a post-doctoral Fellowship at the University of the Witwatersrand, where Dirk van Koop was constantly helpful.

This is the acknowledgement or something like it that (forgive me) I would have liked to have written, for this study was carried out far from the main and secondary sources of documentation, with far from adequate funds and with little of the expert help that a work like this would normally have required. The help therefore received during its preparation was doubly appreciated. Miss Joan Finlay, a wonderfully generous school teacher (now retired), by making her London home and her hospitality available for two weeks, allowed me to acquire most of the secondary material that was available in England. The French and the South African postal systems; and the very co-operative official, university and public libraries of South Africa; ensured *access* to the material available from South Africa.

Christopher Saunders displayed a constant interest in my study, and helped by supplying me with photocopies of secondary material that I discovered I had to consult at the last-minute. David Henige, the editor of *History in Africa* - the only academic to have had a direct hand in this study - generously, tactfully and wisely read and commented on chapters one, four, five and seven.

My late mother made the funding of this study possible with the bequeathal of her prized gold necklace. My wife, Pierrette Nadeau, helped throughout as proof reader and fan.

Niort, France
November 1988.

8

INTRODUCTION

We want a history book on the Zulu nation... Present books on the subject are from the pens of Europeans who, biased on the side of their own people in these things, too often present the Native at a disadvantage. Why should we be told so often of these 'cattle-stealing savages wantonly attacking unoffending white farmers'? Surely you Zulus have some explanation of your own for all this, and there must be another side to the question.

D.D.T. Jabavu[1]

Peter Geyl urged historians 'to track down legends and to show up myth'; while Leonard Thompson reminded them to 'consider the extent to which a myth is an accurate account of an actual historical event or process'[2]. A myth, as far as this study is concerned, is a version of history set out by the victorious to grace their motives, to laud their actions and to exempt their crimes; in brief, it is the rulers' version of the past put together to justify and exonerate their oppression of the ruled. History, in almost every part of the world, portrays the defeated as having been wicked and the triumphant as having been righteous. This particular type of history is rife in the story of European settlement in the Americas, in Australia and New Zealand, and, of course, in Southern Africa. We all know (mainly because of John Wayne and John Ford) of the good settler and the bad Indian in American history. In South Africa this good settler and bad native story of the past — what Thompson calls, 'an old-fashioned, pigmentocratic history syllabus' [3] and what perhaps should be called whitewash history — still constitutes the staple diet of school history lessons. And, in spite of the works of the liberal historians (E.A. Walker, J.S. Marais, W. de Kiewiet and W.M. Macmillan), the old influence persists. This is notable in the story of Hintsa's death, Retief's destruction at the hands of Dingane and the siege of Makapaan's Cave. Other events and issues, less dramatic perhaps, also haunt the collective historical conscience like an incubus. A myth, less obviously, is also, for the purpose of this study, a historian's interpretation of the past in order to sustain a pet and particular analysis of the present. Past is past and present is present, but the twain do meet and can never be separated. The past lives on in the present through genes and culture, through ideas and traditions; and the present, because the past has to be filtered through a temporal present, lives on in the past. That is why we have a changing past and that is why a new generation escape the law of temporality. Thompson shows how the interpretative fortunes of the minor episode of 'Slagtersnek' changed over the years[4]. *All history is contemporary history*, but what a historian should never forget is that what is now in the past was once in the future. This study is an antidote to settler history, and also to careless and over enthusiastic present-minded history.

2

While each of the eight chapters is a challenge to the common wisdom of official South African history, they are nevertheless a product of circumstance and accident or, more to the point, of personal history. To study the historian before his history is good counsel. It is therefore appropriate to explain the initial inspiration for these various essays.

A pamphlet and attendance at a Pretoria parade marking the three hundredth anniversary of Van Riebeeck's landing at the Cape constituted the basic ingredients of the first part of this study. The pamphlet accused Van Riebeeck of being a petty thief — he was, its author stressed, caught red-handed stealing his employers' goods and shipped back home in consequence [5].

Years later, a patient reading of every entry of the Van Riebeeck journal led me to the conclusion that Van Riebeeck was not particularly fond of the Khoi and that his designs against them were questionable. A few years later I was surprised to find that David Livingstone, after reading a particular entry in the journal, arrived (more than a century earlier) at the same conclusion. Within the covers of the same volume in which Livingstone's article appeared, a South African historian took issue with Livingstone and condemned his reaction as being careless and biased. To someone who had not carefully read every entry in the journal and seen how Van Riebeeck's ideas and attitudes to the Khoi had formed and developed on a day-to-day basis, the historian's argument appeared plausible. The thought occurred then that where opinion was so diametrically opposed it would be interesting to see how historians — past, recent and contemporary — had themselves reacted to this controversy. And thus was born the first chapter of this study.

It is possible that some readers might object and claim that the subject is not a running issue; that (because the historians are lined up into those who supported and those who opposed the Livingstone view)

Shula Marks is wrongly classed; and that the chapter peddles a great man version of history. Such objections, however, would be specious; for the first fails to note that Van Riebeeck's statue still stands in Cape Town, that his relation to rands and cents is even more exclusive than is Washington's to dollars and cents, that the Afrikaner nationalists linked him directly to the Great trek[6] and that he is, for better or worse, white South Africa's premier hero — or as one of their number put it, 'the Founder of European civilization in South Africa'[7].

Shula Marks has written a fine article on Khoisan-Dutch relations during the seventeenth and eighteenth centuries, a more extensive period than that covered in the relevant essay here; so her focus — on the particular area selected for investigation — was understandably less sharp and less pointed. This might explain why an incorrect date makes her an *unwitting apologist* for Van Riebeeck[8].

Does the chapter sanction the great man theory of history? Hardly; for it investigates not a man but his policies — his *principle*. But even if it did it would not matter, for there are many rooms in the mansion of history. The recent biographical study of Sol Plaatje is good history[9], and even those in France who continue the *Annales* tradition of history nowadays write biographies[10]. Finally, it is easy to forget that historical writing is also prone to fashion and to conformity — that convention is also, in a certain sense, an element of myth.

The pro-settler historians, G.M. Theal and G.E. Cory, and the pro-Afrikaner historian, G.S. Preller, condemned the Fiftieth Ordinance as a bad law because it made the Khoi the equal of the white man. W.M. Macmillan in the 1920s reversed the trend of their perspective by arguing that the Fiftieth Ordinance was a positive and successful measure. However, a special study of Macmillan revealed that what he was saying about the law; that is, about the changes it wrought, was in itself a distortion. Theal and the others were wrong as well. But identifying this distortion and expressing it was another matter. A book by Nosipho Majeke (actually Dora Taylor)[11] titled *The role of missionaries in conquest*[12], and L.C. Duly's articles 'A revisit with the Cape's Hottentot Ordinance of 1828'[13], revealed that here, too, there was a misleading conflict of conservative and liberal interpretations. Susan Newton-King also added a new dimension in her study[14] where she argues that the Fiftieth Ordinance was passed to increase the labour needs of the colonists. This might indeed have been the case, but what the law was designed to do, and what it actually accomplished, are two different things. But it seems that Susan Newton-King herself

11

has doubts about her thesis; she fails to refer to Duly's seminal article and admits that 'legislation designed to restrict or facilitate the mobility of servants had only a partial relevance to actual practice'[15].

The question seemed to be not one of whether the law had been good or bad but rather, whether taking into account its very short existence, it had been effective or not. Legislation, if not sustained by consistent law enforcement and education, does not in itself alter social malpractices. In 1963, when the United States was celebrating the centenary of the abolition of slavery, James Baldwin, the late American writer, remarked that the black Americans were 'celebrating one hundred years of freedom one hundred years too soon'[16]. The wisdom of his remark, and awareness of the conflicting settler, liberal and radical interpretations shaped the form and contents of the second chapter.

Dr John Philip, school lessons emphasized, was a missionary crank who believed that black and white were equal. He was judged less of a crank than were Johannes van der Kemp and John Read because unlike them, he did not go so far as to marry a 'Hottentot'. The emphasis then on racial separation and racial differences (in the first years of the fifties) was hard and sharp. Philip's book, *Researches in South Africa*, was an indictment of the Colonial Government and the settlers' treatment of the Khoi and the San [17]. It was also a plea for racial tolerance. Yet, surprisingly, Macmillan vaunted Dr Philip as a segregationist. A segregationist (to my mind) is *ipso facto* a doctrinaire or a colour-phobist racist. He either believes that there is an unbridgeable biological difference between races or he simply cannot tolerate people who bear a different pigmentation from his own, or more sophisticatedly, he might hide his biological or colour superstitions under the respectable cover of cultural autonomy. All of these sentiments were foreign to Philip. So, how was sense to be made of Macmillan's judgment?

Effectively, there were several explanations; there was little agreement about the definition of 'segregation'; segregation embodies separation but separation does not embody segregation; and Macmillan was convinced that his own brand of segregation was being advocated by Philip a century earlier. Macmillan had urged Hertzog's Government to accord citizenship to the small number of blacks who had already become urbanised. These black citizens, he reasoned, would constitute a minority and would not disturb or threaten the monopoly of white political power. On the other hand, the numerically overwhelming blacks still in the rural areas should be encouraged to stay on the land by according them more acreage and more credit. Arguing retrospectively, Macmillan stressed that *if* Dr Philip's policy of trying to preserve the lands of the various tribes had succeeded, South Africa would have been naturally segregated and there would never have been the then black pressure on the white urban centres. Philip was therefore, in Macmillan's eyes, the greatest segregationist of them all. Chapter three investigates this claim.

Dr John Philip's ideas about how relations should be forged in the Cape with the Khoi and, on the borders, with the Xhosa and the Griqua, in the area beyond with the other African peoples, were formulated before 1834, but Macmillan claimed Philip was a segregationist in the 1920s. The chapters in this study follow a chronological order. It was therefore necessary to decide whether this chapter was a case study of the 1920s or a case study of the 1820s. Since the subject is 'segregation', in the case of Dr John Philip, it seemed best to consider it as an 1820s' issue.

Several Plain Indian chiefs, I discovered in the late 1960s, were killed while under the protection of the U.S. Government forces, and killed under circumstances that were suspicious and controversial — killed *while trying to escape*. The most notable of these victims was Chief Crazy Horse, the man instrumental for the defeat of General Custer at the Battle of Little Big Horn in 1876. Settler history in the United States resembles, in many ways, South African settler history, and the question arose: was not an important African Chief killed under circumstances equally suspect? As anticipated, there was: Hintsa, the Xhosa paramount Chief, was killed - while trying to escape. But since Hintsa was killed in 1836, South African history had stolen a march on its American counterpart. And yet, unlike Crazy Horse's, Hintsa's death did seem genuinely untoward. E.A. Walker said so in his *A History of Southern Africa*[18] and so did S.M. Molema in his *Bantu Past and Present*[19]; and so did Macmillan[20]; but Macmillan did mention a crankish Dr Campbell who claimed that Hintsa was killed in cold blood. This roused suspicions. Research indicated that an unpublished doctoral thesis by J.G. Pretorius, 'The British humanitarians and the Cape Eastern frontier 1834-1836'[21], had examined the controversy surrounding the killing. Two further studies by A.L. Harrington and J. Peires[23] followed suit. But these, including Pretorius's study, fitted the death into a wider and more general context. A survey of the literature — and it is well to recall that Hintsa at that time was one of the four top leaders of black South Africa (Dingane, Mzilikazi and Moshoeshoe were the others) — revealed that no historian (a lacuna possible perhaps only in South Africa) had devoted a single serious and specific essay to his untoward end. It was also noticeable that Pretorius, Harrington and Peires' versions each respectively contained information that the other two did not contain, and each respectively suffered, because of the particular approach, its own documentary gap. It was apparent that a synthesis of the three versions was required, and any document that had been overlooked needed to be consulted and incorporated into the synthesis, and since each historian uses evidence in his own particular way it was necessary to personally examine every document so that the story would be as complete as possible. A further decision was made to concentrate exclusively on the period of Hintsa's detention. The task was to set out consciously, like a photographer in his dark room who enlarges a portion of a photograph so that he can identify a blur or a spot, to gather as much detail on every incident as was possible and see if it was not possible, in this way, to get nearer the truth.

But there comes a time when documentation runs out. What does a historian in such circumstances do? Hintsa came to the British camp on the assurance that his safety would be guaranteed. But almost as soon as he entered the camp he was detained and ransomed for a considerable amount of cattle. Yet hardly any cattle came in. What were Governor D'Urban and Colonel Smith to do with their hostage? It's possible (and without being tendentious) to express this another way: what does a kidnapper do when the ransom he demands is ignored? None of the previous historians asked this question. Of course, there are those who will say it is no business of the historian to ask such questions and who will counsel: stick to the sources, and if the sources run dry, plead ignorance and say no more. This is good orthodox wisdom but there are times when a historian has also to use common sense and imagination. Resort has to be made to careful and undisguised speculation; that is, to guesswork. Guessing is, after all (as A.J.P. Taylor put it), 'the only way of explaining when solid evidence runs out'[23]. In such an essay the reader is forewarned of the historian's intention, the historian's cards are on the table. The aim, as stated, is to be as thorough as possible.

A Xhosa-speaking historian will one day, with the help of oral tradition, provide further details and will at the same time relegate the present essay to legitimate redundancy. This chapter, in the meanwhile,

14

must serve as the first *complete* account of how Hintsa died.

Dr Louis Herrman's article on Sir George Cory led to the trail of the Retief-Dingane treaty[24]. This was later supplemented by the newspaper report of Cory's 1923 declaration that the treaty was a fake of some ten months (after Retief's death). The logic and the evidence upon which he had based his conclusion appeared fool proof, so his public backing down some months later was puzzling. This was way back in 1973 and ever since, documents and books on the period have been accumulated and analysis of the various aspects of the problem ignored by the sources have been extended − the result is chapter six[25].

If there was one part of school history that remained dramatic and vivid, it was the story of Retief's encounter with Dingane. Dingane was obviously the cad and miscreant, and Retief the obvious hero and knight. It seemed no matter how you looked at it Dingane's action was too perfidious and too recreant to be anything other than pure mischief. An acquaintance with international law, however, brought home the realization that Retief's very entry into Zulu territory had a whiff of gunpowder about it. But making sense of Dingane's action on that fateful Tuesday of 6 February 1838 seemed to be beyond logic and common sense. An article titled 'Dingane: A reappraisal'[26] provided a sense and a logic of sorts: Dingane had Retief killed because this was the only way he could obtain firearms. It is an argument, yet it is rather frail, for it ignores Dingane's sharp awareness that guns required powder, lead and maintenance. Killing Retief did not resolve this fundamental problem. The puzzle remained, until attention was aroused by a series of curious facts: Retief and Dingane met on a Sunday; after the meeting, Dingane sent in haste for his own favourite interpreter; and Dingane's army, when it fell upon the Trekker camps, was surprised by the scale and numbers it encountered − all of which seemed to belie the charge of premeditation. The realisation then dawned that it was because of the unquestioned acceptance that Dingane had made up his mind to kill Retief, even before Retief reached his capital, that had been the barrier to making sense of the Zulu Chief's action. Once the premise of premeditation was lifted an entirely new interpretation became possible.

This case study also posed a chronological problem. Was it to be placed before or after the treaty chapter? After − most will say, for the treaty was signed and then Retief was killed. Before − a few will say, for Retief was first killed and then (ten months later) the treaty

15

was signed. This was not an easy problem to solve. At first it seemed appropriate that the treaty chapter should come after but, on reconsideration, Dingane's final reaction to Retief's presence in Zululand makes better sense if the problem of the treaty is examined first. So strict chronology in this instance has given way to the coherence of greater clarity.

In June 1944 an SS regiment encircled the quiet village of Oradour-sur-Glane in France, rounded up the inhabitants, led the men to a garage and mowed them down with machine-guns; they then led the women and children to the church, ordered them in, bolted the doors and set a torch to the building and left the rest of the village smouldering in flames. Some six hundred and forty-two people were killed[27]. But the village, though scarred, broken and blackened, stands and is today a museum. A visit there in 1965 was the first step to the seventh essay in this study.

A few years later, in March 1968, the My Lai massacre in Vietnam came to the notice of the world's press and media. There, American soldiers entered a village and brutally killed three hundred and seventy civilians. Later knowledge of the Wounded Knee massacre of December 1890 when at least three hundred Plain Indian men, women and children were killed[28] completed the grim catalogue of atrocities. A similar massacre occurred in South African history. Confirmation of it came from a popular and modest source, E. Rosenthal's *Encyclopaedia of Southern Africa*[29].

However, if Wounded Knee claimed some three hundred victims, My Lai four hundred and Oradour seven hundred; the massacre at Makapaan's Cave, as the Trekkers themselves admit, claimed some three thousand victims. But in the three non-South African massacres the victims were surprised; in the Transvaal, the victims anticipated an attack and did effect some resistance. In the three massacres the action of killing begins and ends within hours; in the Transvaal it lasts for weeks. Other differences can also be distinguished but the significant point is that most of the deaths in the Cave massacre were supposedly caused by thirst and hunger. The close investigation in the chapter casts doubt on the traditional version of the siege.

Gandhi was never mentioned at school, but a huge portrait of him adorned one of the walls of the school building. It was from Sarah Gertrude Millin (another popular reference) that the first complete account of Gandhi's struggle in South Africa (within the span of a few pages), was obtained. Gandhi, according to her, 'was struggling against

Smuts for the rights of South African Indians'[30]. This is what writers of popular and serious works on Gandhi have almost all claimed, and continue to claim. A recent publication, for instance, states that the Indians were mobilised in the 1890s and that their energies 'were channelled into a concerted movement which aimed at eradicating the various disabilities from which Indians of all castes, classes and creeds suffered'[31]. A doctoral study, however, reveals that the Indians were divided during the time of Gandhi; and, while it claims that at a certain moment of the struggle 'Gandhi was still simply a representative of the merchants'[32], it does not inform the reader just what motivated and drove Gandhi with such force and fortitude against the various governments in South Africa. In the end the reader learns, somewhat disappointingly, that Gandhi was motivated by a 'purely ethical ideology' and that his true concern was for 'moral individuation'[33].

No one can ever have the final say on such an important subject as Gandhi's formative years in South Africa, but some neglected considerations in chapter eight have been brought into focus. These, at least, present him with more realism than has hitherto been the case.

1 WAS THE 'VAN RIEBEECK PRINCIPLE' A PLEA FOR PEACE OR A PLEA FOR PLUNDER?

> The importance of a historical event frequently lies, not so much in the extent of its influence upon contemporary thought and action, as in its propaganda value for a later generation.
>
> V.T. Harlow[1]

The Dutch Reformed Church in Cape Town celebrated the bicentenary of Jan van Riebeeck's landing at the southern tip of Africa in 1852, and since the Church elders considered that the Dutch Commander represented not only a trading company but also Christianity, it feted on the same occasion the bicentenary of the introduction of Christianity to South Africa. David Livingstone,[2] who was in Cape Town at the time, found the equation too gross and too abject. He protested:

> This observance evinced no small amount of moral courage, for we find from the journal of this same Van Riebeeck that in his person were associated the introduction of Christianity, *plus* a principle fraught with lamentation and mourning and woe. We see the apostle of peace on earth and good-will to man utterly unable to restrain his greedy soul when viewing the herds of Hottentot cattle quietly feeding adjacent to the fort. He wonders at the mysterious dispensation of Providence, by which such fine animals had been given to the heathen . . . {and} coolly records his calculations as to how many of the Hottentot *'cattle might be stolen with the loss of but a very few of his own party'*. This is the first enunciation of what we call the Van Riebeeck principle. This unfortunate obliviousness of the rights involved in *meum* and *tuum* has been a prominent feature in the history of the border Boers during the last two hundred years . . . and when we find that this moral monstrosity is endorsed by the Church we stand mute with amazement[3].

When, one hundred and twenty-two years later, *David Livingstone's South African papers 1849-1883* was published, Dr Anna Böeseken (sometime head of publications, Government Archives, Cape Town;

and historian) had an opportunity to comment on Van Riebeeck's Khoi policy[4]. The volume carried the text of Livingstone's 1853 essay, 'Trans Vaal Boers and slavery' - the text in which he first employed the term, 'the Van Riebeeck principle'[5]. 'Appendix 3', in the same volume, had a two-page article by Dr Böeseken, 'The Van Riebeeck principle and practice'.

Livingstone was undergoing an operation in Cape Town and he must have had time then, Dr Böeseken speculated, to look into Donald Moodie's *Record*[6]. But either his examination of the *Record* was careless or his interpretation was dishonest, for how else could he have come out, she protested so violently against 'the Van Riebeeck principle or practice'? Dr Böeseken admitted that Van Riebeeck did not particularly care for the Khoi; that he meditated on the *possibility* of taking their cattle without incurring any losses. But the 'jaundiced and unfair' Livingstone transformed these 'musing' of a 'harassed Commander' into a general principle. If he had only considered 'the full background' of Van Riebeeck's Cape Appointment, and if he had examined Moodie with greater care, he would have seen that even after the Khoi had killed a 'European herdsmen' (*sic*) and stolen almost all the Company cattle, which had been legitimately obtained through barter,

> Van Riebeeck gave strict instructions to his men that 'no one, on meeting here at the Fort or elsewhere . . . shall do them (the Hottentots) any the least harm or injury . . . but shall on the contrary show them every kindness and friendship'. (19th [actually 21st] October 1653, Moodie p. 37). In practice the Van Riebeeck principle was an attempt to maintain peace at all costs[7].

The idea of the Van Riebeeck principle, if not a controversy before certainly became one after Dr Böeseken's fierce defence of Van Riebeeck, and after her sharp attack on Livingstone. R. Elphick, in his study of initial white settlement at the Cape, pointed to the contradictory opinions of C.F.L. Leipoldt[8] and Theal[9]. Leipoldt, he indicated, argued that Van Riebeeck's generosity was real, while his vindictiveness was an artificial response to the anti-Khoi-Khoi clamour of his subordinates'; while Theal' felt that Van Riebeeck's inmost inclinations were toward a violent solution, and that he pursued the policy of kindness purely out of a determination to obey orders'. But he believed that 'Both of these interpretations ignored a considerable body of evidence', for Van Riebeeck's response to the Khoi was 'at its deepest level dualistic'. Sometimes his attitude to the Khoi was dominated by 'totalitarian fantasies' and sometimes by 'tolerant affection'[10].

An examination of the various opinions concerning 'the Van Riebeeck principle' clearly suggests that there are essentially two views: the Livingstone view (supported, to a great extent, by Theal, E.C. Godée-Molsbergen — in the Dutch text[11], I.D. MacCrone[12], H.M. Robertson[13], and Margaret Spilhaus[14] which sees Van Riebeeck as an incorrible advocate of extreme and iniquitous measures; and the E.B. Watermeyer view[15] (buttressed by the writings of Leipoldt, A.J.H. Goodwin[16], Godée-Molsbergen — in the Afrikaans text[17], Shula Marks - to an ambiguous extent[18], and of course, Dr Böeseken) which argues that Van Riebeeck's harsh proposals were either 'musings' or one-off affairs or reprisal for the killing of a herd-boy - proposals, in sum, made under extreme pressures and exceptional circumstances[19].

It would have been possible, initially, to argue that there was a third view, that of R. Elphick's, which holds that Van Riebeeck's Khoi policy was 'dualistic': now 'in the grip of totalitarian fantasies'; now in the effusion of 'tolerant affection born of the highest principles of religion'. But two years after having formulated this dualistic view, Elphick aligned himself with the first of the two views: Van Riebeeck *repeatedly* appealed to the directors to let him enslave the Peninsulars [that is, the Goringhaicona, the Goringhaigua and the Gorachouqua] and confiscate their cattle[20].

One of these two views is more veridical than the other. The question is, which one? Or, to put it another way, whose interpretation of 'the Van Riebeeck principle' was closer to the truth, Livingstone's or Dr Böeseken's?

1

Can Dr Böeseken's refutation of Livingstone's charge be sustained, as she claims, by *the full background of Van Riebeeck's activities at the Cape*? To appreciate that background it is necessary to answer two fundamental questions: why did the VOC choose to establish a station at the Cape; and why did they select as overseer of the project?

The VOC had no intention of colonizing the Cape. What they sought was a victualling station where their ships, plying between western Europe and eastern Asia, could stop, and where their crews could rest and renew their supplies of water and fresh food. The Council of XVII, the directors, reminded and re-instructed Van Riebeeck as late as April 1658 that the promotion of agriculture and stock-breeding was his prime task and chief object, and that everything else was secondary and had to be set aside for the present[21].

Van Riebeeck had previously been stationed in Tonkin (northern Vietnam). His talents there as a merchant brought in handsome profits for the honourable Company. But, like many others, he indulged in some private trade, cashed in on some of the takings, was caught out, fined the equivalent of two months salary and ordered home early in 1648[22]. On his way back, he called at the Cape and remained there from 10 to 28 March 1648; he therefore had occasion to acquire some practical experience and knowledge of the Cape.

When he reached the Netherlands he hoped the XVII would review his case and tax him with leniency. The hope was vain; he was discharged[23]. When the Company, however, seriously considered establishing a station at the Cape, they invited Van Riebeeck to comment on a memorandum that favoured such a venture[24]. Van Riebeeck commented positively and appealed for the assignment of establishing the station to be given to him: 'We will hope and Pray God Almighty to grace us with foresight and understanding, so that we may become capable of conducting your affairs there, for the best service and profit of the Honourable Company'[25].

Van Riebeeck's willingness to undertake the Cape assignment was an obvious act of penitence; and the Company's decision to accord him the task was both an act of grace and an order of penance. But Van Riebeeck expected his stay at the Cape to be brief; for within weeks of his arrival he requested to be transferred to India[26]. He had, of course, signed a contract to serve at the Cape for five years but he doubted that he would be asked to stay there for the full period. On 14 April 1653, for instance, he wrote to the XVII in this vein:

I most humbly, respectfully, and earnestly pray, that your Honors will think of removing me hence to India, and to some better and higher employment, in order that in due time, and in consideration of better services than I can render here, I may earn promotion; for, among these dull, stupid, (botte, plompe) lazy, stinking people, litle address (subtylteyt) is required as among the Japanese, Tonquinese and other precise nations thereabouts, who, as I have sufficiently experienced in my ten years service, give enough to do to the brains of the cleverest Dutchman; and here there is nothing to be done, except to barter a few sheep and cattle, in which little address is required[27].

Ultimately his posting to the Cape lasted not five but ten years. He was, in truth, deprived and barred from the rich pickings and experience of the East for a full decade, which in his eyes (and in fact) was severe punishment, indeed.

Van Riebeeck came to the Cape resolved to make a quick and distinct success of his assignment. His energy and loyalty in carrying out Company policy was second to none[28]. Growing the requisite agricultural products proved more formidable than at first anticipated, but he ensured a positive and promising beginning. Securing and, above all, ensuring a regular supply of fresh meat, however, proved elusive. In the ten years of his stay, he never quite succeeded in establishing a system that would make the Khoi reliable and consistent suppliers of the livestock that sailors on the Company ships required, demanded and, sometimes, threatened to do violence for[29].

The XVII had issued Van Riebeeck with strict instructions not to antagonize the indigenes. They did this not because of any intrinsic respect for the safety and welfare of the African aborigines (which does not mean they were indifferent to it), but because they knew hostilities, in the long run, encouraged expenses, jeopardised trade and compromised profit. As the directors of the Delft Chamber pointedly observed (in 1644):

A merchant would do better to increase his talent and send rich cargoes from Asia to the Netherlands, instead of carrying out costly territorial conquests, which are most suitable for crowned heads and mighty monarchs than for merchants greedy of gain[30].

Van Riebeeck, anxious to please, wholeheartedly accepted the precepts and consigns of his directors. He did everything possible to win the confidence of the Khoi and to forge an agreement that would make for a regular and smooth supply of mutton and beef. The first tentative bartering rounds were promising, but thereafter his every endeavour to establish the exchange on a fixed period, proved abortive and, in time, gave rise to vexing frustration.

The meat demand of a victualling station belonging to what was one of the richest companies in the world[31], was disproportionate to the herd and flock supply of the very modest Khoi. Van Riebeeck, a man with a rich merchant background, could not understand the Khoi's reluctance to honour the sanctiment of sale and purchase. Their failure to conform to the law of supply and demand (or demand and supply) struck him as a dereliction, a delinquency, and, even, a damnation.

The XV11 and superior officers (the Commissioners) visiting the Cape station urged Van Riebeeck to treat the Khoi with more friendship. They were convinced that if only sufficient amity were exercised, sufficient stock would be forthcoming. In this they were mistaken, for the stock meant everything to the Khoi: their livelihood, their wealth, their status and their place in tribal hierarchy. They did not mind bartering their surplus or diseased stock, but their regular and healthy stock was essential for breeding and natural increase. Friendship or diplomatic skill, no matter how much of it Van Riebeeck could muster, was powerless against the simple reality of the Khoi economy[32]. Milk was an essential element of their diet but the milk yield of their stock was low: ten cows provided enough for on adult; ten ewes enough for one child. With the exception of the Goringhaiqua, who had more sheep than cattle, most of the tribes were endowed with the respective ten to one ratios[33].

It is doubtful if Van Riebeeck ever grasped what the herds and flocks meant to the Khoi. To him they seemed to be no more than moveable property and therefore subject to barter and sale; whereas to the Khoi they were an essential food source. The controversy surrounding Van Riebeeck's Khoi policy fixed on this fulcrum of misunderstanding of divergent needs and disproportionate wants, of subsistence supply and commercial demand.

To complete his penance at the Cape, Van Riebeeck had to transform the settlement into a viable victualling station, and viability meant, first and foremost, a capacity to provide a regular and sufficient supply of fresh meat. The animals capable of meeting this twin demand were there, but they were under the ownership of the Khoi. The Khoi possessed the one commodity (even though it was not gold or diamond, uranium or petrol) that was of value to the Dutch. They enjoyed a 'monopoly' that they neither sought nor wanted[34]. To procure this valuable commodity, Van Riebeeck was prepared to barter. The Khoi were willing to barter the stock they judged surplus to their needs. Propositions concerning this fundamental contradiction feature prominently and regularly in entries made in the Company journal, in correspondence between Van Riebeeck and the XV11 and in despatches between the XV11 and Van Riebeeck. The three indispensable printed sources containing this information are: Moodie's *Record*, Leibbrandt's *Precis of the Archives of the Cape of Good Hope* (which reprints the letters received and despatched from the Cape) and an up-to-date and complete edition of the *Journal of Jan van Riebeeck* (the Company record of Van Riebeeck's command from December 1651 to May 1662)[35].

3

Godée-Molsbergen refers to 13 December 1652 as the date when Van Riebeeck first enunciated (what Livingstone would term) 'the Van Riebeeck principle'. The journal entry for that day is also cited as a reference by Goodwin and Böeseken, and it is important to be well acquainted with the contents of this crucial entry.

The entry first points out that the Goringhaiqua approached the fort with thousands of cattle and sheep, and came so close that their herds almost mixed with the Company's stock. But bartering initiatives proved disappointing and only a few animals were obtained. 'It is very sad', it noted, 'to behold such fine herds of cattle and to be unable to purchase anything worth while'. More copper and friendship were proffered, but to no avail. Were they (the entry wondered) glutted with copper or were they affecting reluctance out of envy or mischief? There was no way of knowing. The entry then continued in this manner:

It would be a pity to see these herds leave without being able to do further trading. To-day we had ample opportunity of depriving them of 10,000 head of cattle had we been allowed to do so. If we are ordered to do this, it can always be done at some future date; this would suit us even better, for the Saldaniers[36] trust us more as the days go by. Once we had possession of so many cattle, we could maintain an adequate supply by breeding; moreover we should have no fear of the English touching here and spoiling the cattle trade with the natives.

The entry (made eight months and a week after landing) went on to describe the justification for such action, its technical feasibility and its chance of succeeding without recourse to physical violence:

> These people daily give us sufficient cause by stealing and carrying away our possessions; we are so often subjected to this that we have enough reason for taking revenge by capturing them or their cattle. If one cannot get the cattle from them by friendly trading, why should one then suffer their thieving without making reprisal? This would only be necessary once: with 150 men ten or twelve thousand cattle could be secured without the danger of losing a single person. On the other hand many savages could be captured without a blow as they always come to us unarmed; they could then be sent to India as slaves.

These considerations were only referred to 'in passing' the entry stressed, and owned that for such approaches to become policy, more reflection and maturer judgement were requisite. It was added, however: 'It could be considered and deliberated more fully later on, after more experience, in the event of our receiving higher orders to that effect'[37].

This was a chilling proposal for equipping the victualling station with a guaranteed supply of fresh meat. But it could have been no more than a 'musing', for the task of setting up a station in a virgin environment was not an easy one. Besides, there was a host of problems that confronted him daily: the character of the soil had been misread, the force of the wind had been underestimated, the wild animals were more daring than anticipated, the men were difficult to control and there was a general shortage of tools, material, fuel and food. Van Riebeeck had expected so much (with the arrival of the Goringhaiqua) and had, in the eventuality, received so little, that he gave way in a moment of rank frustration to an inconsiderate and rash utterance. The 13 December entry is there. It is evidence — documentary evidence. It cannot be wished away; it did record an infamous reflection but this did not indicate Van Riebeeck's real and general Khoi policy — or did it?

On 19 October 1653, a band of Khoi killed a Dutch herd-boy and made off with his charge of cattle. Van Riebeeck suspected, though he had no proof, that Herry[38] had something to do with it. How Van Riebeeck set out to deal with this affair provides a microcosm of his thoughts and strategy – his real Khoi policy.

Initial attempts to recover the cattle proved vain. Two days later Van Riebeeck, manifesting level-headedness and calm leadership, issued a proclamation, which, contrary to common expectation, forsook hot-blooded vengeance and heeded the consequences of hasty reaction[39]. Böeseken quoted a passage from the proclamation in order to repugn Livingstone's charge. Her citation, however, because it is incomplete, gives the impression that Van Riebeeck was forgiving and forbearing, but the full version (the words in capitals and bold type are the ones that were omitted) reveals:

> No one, on meeting, here at the Fort or elsewhere **ANY OF THE INHABITANTS, WHETHER SALDANHAMAN OR WATERMAN THE STEALERS OF OUR SAID CATTLE, AYE EVEN OUR LATE INTERPRETER HERRY, APPARENTLY THE CHIEF AUTHOR OF THE ROBBERY? AND ALSO ABSENT,** shall do them on that account, any the least harm or injury, but shall on the contrary show them every kindness and friendship, **AYE MORE THAN EVEN HERETOFORE, AS IF THE LATE OUTRAGE HAD NEVER HAPPENED, OR AT LEAST WAS TOTALLY FORGOTTEN BY US; SO THAT THE SALDANHARS BE NOT THEREBY FRIGHTENED FROM COMING TO US AGAIN, BUT THAT, OBSERVING OUR GOOD NATURE, THEY MAY BECOME THE MORE ATTACHED AND ACCUSTOMED TO US, SO THAT WE MAY, NOT ONLY SPEEDILY PROCURE OTHER CATTLE FROM THOSE DAILY EXPECTED HERE, AND TRADE WITH THEM, BUT ALSO THAT WE MAY CONTINUE THE MORE SAFELY TO FREQUENT THE ROADS IN ALL DIRECTIONS**[40].

Van Riebeeck was not suggesting that bygones by bygones, but was advocating that the more general and long-term interest not be put at risk by hasty and dramatic reaction. Besides, he had already had some knowledge of how the potential cattle suppliers reacted; for on 18

November 1653 the journal expressed the fear that the Goringhaiqua, hearing of the killing, would not venture close to the fort even though they were entirely innocent. Van Riebeeck deemed it necessary therefore to play down the crime lest a too vigorous showing of outrage risked scaring away the all-important stock suppliers. His outward reaction, there is no doubt, was pacific and placatory. His policy, for all that, had little to do with pacifism or Christian charity; on the contrary, there was a very earnest, very Realpolitik logic to this expressed leniency. He made his intention clear three months later when he admitted that it was difficult to witness the thieves passing with the stolen cattle right before their eyes, and to have to pretend friendship when it would be quite legitimate to practice revenge. Then he expressed his 13 December thoughts once again, emphasizing that they could obtain twelve to thirteen thousand cattle and some five to six hundred sheep with the use of fourteen or fifteen men and without having to strike a single blow[41].

Later, in the same entry, the identical design was reformulated; though coupled this time with the idea that since trade with the Khoi was never going to prosper, it was just as well that the deed be done now so as to solve, once and for all, the problem of securing a reserve of fresh meat. The entry also went on to note: 'It would perhaps be a better proposition to pay out this guilty gang, taking the cattle to use for refreshment and our own use, . . . and their persons as slaves for fetching firewood and doing other necessary labour'[42].

Van Riebeeck, in a later despatch to the XV11, noted that Herry had convinced the Goringhaiqua that revenge would befall them as well as his own tribe. But Van Riebeeck indicated that a delegation visited the Goringhaiqua and assured them that this was not their intention. Cautious bartering resumed. But Van Riebeeck — contrary to the pledge and to the assurance — did seek revenge against both the Goringhaicona and the Goringhaiqua. He addressed the XV11, referred to the journal entries of 28 January and 8 April 1654, and stated that the two tribes were allied, and that the Company's stolen cattle were identifiable among their herds. He once again sought specific permission to attack the tribes. This time, however, he emphasized:

We shall confirm them as much as possible in their confidence in us by every kind treatment, . . . This, however, we only do to make them less shy, so as to find hereafter a better opportunity to seize them

27

with all their cattle . . . with which live stock the Company would be at once, and by breeding almost for ever, supplied with cattle enough, and could derive good service from the people in chains, in killing seals, or in labouring in the silver mines, which we trust will be found here[43].

The XV11 sanctioned severity towards the actual culprit responsible for the herd-boy's death and banishment for Herry, and they allowed that the loss of the Company's cattle had to be made good, but they were cautious about venturing any further. They called on Van Riebeeck to use 'lenient measures' and to win the friendship of the Khoi. But they prudently suggested that if friendship failed and violence was committed again, he might apply more rigid measures and see whether these new policies would not better check and keep the Khoi to their duty. This counsel was nevertheless tempered with prudence: 'In this, however, it is necessary to use wisdom and discretion'[44].

Van Riebeeck, the men of action — the man on the spot — politely told the XV11 — the man sitting in their armchairs in the Netherlands — that they were talking through their hats. After explaining why their way of settling the matter would not work (the tracing of the herd-boy's killer would be impossible, and taking only the cattle that were lost would rouse hostility to the same degree as if all were taken), he yet again sought permission to put into practice 'the principle' he so much coveted.

We should take them and their cattle into our power. The Honourable Company would have enough from the encrese (sic) to supply the ships with fresh meat . . . and could get good service from the men on the Islands in killing seals, on the flesh of which we could maintain them without any other food, and might send away the women and children to Batavia[45].

The XV11 replied that recourse to such extreme measures must be approached slowly and only if matters become desperate[46].

5

From March 1657, Van Riebeeck would refer to a policy of trying to transform the entire settlement into a fortress by blocking up the mountain passes with a series of redoubts — a project which would exercise his mind hereafter quite considerably. He hoped that Rijklof van Goens[47] (who was soon to visit the settlement) would approve his plan[48].

Van Goens arrived at the settlement on 16 April 1657, stayed for a spell, inspected the station, read the copies of the various despatches and became wellacquainted with Van Riebeeck's thoughts on Khoi policy. He concluded there were three ways of settling relations with the Khoi. First, they could try to intercept, by means of fortifications and guard houses, the communications between the Goringhaiqua and the Goringhaicona; second, they could seize, kill or banish them; and third, they could live peacefully and co-operatively with them by gaining and keeping their friendship.

The Commissioner admitted that he had a preference for the first of the three options, but deemed it too expensive. The second, which Van Riebeeck favoured, he judged 'barbarous and unchristian' and abhorrent to God; he also noted that it was contrary to the instructions of the XV11. The third, he thought worthy, but the Khoi seemed so 'brutish and savage' as to render it quite impracticable. He ruled in favour of the first option but instructed Van Riebeeck to await the specific approval of the XV11. In the meanwhile he advised him to win the Khoi's confidence[49].

Thus once again Van Riebeeck had his request to act upon his policy turned down. This time, however, insult was added to injury: his policy option was qualified as being barbaric. Van Goens did, for all that, leave the door open: he suggested that Van Riebeeck could apply his policy of righteous revenge in a carefully defined and strictly limited way:

> Should it happen that they again do us a serious wrong by theft — the case deserving it, but not otherwise, you should instantly lay hold of some of the people of Herry, . . . or those you may deem to be guilty, and place them on Robben Island, until they point out the actual offender; and on that being done, you should release the others, and banish the culprit to work for us on the said island for 2 or 3 years; at the same time, apprising the chiefs of your proceedings, so as to cause as little estrangement as possible[50].

After Van Goens' visit, Van Riebeeck still clung to his own favourite solution. He now proposed confining Herry and the Goringhaicona, with their stock, within the Hout Bay area by blocking up the passes. In a despatch to the XV11, he elaborated this plan with enthusiasm: after stating that he would require about five redoubts to shut Herry and his followers behind the mountains and to control their movements, he observed:

> Consequently, they could there be held under good subjection having enough of good pasture for thousands of cattle and sheep, out of the increase of which you could draw great supplies, always taking out in proportion to the increase, and that for brass and tobacco by way of barter, and allowing them — that is to say the men — to pass out freely to fetch other cattle from the interior for brass and tobacco, thus acting as traders for the Company; but confining all their cattle within the said enclosures, and leaving there so many, that the men (when out buying other cattle for the Company or for themselves) and always longing for their wives, and for their chief riches so closed in, would continue supplicants for their cattle[51].

Enthusiasm for the project, however, was short-lived. From five redoubts he now calculated he would need ten or twelve - or even fifteen[52].

Commissioner Joan Cunaeus[53], on his way from Batavia, visited the Cape station in March 1658. He thought the redoubt plan was too costly and that it would not work: he advised its abandonment and urged instead (in his official instructions) that Van Riebeeck solicit the co-operation of the Khoi by kindness rather than by imprisonment[54].

6

Van Riebeeck proposed a variant of his 'principle' to the XV11 on 31 March 1658. According to him, Herry and Doman[55] (the respective leaders of the Goringhaicona and the Goringhaiqua) suggested they and the Dutch should jointly attack two neighbouring tribes and deprive them of all their cattle. Van Riebeeck described the proposal, noted that the designated tribes — the Chariguriqua and the Chorachouqua[56] were 'very rich in cattle', that they bartered only their 'lean, old, or sickly' stock and that they were, besides, a 'very great annoyance'. He concluded: 'The scheme appears to us feasible

30

enough'[57].

While he was still entertaining this idea, a despatch from the XV11 informed him that they had seen Van Goens' instructions, and that they had found them sound and wise. They dryly instructed him to regulate his conduct by them until they saw occasion to direct him otherwise[58].

In a further despatch, about five months later, the XV11 reiterated their disapproval of his disparate but consistently hostile proposals concerning the Khoi. This time, however, there was — for the first time — an evident tone of rebuke in their instruction:

> The ill will of the Hottentots must be in some measure overlooked, and submitted to and although they will not consent to any trade, we are not to take their property from them by force, as we do not perceive that adequate ground have at least as yet, been given for that course[59], meanwhile we must direct our attention to breeding, so that we may in time subsist upon oxen, cows and sheep, of our own[60].

These explicit instructions did not, however, prevent Van Riebeeck from acting otherwise.

7

Van Riebeeck informed the XV11 (15 January 1659) that, at last, the Company's settlement had an ample supply of sheep and cattle. He also reported that he had finally settled accounts with Herry, the Goringhaiqua and another neighbouring tribe. He had acted, in part, on the premise of his 'principle' and in part, on Van Goens' instructions. He captured Herry and the Goringhaicona, deprived them of all their cattle, banished Herry to Robben Island and then released the other members of the clan. He ended his despatch with an earnest plea for horses. He was convinced that with an armed and mounted force of twenty men he would be able to 'master' all the Khoi clans, especially the Goringhaiqua and the Gorachouqua, who were particularly rich in cattle[61].

In a later despatch, he confidently informed the XV11 that everything was now going well: trade was better, the Company was rich in stock and security was assured. He emphasised that the Council had adopted the resolution to deal with Herry; and he then went on to

31

describe how Herry was first enticed with fair words into his office and then arrested; and how his soldiers thereafter, with concealed weapons, surrounded his clan and secured all their stock. He ended his despatch with a plea, once again, for horses.

Before his last message reached the Netherlands, counter recommendations, however, were already on their way. These emphatically instructed him to keep expenses down, not to expect the receipt of horses and to pursue the established policy of trying to win the confidence and friendship of the Khoi by peaceful persuasion and by legitimate trade[62].

Van Riebeeck must already have sensed that the policy he was convinced would work best was never going to be sanctioned by the XV11. Before the despatch bearing the recommendations could reach him, he turned to the Governor-General and the Council in Batavia. Like himself they were men on the spot who would (he must have believed) understand his position and sanction his principle. So he complained that the Goringhaiqua should be smitten and deprived of their cattle. He stated diplomatically but boldly that patience and kindness could not work with the Khoi, and that on that account he sought a mandate for the use of harsher methods. He ended his plea by expressing the hope that matters would not come to a head before he received their reply[63].

But before the Batavian authorities could respond, Van Riebeeck was already informing them that he was — without intending it — at war with the Khoi. He once again emphasized that previous hopes that the Khoi might be won over by kindness had proved vain — the only way to deal with them was 'by force and through intimidation'[64].

8

When the XV11 learnt of the war, they could barely conceal their displeasure. Implicitly and reproachful, they observed (on 21 August 1660):

> We have, for some time back, and especially since the banishment of Herry, and the capture of his cattle, felt rather uneasy upon the subject, and apprehensive that the Caepmans or Hottentots would endeavour to give us an unexpected blow, and we should, therefore, have been better pleased if, with reference to what has been done

to Herry, we had exercised our patience a little longer. Our sentiments upon that subject you must have seen from our former letters; and we now find, God better it! that our fears and apprehensions were not without cause. The discontentment shown by those people, in consequence of our appropriating to ourselves — and to their exclusion — the land which they have used for their cattle from time immemorial, is neither surprising nor groundless.

Turning towards the matter of the free colonists, the XV11 noted that their act of treason gave no proof of great contentment — in 1660 forty-four out of a total of seventy stole away on ships sailing back to the Netherlands. They also stressed that the affair, with others, diminished the hopes they had entertained for the Cape station.

They also commented on the system of price fixing concerning purchases and sales to the free colonists. Here they found that all the corn the free farmers grew was bought by the Company and then sold back to them with a price increase of twenty-five per cent. The XV11 considered this nothing but 'exaction and extortion'[65].

Having stated all this, they responded to the Commander's oft repeated transfer request, in what was a manifestation of rebuke rather than reward[66]: 'At the urgent request of the Commander Jan van Riebeeck, and upon other considerations us thereunto moving, we have thought fit to consent to his *removal* from the Cape'[67].

9

In the beginning Van Riebeeck had urged outright treachery: the Khoi's confidence should be won, their vigilance should be dulled, their cattle should be confiscated and their liberty should be cancelled. Later he considered bringing the Goringhaicona, with their herds, under the jurisdiction of the Company, and of detaining them within the barred province of the settlement. After that he contemplated an open and joint attack, with the Goringhaicona and the Goringhaiqua, against the Gorachouqua and the Chariguriqua. And finally, he envisaged imposing a protective tribute relationship - by providing a regular supply of sheep and cattle, the Khoi would earn the right not to be molested by Dutch guns and horses. Thus after nearly seven years, though there were shifts in emphasis, there was no shift in Van Riebeeck's fundamental strategy for dealing with the Khoi and for obtaining the requisite supply of sheep and cattle.

These were not the reveries of a turn-the-other cheek Christian, but the tough and matter of fact logic of a seventeenth century Dutch merchant with east Indian experience who, checked in his ambitions, was anxious to succeed at all costs — and success (at the Cape) meant solving the Company's shortage of live stock[68].

The full background of Van Riebeeck's command, and his own testimony over a period of seven years or more, leaves little doubt that his principle was neither a musing nor a stray thought — nor even the outcome of a herd-boy's death — but a pitiless policy announced with candour, stated with consideration and pleaded with conviction.

2 WAS THE 50TH ORDINANCE A CHARTER OF KHOI LIBERTIES?

'It makes the Coloureds, the Hottentots, the Bushmen the exact equal to us Boers. They have all the rights we have. No further apprenticeship of the young. No work contracts. They don't have fixed abodes. Magistrates can no longer whip them as won't-works. From now on, damnit, Van Doorn, a man of color has all the rights I have'.

James A. Michener[1]

The Cape Khoi in 1659 (seven years after the landing of Van Riebeeck), fearing that Dutch settlement jeopardised their independence, attempted resistance[2], won an immediate respite but lost − in time − their herds and their lands; and succumbed over a 150 period to the inevitable concomitants of European incursion: immigrant disease and imported dram[3]. Those that survived the ravages of illness and alcoholism were driven by necessity to labour under the unregulated control of their farmer masters. Physically they were within the colony, but legally they were in a no man's land; they were subjects but there was no statutory acknowledgment of their position.

In 1809 the British administration at the Cape put an end to their ambiguous status by bringing them under colonial jurisdiction. The law in question was known as the 1809 Proclamation[4]. The Proclamation had provisions that, ostensibly, protected the Khoi labourer against his white master[5]. But the 'pivot' of the Act was its pass law provisions[6]. Its main effect was to deprive the Khoi of their liberty, which − whether nominal or not − gave them, at least, freedom of movement, and hence a bargaining counter in the labour market.

A further law in 1812 made those children of the Khoi who had been born and raised (up to their eighth year) on the farm where their parents worked and lived, liable to a ten year apprenticeship under the employing farmer[7]. An 1819 law applied a similar provision to orphan children of the Khoi and to the orphans of free blacks − San children, for instance, who had lost their parents during a clash between farmers and their elders, could be (and were) kept as servants

35

until eighteen years old[8]. These various proclamations fettered the Khoi.

Settler society (on the claim that labour, under white masters bestowed upon the aborigines the rudiments of civilisation) was convinced that these measures were passed in the interests of the Khoi themselves; whereas critics — notably missionaries of the London Missionary Society, especially its resident director, Dr John Philip[9] - viewed them as oppressive laws even harsher than those which applied to slaves.

In a 1828 law, the 50th Ordinance, was passed which repealed the anti-Khoi proclamations. The Ordinance, raised the ire of most settlers, but among the missionary friends of the Khoi and the Khoi themselves, it raised hope and was looked upon as the Khoi *Magna Charta* - their 'charter of liberty'[10].

How have these contradictory responses to the 50th Ordinance been reflected in South African historiography? Theal regretted the Ordinance[11]. A long line of historians (partisans of the settler cause[12], of Christian national education[13] and of segregation[14] concurred. W.M. Macmillan welcomed it[15]. J.S. Marais believed it was a mixed blessing[16]. N. Majeke (Dora Taylor) judged it a dual measure pointing 'forward to capitalism and backward to serfdom'[17]. Susan Newton-King thought it represented the intervention of the colonial authorities in the labour market to ensure the new British sheep and cattle farmers an adequate supply of herders and domestic servants[18]. With the exception of Dora Taylor, historians from Theal to Susan Newton-King all assumed, whether they thought it positive or negative, that the 50th Ordinance was, if not emancipatory, at least a liberalising measure; or saw it as a law that marked 'a turning point in the history of the Cape Colony'[19].

By the time the Ordinance was repealed in 1842, fourteen years after its promulgation, Macmillan considered that its work had been done, that its principles had been established, that it had placed the Coloured population of the Colony 'on a footing of complete legal equality with Europeans' and that it had given them 'at least the full protection of the ordinary law of the land'. The Cape therefore ceased to know any 'legal distinction' between 'white' and 'coloured'[20]. Hence 'the first battle for non-European rights' was crowned with victory[21].

In championing the cause of the Khoi, Dr John Philip sought, in essence, a single reform: freedom for the Khoi to bring their labour to a fair market[22]. This, of course, meant that he considered there ought not to be legal discrimination between the Khoi and other Colonial subjects. If he, and after him Macmillan, favoured the reform that would allow the Khoi fair remuneration for fair labour, it was because they believed, in addition to their humanist sentiment, that the habit of considering the Khoi (in Philip's celebrated phrase) only as 'producers' and not also as 'consumers' kept the farmer and the labourer poor and backward. The farmers, guaranteed a cheap but ill-trained labour force, were content with farming methods that were outdated and poor in yield; while the low-paid Khoi underconsumed, failed to improve their living standards and deprived the economy of the incentive indispensable for growth and improvement[23]. The 50th Ordinance was thus the harbinger of a threefold promise: a legal promise — the full protection of the law; an economic promise — an improved standard of living; and a political promise — no legal distinction between white and Coloured. How far and to what extent did the Ordinance keep faith with these promises?

1

The Ordinance was published in *The Cape of Good Hope Government Gazette* (25 July 1828) with no further reminders or correspondence. And after July 1828 no emphasis was laid on its terms either to the different Government departments and officials or to the general public.

In a community in which the literacy rate and media circulation were low the Ordinance's existence risked being little publicized and little known. The Khoi near and in the mission stations did know about the measure and welcomed it. An old man at the Kat River missionary station, for instance, safeguarded a copy of the Ordinance in his Dutch Bible, stating that it was 'God's word that taught us how to make right use of our privileges'[24]. But even those Khoi ignorant of the Ordinance's existence, but serving masters who *were aware* of it, were treated better than they were before the passing of the Ordinance. Philip in 1832 explained that this was so because the masters knew that if their servants escaped, they would not be able to apprehend them and bring them back to their farms. He found that these Khoi were better dressed and fed, that their masters' authoritarian manners towards them were mitigated, that they could enter their masters' houses without having to fawn and scrape, and that the relationship between master and servant was generally quite different from what it had been

37

in 1825[25].

Evidence seems to suggest that between July 1828 (when the Ordinance was passed) and May 1834 (when the draft of a vagrant law was published in colonial newspapers) — that is, in the first six years of the Ordinance's existence — the conditions of the Khoi were, in important respects, improved. The missionary J. Kitchingman, in a letter dated 13 June 1834, noted that under the old system the Khoi often complained of having received physical punishment but that a visit to Bethelsdorp two years later failed to produce a single complaint of this kind[26].

Where knowledge of the Ordinance's existence was known by both the farmer and the Khoi, wage rates and standards of treatment were almost certainly improved. Where only the master knew of the Ordinance's existence, wage rates and treatment were also markedly improved. But where master and servant were totally ignorant of the Ordinance's existence, matters — it must also be assumed — proceeded much as before. It may be that a great many fell into this latter category — perhaps even a majority.

Whatever the case, it must be noted that the machinery for enforcing the provisions of the Ordinance was totally lacking. Prior to 1828 the two officials who intervened most frequently between Khoi servant and farmer master were the fieldcornet and the landdrost (the chief district officer of the Government). Both these officials benefitted from the pre-1828 conditions, for these armed them with the power to recruit and distribute Khoi labour. The fieldcornet and the landdrost, with the necessary knowledge and proximity, were in a position — if so instructed and leaving aside the consideration of personal inclination — to ensure that the provisions of the 50th Ordinance were known, implemented and respected. But the Ordinance's application and control were removed from the jurisdiction of these two men-on-the-spot officers and placed under the jurisdiction of the justice of the peace and the clerk of the peace[27]. The justice of the peace and the clerk of the peace registered contracts, examined the procedures for adjusting relations between farmer employer and Khoi employee, and obtained (where this was applicable) legal redress. The records of these officials should indicate how master-servant relations had evolved since 1828, and how in effect, the 50th Ordinance was functioning — but their records are curiously silent. Why?

Both the justice of the peace and the clerk of the peace were too remote to exercise, in any meaningful way, control or jurisdiction. They were confined to a single village within a single district that in every instance was large an extensive. Administration and administrative justice for both master and servant were more trouble in terms of time, money and energy than were worth the complaint, the injury or the injustice suffered. As the justice of the peace of the Beaufort District observed:

> The residences of some of these parties are 350 miles from the chief town; many of them reside at 150 miles, and by far the greater number at from 70 to 100 miles distant: facts sufficient to account for the little business before the Circuit and Magistrates' Courts. Parties either admit to the evils such a state of things cannot fail to produce, or in cases of petty thefts, ill-conduct of servants, etc., they take the law into their own hands, and inflict such punishment, as they think fit. The persons thus illegally punished are prevented, for the same reason, from taking their complaints to the proper authorities, deterred also by the fear of being overtaken on the way, and again punished[28].

When it was mooted, with the publication of the draft vagrant act, that the 50th Ordinance risked being annulled, fieldcornets in numerous districts started issuing passes and arresting *vagrant* Khoi[29]. In some instances, matters became even worse than they were prior to 1828, as the memorial by the Khoi of the missionary station of Pecaltsdorp attested:

> The people of Dyzel's Kraal, the grazing place of the institution, were prohibited from leaving the grazing even to see their families at the institution, without a written permission; the cattle-herds are not allowed to go abroad into the fields with their cattle without a written permission; an exercise of authority which was never attempted by those local authorities, in relation to a missionary institution, in the worst period of Hottentot oppression, 'before the passing of the 50th Ordinance'. We have even in that dark period no instance on record of passes having been required from our cattle-herds, or of the field-cornets exercising such an authority over our people without a reference to the missionary; but not only are the cattle-herds required to have passes, but the head of the institution, Jonas Botha, who this year paid 15s direct taxes to government, and whose personal property is equal to that of many of the boors,

was prohibited from leaving the grazing-place to visit the institution without a written pass or permission[30].

The draft vagrant act, perhaps because of the strong opposition of Philip, the missionaries and the Khoi themselves [31] — or for whatever reason — never became law, but its provisions[32] reveal that its principal object (and it should be noted that the settlers throughout the period 1829-1834 appealed for such a law)[33] was to favorably secure for the master the necessary amount of Khoi labour. Judge William Menzies framed the 1834 draft act which, it has justly been said, echoed the Proclamation of 1809[34]. Macmillan condemned the draft act out of hand[35]; yet he welcomed the Masters and Servants Ordinance of 1841 which, while formally eschewing colour distinction, emphasized the difference between master and servant and weighted that emphasis in favour of the master. Class, apparently, had replaced colour, but in the Cape, at that time, the term *servant* was synonymous with Coloured or black; while *master* was synonymous with white[36]. Judge Menzies, the author of the 1834 draft vagrant act, helped frame the Masters and Servants Ordinance of 1841, and in doing so was, perhaps, the very first to frame legislation which *proposed* equality but dispensed inequality[37].

Six years were, of course, insufficient to alter a tempered tradition and a hardened habit: the settlers had behind them one hundred and seventy years of experience of being masters to black slaves and a near twenty-year sanction of a pass-labour law; besides, the 1809 Proclamation merely endorsed and legalised what had already become current practice[38]. And during the six years spanning the hey-day of the Ordinance's existence (1828-34), the old spirit of the farmers was kept in check but hardly extirpated. For the farmers, mainly Dutch, in response to an 1848 inquiry concerning the Masters and Servants act, called for an extension of the terms of imprisonment for breach of contract by servants as well as physical punishment: the stocks, flogging, solitary confinement and hard labour on the roads; appealed for an extension of the jurisdiction of the Magistrate, the Justice of the Peace and the fieldcornets; favoured a vagrant law empowering constables and fieldcornets to arrest and punish any *coloured person* without a fixed abode on the spot; asked for an extension of the period for labour contracts, which would prevent *coloured persons* living or congregating independent of *Europeans* ; demanded the registration of all *natives* and solicited the creation of a rural police for the suppression of va-

40

grancy[39]. But these sentiments and all that they imply were not exclusive to the Dutch. J.M. Bowker, one of the British settlers' leading spokesmen, in 1844 appealed (in a letter to a British official) for a similar draconian law:

> A vagrant law is much wanted in this colony... The present system which has induced the monthly hirings and knockabout lives of the Hottentots, alike interface with their health, morals and civil improvements. The here-today-and-gone-tomorrow system of Hottentot service, begets a carelessness of the master's property on the one part, and a carelessness of the health, morals and comfort of the servant in the other. Can nothing be done to induce a more permanent systems of labour?[40].

At no time between 1828 and 1853 (when the settlers obtained control of the Cape legislature) did one for the other of the Khoi's white compatriots fail to remind them that their *freedom* was foredoomed. 'How often some of us have already been taunted by being told we have been long enough our own masters', so lamented the Khoi at the missionary station of Theopolis[41]. And as a missionary in June of the same year warned: 'Years must elapse, and perhaps generations, before, the old spirit (of the masters) would be prepared to call it a day'[42]. In dealing with legislation that goes against the force of tradition and prejudice, it should be recognised that legal measures or revolutionary statutes cannot in themselves efface the spirit of the privileged sector of a community that is stubbornly and sometimes perversely apposed to the rights of the underprivileged. As a fieldcornet, Cobus Fourie, told the residents of the Kat River Settlement in January 1851: 'Bear in mind further that Government cannot remove the prejudices against colour and class — on which you lay so much stress'[43]. Legal equality between 1828 and 1842 was restricted and truncated — was, in effect, alienated.

2

When the Khoi question 'ceased to be a question of politics', the Khoi ceased to be the main labour force of the Colony. Ordinance 49 of July 1828, though initially greeted as a mischievous law because settler opinion thought it gave the trans-frontier tribesmen leave to steal in

the Colony[44], was nevertheless instrumental in providing an early alternative to Khoi and slave labour[45]. It (and bear in mind that it was
not applicable to the Khoi) allowed the Xhosa and other tribesmen,
with the issue of passes, to enter the Colony and to contract themselves
to farmers for short intervals[46]. It was no accident that the law was
passed three days before the 50th Ordinance[47]. The Legislative
Council reversed a policy, dating from 1809, of barring the Xhosa from
entering the Colony. This law recognised, to a limited extent, interac-
tion and even co-operation, but its primary purpose was to meet the
labour demands of the colonists by substituting the free movement of
the Khoi with the restricted movement of the Xhosa and other
blacks[48].

The Khoi after 1809 and before 1828 were the Cape's principal
source of cheap labour. After the passing of Ordinance 49 and of Ordinance 2 of 1827 (which, with slight changes, 're-introduced some of
the old provisions of the Pass Law' for the trans-frontier tribesmen)[49], the Khoi lost their former dominance in the labour market.
By providing an alternative labour supply, Ordinance 49 progressively
and effectively cancelled out the rewards of free labour. Philip had
hoped that the Khoi, by selling their labour in the best market, would
prosper and thereby effect the transition from nomads or pure pasto-
ralists or a combination of both to real peasants and veritable farmers[50]. But even before the 50th Ordinance — even before the 1820s
— non-Khoi and non-slave labour was already part of the Colony's
economic system. Tribesmen who had broken away from their communities established a rough and ready clientele relationship with their
farmer masters. The white farmers granted black tribesmen rent-free
land in return for services. These early black labourers made, according to one source, 'very faithful servants' and were (in some respects)
'better' than the Khoi[51].

Later (between 1824 and 1825) some 10,000 Bechuana were brought
into the Colony[52]. Later still, trans-frontier tribesmen, mainly young
men, came to work for the farmers for limited remuneration[53]. The
presence of these early 'migrant' workers, who were not protected by
the provisions of the 50th Ordinance, caused a gradual drop in Khoi
wage levels and a progressive decline in the demand for Khoi labour.

Even more important to the undermining of the economic promise
of the 50th Ordinance was the Sixth Frontier War, and the so-called
liberation of the Mfengu[54]. Ordinance 49 allowed a limited number
of trans-frontier tribesmen to enter the colonial labour market, but now

(at the end of the 1834-35 Frontier War) the Mfengu entered the Colony — with official blessing — in one feel swoop. J.E. Alexander, aide-de-camp to Governor D'Urban during the War, who witnessed the entry of the Mfengu into the Colony, enthused that they were bound to provide what was urgently required: farm labourers, herdsmen and shepherds[55].

Some land was, at first, set aside for the Mfengu in the district of Peddie and later in Victoria East[56]. But this did not prevent these 1835 settlers from moving into the interstices of colonial territory and into the mission stations[57]. They found refuge, notably at Theopolis and, to a limited extent, at Bethelsdorp and at the Government sponsored Kat River Settlement[58]. Others moved into the towns of Uitenhage, Port Elizabeth and Grahamstown[59].

The presence of these new settlers glutted the labour market. An early report from Theopolis, for instance, cited the case of a farmer who habitually employed the Khoi at a rate of 1s 6d a day for seasonal harvest work offering only 1s a day on the premise that he could get all the labour he required by engaging Mfengu at the lower rate[60]. By 1849 the Mfengu had become indispensable to the rural settlers and to town folk of Grahamstown[61]. Over the period 1835-51, the Mfengu effectively replaced the Khoi as workers in the towns, as labourers on the farms and a soldiers in the army[62]. So great was the displacement that the Khoi became openly resentful of Mfengu competition and accused them of usurping their position of favourite *coloured* people of the colonists[63].

Another labour law, Ordinance 3 of 1848, introduced an indentured system of labour where whole families of Xhosa were assigned to unknown employers for unspecified wages[64].

After the frontier wars of the 1840s many Xhosa became landless. They also took refuge in the Colony, swelling the labour market. But of greater import still was the mass cattle-killing of 1857, for in its aftermath a new employment act was passed[65]. This facilitated, mainly for the white farmer, the engagement of huge numbers of labourers willing to work for a pittance. It is estimated that anything between thirty-three and forty thousand Xhosa took service with the colonists by 1858[66]. All of this rendered the Khoi superfluous in the settlers' ever eager need for a plentiful supply of cheap, unprotected and closely controlled labour.

The economic promise, though compromised by the competitiveness of black labour, could still have been kept if the Khoi had been granted a dispensation in land. But apart from the inadequate experiment of the Kat River territory — the enthusiastic way the Khoi moved to this area demonstrated their critical need for extra land[67] — nothing was done to meet Khoi needs in this regard. In 1838 (a decade after the passing of the 50th Ordinance) the Wesleyan missionary, W.B. Boyce noted:

> The fault of the 50th Ordinance, is its *imperfection* as a measure of justice to an injured people . . . This sort of justice cost the Colonial Government noting beyond the trouble of compiling the document so pompously termed 'the charter of Hottentot freedom'. Like all half measures which aim at alleviating symptoms rather than . . . cure it has failed to answer the sanguine expectations of benevolent men, and the reason of this failure is obvious. Hottentots had only one-half of their wrongs redressed; they were restored to liberty and freedom of action, but they were not placed in the possession of land or other property, as some compensation for the whole colony and the numerous flocks taken from their ancestors[68].

Boyce advocated a special enquiry to investigate how much and what lands would be required for the Khoi, as well as how much funds were necessary to purchase such lands, but nothing came of his suggestion. The Khoi were left to fend for themselves.

Even more revealing of the economic promise was Philip's 1845 observation, and lament, that the white colonists were determined to depress the economic and social position of the Khoi[69].

If Ordinance 50 was a bonus bestowed on the Khoi with one hand, Ordinance 49, the *liberation* of the Mfengu and the non-Khoi labour laws of 1837 and 1857, and the failure of land provision was the same bonus retracted with the other.

3

Impoverishment among the Khoi was not uniform, for a few who took to transport riding, metal work and building did prosper[70]. The white settlers, notably those of Grahamstown, who were always complaining about the vagrant and indolent character of the Khoi, detested these prosperous Khoi more than they did the vagrants[71]; and it was these settlers, probably in the early years after the passing of the 50th Ordinance, who wanted their children to be educated not in the missionary schools but in the secular and superior Government-funded English schools[72]. The principle of legal equality meant that these schools were open to all — as indeed the Government insisted they were - but in 1832 the settlers succeeded in preventing the entry of the Khoi children to the Government school of Stellenbosch[73]. Attendance by Coloured children at new Government schools established during the 1840s became increasingly difficult[74]. It is therefore no surprise to learn that these Government schools were by 1861 the exclusive preserve of white children[75].

Flagrant discrimination operated in other areas as well. During the frontier War of 1834-35 Khoi men were called up along with their white compatriots to serve in the commando forces. But once the War was over, the white members of the commando were released, thus allowing them to attend to their ploughing and sowing, while the Khoi members were retained and ordered to build new forts — some were kept on for as many as twelve months[76].

Further, it was the custom to make good the stock losses suffered during frontier clashes by distributing the animals that had been seized from the Xhosa, but the Khoi, though their losses were in proportion every bit as severe as that of their white neighbours, were always the last and the least compensated[77].

In 1845 Philip observed that the enemies of the Khoi within the Colony, having failed to shackle their 80,000 Khoi compatriots with a vagrant act, were surreptitiously using the municipalities to gain power to force the Khoi to live on their lands by preventing them from living in the villages and by denying them the right to use the common lands as grazing fields. Philip feared that if they succeeded, the only freedom left to the Khoi would be in the mission stations[78].

Later, as a result of the Eighth Frontier War, the Khoi suffered such disastrous economic losses that a far smaller number qualified as voters for the Cape legislature. But even those who did qualify faced obstacles, for the law guaranteeing equality was, sometimes, violated in the actual act of voting. How extensive this practice was is uncertain, but a number of Khoi servants who refused or failed to use their vote to back the farmer-master's own choice of candidate were harassed by their employers, while Khoi tenants who failed to back their landlord's choice in an election often faced eviction.

In the 1840s, with the governorship of Henry Pottinger and Harry Smith, and with the London Missionary Society's representation by

William Elliot, sympathy for the Khoi among the governing authorities and the missionaries was reversed[79]. Harry Smith appointed Bowker, Godlonton, S. Southey, J.C. Chase and other like-minded enemies of the Khoi to key administrative positions[80], and urged the Legislative Council to consider the passing of a vagrant act[81]. Elliot, the missionary who blandly announced that colonial law protected the black man as well as the white, referred (in 1848) to large masses of *paupers* with little motive for industry crowding together at Bethelsdorp and other institutions[82].

In many respects the situation of the Khoi was even worse than it had been prior to 1828, for in the earlier period the Colonial Government was at least willing to consider their grievances and the missionaries were active in their defence. By 1850, the legal, economic and political prospects of the Khoi were anything but promising.

4

The legal, economic and political predicament of the Khoi in this new situation is illustrated by the fate of the Kat River Settlement. The Settlement was created in 1829, on land that was newly annexed from the Xhosa. Annexation of course, made it the most advanced settlement of the Colony, and consequently the most militarily exposed. The primary motive for this creation was to prevent the expulsed Xhosa from re-inhabiting; that is, reclaiming the disputed area. Actually it was a cost-effective way of replacing the troops that otherwise would have been required to man the border. The Settlement (according to the important testimonies of Governor Cole, Chief Justice Wylde, Judge Menzies, Dr J.R. Innes and George Napier) thrived[83]. But the Sixth Frontier War sharply interrupted its progress. Its inhabitants had to repair to a refuge post and, during their absence, many lost their homes, stock and crops. Many also, as indicated, had to serve on military command for an unfairly long period and many did not receive the cattle reparation that was promised.

Economic recovery was slow and made worse because Khoi farmers could not, like their white counterparts, obtain credit. During an auction of captured live stock, for instance, white farmers were allowed several months credit; the Khoi could bid only if they paid in cash[84].

If the problem of obtaining credit was bad, the problem of overcrowding was worse. In 1842 the Settlement had a population of 4,876;

in 1845 it rose to 5,300 and in 1849 near to 6,000. The Colonial Government used Kat River as a dumping ground; the Mfengu were allowed to live there and so were other Khoi groups that had been dispossessed elsewhere in the Colony. Even ex-slaves by 1838 sought out the Settlement as a place of refuge[85]. Furthermore, since the granting of land was part of the patronage system of government, land was alienated from the Settlement and granted to officials and supporters of the reigning governor[86]. The Khoi protested against such appropriation, petitioned for more land and called for the removal of the Mfengu but the Government ignored their protests and turned a deaf ear to their pleas.

The Seventh Frontier War, as the previous war, interrupted and cancelled the recovery of the settlement, but this time the losses were particularly onerous. Once again the Government showed no sympathy for the plight of its inhabitants. New and burdensome taxation was imposed on some of the property and on wood cutting. This angered the Khoi because the taxation was iniquitous in itself and also because it came so soon after the heavy war losses. Further vexation came with the successive appointments of Biddulph and Bowker as resident magistrates of the Settlement. Both men were notorious for their anti-Khoi views(87).

When the Victoria District was annexed in 1847, the Cape frontier pushed up to the Keiskamma. This effaced the Settlement's status as a buffer zone(88). The strategic change meant that the chances of it being preserved as a Khoi settlement diminished, and its attractiveness for the new British farmers correspondingly increased - it had always been luscious and fertile, now it was safe.

George Christie, Philip's son-in-law, made a tour of the Khoi stations in 1849. He sent the Directors of the London Missionary Society a long report (20 March 1850) detailing the fortunes of the Khoi. His principal conclusion was that the *coloured* people, in recent years, had a profound and grievous impression that the Government was unwilling to heed their claims, to do them justice or to preserve their freedom(89).

When the Eighth Frontier War broke out in 1851, a number of Kat River residents rebelled and joined the Xhosa. During the rebellion James Read, junior and W.R. Thomson, the missionary of the Glasgow Missionary Society, and some other members of the Kat River Loyal Burgher Association hurried to one of the rebel strongholds and pleaded with those present not to take up arms against the Queen. Uithaalder, one of the Khoi leaders, stressing that they were not against the Queen, addressed these revealing words to Thomson:

> Sir, you and Mr Read were both young when you came among us, and you are now both old, and klein Mynheer (young Mr. Read) had no beard when he came to Kat River, and he is now getting advanced in years, and yet these oppressions won't cease. The Missionaries have for years written, and their writings won't help. We are now going to stand up for our own affairs. We shall show the settlers that we too are men(90).

When the rebellion actually occurred, its suppression was pitiless. Though no more than a fourth of the men joined the rebel cause no distinction was made between loyalists and rebels; and, sometimes, no distinction was made between men, women and children[91]. Damage to property was notably wanton: schools, churches and houses were singled out for destruction by fire[92]. After the rebellion, property belonging to those who had remained loyal was indiscriminately confiscated and sold[93].

If the colonists, before the rebellion, had accepted that they enjoyed no legal privilege over their Khoi compatriots, after the rebellion, they scattered that acceptance to the winds. Shortly after the War the Settlement was demolished[94]. By 1853 most of the land was owned by colonists and most of the Settlement's inhabitants were either dispersed or coerced into labour service[95]. The attitude of the settlers - the Khoi's fellow citizens — before, during and after the rebellion negated the claim to *equal treatment*.

Philip went to his grave with the knowledge that his aspiration for an upwardly mobile Khoi population had been a dream[96]. He had never set much store by an independent colonial assembly where power was concentrated in the hands of the settlers[97]; nor, for that matter, did the Khoi — for they feared this as much as they did a vagrant law[98] - but by 1853 such an assembly was a fact. The legal, economic and the political promise of the Khoi's charter of liberties never materialised. The 50th Ordinance was promise — certainly; but practice — in the way Theal, Macmillan or Susan Newton-King envisaged it — never.

3 WAS DR JOHN PHILIP AN ADVOCATE OF 'SEGREGATION'?

He would have done well to remember that the word segregation as South Africans used it had many different meanings.

W.K. Hancock[1]

Dr John Philip[2], as every South African schoolboy knows, was notorious for entertaining fancy ideas about black and white equality. Indeed, it has been claimed that he represented the antithesis of those who believed in the inherent and fixed inferiority of the black races[3]. The early settlers, Philip's contemporaries, were, however, firmly convinced that there was an unbridgeable gap — whether it was religious, racial or cultural — which made it impossible for relations between black and white to be regular, formal or conventional. In 1799, Courage, a Khoi, wanted Dr J.T. van der Kemp — a pre-Philip champion of black rights — to confirm that God created the Khoi, the whites as well as the beasts of the field; for the Dutch farmers, he complained, baited them with the idea that God neither created nor took any notice of them[4]. In 1845 a Swellendam housewife asserted to J. Kretzen, an itinerant missionary, 'but the Bible does state that this people (the Khoi) must serve us'[5].

These convictions might have been inspired by Biblical comparison, ignorance caused by frontier isolation, Middle Ages European beliefs about colour and savagery[6], economic egoism or a combination of some or all of these separate phenomena. The conviction itself, however, was uniform[7]. Later when theorists, advocates and apologists of what was first called *segregation* and then *apartheid* came to make their case they would stress, over and over again, the importance of the fundamental difference between white and black, as if that difference was one not of degree but of kind[8]. F.W. Bell, an early advocate of segregation, was convinced that 'Nature does not mix up swarms of black and white ants. Different kinds go separately'[9]. J.C. Smuts claimed that 'soul' as well as colour separated white from black[10]. J.B.M. Hertzog believed there was no injustice done by according sheep and cattle different grazing grounds[11]. H.F. Verwoerd, during his term as Minister of Native Affairs (1950-58), told a Native Advisory Board: 'The lion and the elephant can live, but they live better apart'[12].

Belief that there was an unbridgeable gap between black and white was not one of Philip's convictions. Theal, for instance, stressed that Philip 'laid down a theory that the coloured races, were in all respects except education mentally equal to the European colonists'[13]. G.E.G. Schutte (in an M.A. dissertation) also supported this view, arguing that Philip claimed 'complete social equality between white and black'[14]. C.F. Kotzé, an orthodox Afrikaner historian, as late as 1975 also emphasized — as pre-1920s South African historiography had done — that Philip was out 'to achieve equality between Whites and non-Whites'[15]. Indeed, Philip is himself on record as stating: 'So far as my observation extends, it appears to me that the natural capacity of the African is nothing inferior to that of the European'[16]. His view on black and white equality is also apparent in a reference to the Rharhabe Chief, Maqoma:

> In treating with such a man, we have nothing to do with his being black, or living chiefly on milk, or wrapping himself in an ox's hide. He is a man of ability and sound sense, and the undoubted legitimate prince of a nation. As such he should be met and spoken with by the governor of the colony, or his proper representatives, on a footing of equality[17].

Yet in the 1920s W.M. Macmillan announced that Philip was an early advocate of 'segregation'. More specifically, he said at a 1923 conference organised by the Dutch Reformed Church: 'That if it was segregation they believed in — separation of the races — their much abused Dr Philip had advocated a system of separation when it was still just possible'[18]. Four years later, he went even further when he declared: 'So far from desiring a sudden and indiscriminate mixing of the races, Dr Philip, it will be found, was the first and greatest *segregationist*'[19].

1

A whole line of writers followed where Macmillan led. In 1928, a year after *The Cape Colour Question* was published, E.A. Walker wrote that

50

Philip was 'a convinced segregationist'[20]. Five years later, A.F. Hattersley opined that Philip's policy was 'one of segregation'[21]. Four years after Hattersley, D.K. Clinton claimed that Philip was 'a convinced segregationist'[22]. Two years after Clinton, R.F.A. Hoernlé declared that Philip 'was one of the earliest advocates of *territorial segregation*'[23]. In 1972, thirty-two years after Hoernlé, J.G. Pretorius argued that Philip favoured 'territorial segregation with a view to protecting one group of the population from the other'[24].

Could a person who evidently made no fundamental distinction between white and black espouse a policy of segregation? Even assuming he did discriminate between the races, Philip argued that the notion that all the nations of the earth had been created of one blood was more simple, beautiful and harmonious than that which vaunted different origins, for this emphasis on differences gave rise to invidious distinctions that encouraged pride and excused oppression[25]. Is it possible, then, that such a person really championed a programme which, in theory at least, is based on the premise that there is — a fixed and fated divide (whether it is race, culture or colour) between black and white? There is clearly a contradiction here, especially in the light of the observation that 'the Christian missionary and the political revolutionist start from the same proposition of the equality of man'[26].

The problem, quite obviously, is one of definition. What did the advocates of segregation between 1923 and 1927 (when Macmillan pronounced Philip a 'segregationist') mean by the term *segregation*? And what was there in the body of Philip's policy proposals that led Macmillan to refer to him as an advocate of 'segregation'?

2

The colonists who left the Cape in the 1830s set up various republics in Natal and in the future territories of the Orange Free State and the Transvaal. Their governing institutions were democratic but racially exclusive[27]. The Transvaal (South African Republic) Grondwet of 1858, for instance, frankly stated that there was to be *geen gelijkstelling van gekleurden met blanke ingezetenen toestaan, noch in Kerk noch in Staat* (no equality between white and coloured inhabitants either in Church or State)[28].

When Natal, which became a British colony in 1843, was granted a legislative council in 1856, provision was made for twelve elected members. The right to vote for such a council was open to all British subjects irrespective of race. Nine years later the same Council passed Natal Law No 11 of 1856, which disqualified most Africans from exercising the franchise and which introduced, not in the letter but in the spirit, and certainly in practice, a racial franchise[29]. Later, when Natal was granted responsible government, a similar law to that of 1856 was passed in 1896 which deprived Indians (without mentioning the term 'Indians') of the franchise[30].

In the Cape, the Colony's Legislative Council in 1836 created municipal boards in towns and villages that provided for a colour-bar-free franchise. Cape Town even had a Coloured wardmaster[31]. But even in the liberal Cape, the argument favouring a racial franchise was topical. When in the 1840s the mainly British settlers sought local autonomy, their franchise proposal was decidedly narrow and exclusive. The vote, they argued, should be the preserve of the Dutch and British inhabitants, for none of the natives of the Colony were intellectually equipped to understand or appreciate its significance; and even if the vote was granted them, they would neither care for it nor value it[32].

During the greater part of the second half of the nineteenth century, though the problem of representation was present and changing in the four territorial entities that were eventually to form the Union of South Africa, it was for all that a secondary urgency. The dominant position of Europe in the world seemed assured, while British imperial forces guaranteed security in the Cape and Natal. Matters were slightly different in the two Trekker Republics — notably in the Transvaal, where the white farmers' conquest was neither uniform nor, until well towards the end of the nineteenth century, uncontested[33]. It was effectively in the first decade of the twentieth century when the four separate parts of South Africa were drawn into a unitary state that the problem of reconciling the democratic principle with the reality of a multi-racial community became truly imperative. Segregation was a political answer to a political problem[34].

3

The various leaders of the Cape, Natal, the Transvaal and the Orange Free State who had hitherto experienced the problem of black and white relations locally had now — with the advent of Union — to come to terms with it nationally. J.C. Smuts had anticipated the problem prior to the Anglo-Boer War, for he stated in October 1895 that the democratic theory of Europe and America was 'inapplicable' to the native races of South Africa, and that it was essential to recognise this truth if any progress was to be made in regard to the Native question[35].

The crucial problem on the eve of the Union was which model was to prevail: the Cape, with its ostensibly non-racial electoral system or the Natal (Orange Free State and Transvaal), with its undisguised racial franchise. That this was the nub of the problem, politically, is patently clear from the discussions that occurred in the National Convention meetings over the question of the franchise. Colonel Stanford (the Cape representative), for instance, argued that the crux of the entire 'Native question' was the franchise, and he urged the Convention to grant the Africans citizenship[36]. J.W. Sauer (also from the Cape) stood out against a differential franchise and pleaded for political equality[37]. Other Cape representatives — J.W. Jagger, F.S. Malan, T.W. Smartt and E.H. Walton — argued in similar vein[38]. The delegates from Natal, the Orange Free State and the Transvaal, however, were dead set against the 'principle' of a non-racial franchise. J.B.M. Hertzog (from the Orange Free State) admitted that he was smitten with anxiety at the potential danger of a constant demand to lower the qualification until the 'native' voter would be in a position to swamp the 'European'[39].

To accept the Cape non-racial franchise whatever its shortcomings was to accept the multi-racial reality of South Africa. This is something white opinion, generally, and white leaders, particularly, could not then (and cannot now) get to grips with.

The coming of age of the mining and farming industries meant there was a greater urgency to bring the African labour force under tighter control. Economics, undoubtedly, was tied up with politics, but the legatees of European colonialism with their military, administrative and economic power sensed their feeble numbers and felt, moreover, an emotional vulnerability. Smuts, for instance, in 1902, gave utterance to this fear — in a slightly different context — when he warned that the exceptional condition of a small white community in the midst of a very large and rapidly increasing black community had created a special code of morality: the whites in their disputes must on no account appeal to the blacks for assistance. This agreement was essential he insisted, if the whites were to continue as the ruling class in South Africa

53

— otherwise the blacks would become arbiters and, in time, the predominating political force[40].

If the democratic principle were adhered to, it followed that in time the exclusive hold of political power, which allowed the legatees of European colonialism a disproportionate share of the country's wealth and resources, would be compromised. Hertzog, in 1929, said:

> In the doctrine of Franchise equality for Black and White, every true South African sees, and rightly so, the existence of his people endangered and threatened, the end of the White man in South Africa . . . unless the Native vote be separated from that of the White man, the Cape Native vote will be the cause of the greatest tragedy in the history of South Africa[41].

It would be a mistake to believe that Hertzog's blunt words were unique to post-Union South Africa and exclusive to Afrikaner nationalism. Lionel Phillips, an English-born South African mining magnate, formulated, in essentials, the same idea as early as 1902 when he suggested that given that black and white could not rule jointly in South Africa, no white person with a knowledge of the subject should hesitate in answering who *should* rule. The numerical superiority of blacks over whites meant that equal voting rights would result in government by the blacks, he said. And if universal suffrage were adhered to, no device, educational or economic, could in the long run avert black rule. Lionel Phillips was more consistent than Hertzog, for he went on to state that if the threat of black rule was to be averted the only way around the problem was to declare the blacks 'a subject race'[42].

4

Whether it was Theophilus Shepstone or James Stuart or Heathen Nichols in Natal[43] , C.J. Rhodes or James Rose Innes in the Cape[44], or Lionel Curtis or Lionel Phillips in the Transvaal[45] who formulated the idea of 'territorial segregation'; whether it was done to 'undermine the African peasantry and to stop the emergence of an African elite'[46], or to ensure the Africans a system of parallel government, or to create a reserve where so-called 'surplus' Africans could be consigned, or to preserve and protect tribal culture from being contaminated by European culture[47] — the point is that 'segregation' was designed to exclude the Africans from the organs of power. Smuts admitted as much in 1917 when he pointed out that South Africa was not yet a white man's country — and noted that there were sensible people who did not think it could be made into a white man's country — but he insisted that an attempt was going to be made to make it one, and that instead of mixing up black and white they were going to keep them apart as far as was possible in *government*. The attempt, he admitted, might take hundreds of years to achieve, but it could in the end solve the 'native problem'[48].

Removing the Africans from the political process ensured that the Africans would not only cease to be a political threat but would also be a source of unprotected and therefore underpaid labour[49]. For both African and European leaders, the key issue of the day was African political representation[50]. E.H. Brookes commented in 1927 that it was difficult to envisage the franchise system of the Cape obtaining majority approval from the European electorate, for the whites were aware that this question of the franchise was relevant for both the present and the future and that what today might appear as a mere act of justice would in the future, whether good or bad, inevitably produce a black majority[51].

Segregation in the 1920s meant denying Africans the right to be fellow members of the South African commonwealth; it meant a denial of a multi-racial South Africa; it meant undoing what history had already done; it meant an attempt to untwist in theory what had already been twisted in practice; it meant, therefore, a denial of fundamental rights in places where the Africans worked and where many were born, bred and buried — it meant, in essentials, defining the status of the Africans exclusively as workers and never as citizens. Political differentiation in every community has always been a means by which a particular section of the citizenry retains for itself a disproportionate amount of the social and economic bounty[52]. In South Africa this particular form of politics took on the guise of segregation.

5

Two basic policies determined Philip's view of black and white relations. Both policies were fixed, it bears noting, to (what Macmillan termed) Philip's 'profound belief in the potential equality of the races'[53]. First, there was the problem within the confines of the Cape Colony: how were relations to be ordered between settlers and, most notably, the Khoi? And second, how were *border* relations to be ordered between the settlers (especially before the Trek movement of the late 1830s) and the trans-Colonial tribesmen?

As far as the Khoi within the Colony were concerned, Philip advocated total, legal equality:

> We ask for no new laws: we simply ask that the colonists, and the different classes of the natives, should have the same civil rights granted to them. The liberty we ask is not an exception from the law, but its protection; and the law grants no rights to the colonists which it may not extend with perfect safety to all classes in the colony. Denial of such a request cannot be justified[54].

And when he was asked to state his case on behalf of the Khoi, in a single sentence he replied (as indicated already) that all he required was for them to bring their labour to a fair market[55]. In a letter to T.F. Buxton (1 July 1828) he broadened his plea, stating that what was required not only for the Khoi but also for the indigene was the liberty to bring their labour to the best market[56].

Philip defended the existence of the missionary institutions because he believed they afforded the Khoi, under the prevailing adverse conditions, a limited space of freedom and security[57]. His call for their continuing existence, it might thus be (and has been) argued, was his way of advocating a policy of segregation[58]; but Philip, as early as 1824, discounted the eventuality of such an interpretation by declaring that he hoped Khoi institutions would be unknown in the Colony, that the power of division would be broken and that all the inhabitants would be blended into 'one community'[59].

Furthermore, when a section of the Cape's white population (including Philip's son-in-law, John Fairbairn) appealed to London for self-government, Philip opposed the constitutional change, arguing:

> The influential people among our Colonists have but one idea of liberty, and that is the liberty of oppressing all beneath them: and till they are more enlightened and liberal on this subject, I must deprecate a legislative assembly as one of greatest curses that could come upon the country[60].

Philip's Khoi policies and his internal Cape policies cannot, therefore, be justly described as segregationist.

6

Philip's other basic policy was addressed to what he called: 'Colonial policy' or 'the aboriginal tribes living on or near our borders' or 'our frontier affairs' or 'the tribes beyond the frontiers of our colonies'[61] in sum, to the Colony's foreign affairs.

His basic policy, in this instance, was to prevent the white settlers, the subjects of the Colony, from encroaching on and taking over piece-meal and wholesale black tribal territory. He was aware that the farmers paid scant honour to the indigenes' right to possess and own land. He quotes a Dutch farmer who, on being asked where the northern boundary of the Colony was, replied: 'We colonists are not nice in these matters: all is colony to us where we can find a good spring of water, and pasturage for our cattle'[62]. The British settlers with their racist, survival-of-the-fittest doctrine were no better, or perhaps even worse in their attitudes than were the Dutch farmers[63]. J.M. Bowker, who expressed the sentiments of many of these recent settlers, compared the Xhosa to springboks: there was a time when the plains of the Cape were covered with springboks, they disappeared and no one regretted it because they were replaced by marino sheep, whose fleeces provided employment for thousands. Were not the sheep, he asked, better than the springbok[64]?

Philip, looking at the past record of colonial expansion made at the expense of the Khoi, then of the San and then of the Xhosa, warned in 1828 with remarkable prescience:

We shall proceed, if the present system is continued, till having treated all . . . − the tribes as some of them have been dealt with, we come to fix the boundary of the colony at Delgoa Bay, and then we shall order out our commandoes against the inhabitants of Mozambique[65].

The farmers, at certain seasons of the year, had taken to the habit of leaving the Colony with their sizable stock of sheep and cattle. They argued that they entered extra-colonial territory only in bad seasons and only temporarily. Philip pointed out that these were bad seasons for

57

the Xhosa as well. And a rough calculation (fifteen hundred farmers each with at least a thousand animals) revealed that a maximum of one and a half million cattle, sheep, goats and horses invaded Xhosa territory. Such an invasion denuded the pasture and left the tribesmen in a state of utter destitution. This process, Philip argued, was 'cruel robbery' which brought in its wake 'starvation and death'. The Dutch farmers complain, he observed, that their cattle are lifted by the tribes 'beyond the boundary', yet when they received their land from the government they were aware of its soil and climate, aware that it was subject to drought and aware of the number of sheep and cattle it could carry. In spite of this, they overstocked their land and made no provision for extra grazing land within the Colony because this would have made for additional expenses. And it was this sheer avarice, he said, which made for the invasion and resulted in robbery and murder. The authorities argued that the state of the country was such that the movement of the farmers could not be effectively controlled. But, Philip countered, if this was so then means must be found to stop the evil. And the British Government should not condone the theft, destruction and 'invasion of peaceable countries' and the dispossession of entire tribes of fellow men[66].

Philip argued that friendly relations could be achieved very rapidly if proper agents were appointed to prevent farmers from illegally entering Xhosa territory. He made a final plea for a change in colonial policy; arguing that peace would be impossible if the farmers were not restricted to the Colony and if a permanent stop was not made to the encroachment of the territory belonging to the Xhosa[67].

Later when his various pleas fell on deaf ears, he would — as a second-best solution declare that he did not mind the territory of the Xhosa and the other indigene becoming part of the Colony, provided the inhabitants of these territories had their land secured to them — what he opposed and objected to was dispossession[68].

Once the Trek movement got underway, fear of dispossession and knowledge that the British Government did not want (for mainly financial reasons) to extend the area of its control led Philip to advocate a series of treaty states with the Griqua Chiefs, Kok and Waterboer, and with the Sotho Chief, Moshweshwe. Here again it might be argued that in trying to make these Chiefs vassals of the British Government he was, in effect, fashioning a sort of reserve system — an early version of the Bantustans. But was this so? In referring to the treaty with Kok, Philip pointed out that it would educate the Trekkers to respect the

Chief's authority, prevent them from attacking him and demonstrate that he had the protection of the British Government[69]. But in this instance, too, his concern was to avert dispossession.

There was not only a near-century divide between the policies of Philip and the policy of segregation, but also a world of difference between respective circumstances, necessities, ideas, aims, fears and inspirations. It should not be forgotten that 'circumstances are also facts'[70]. But the fact of circumstances, in Philip's case, was ignored. Philip did not for a single moment contemplate the withholding of political power and the discriminatory allocation of territory to a multiracial community that was essentially one. His call to halt settler expansion — settler-land grabbing — was to preserve not so much a political system or a political advantage, but the lands that the various African tribes effectively possessed and which were indispensable for their sustenance, their evangelisation and their progress. The promiscuous entry of the settlers on the tribal lands would, he feared in a matter of time, leave the tribesmen destitute of land and defunct of stock. What motivated Philip was the consternation of a well-armed minority dispossessing an ill-armed majority; not the fear of the majority principle inherent in democratic government[71].

7

Macmillan was the first and the last historian to work with the Philip Papers. Descendants of Philip sent the entire collection to him in 1920. Eleven years later, in December 1931, the total collection was consumed in a fire that gutted part of the University of the Witwatersrand's library[72]. After years of work with the Papers, Macmillan must have been in a position to know what he was talking about when he claimed that Philip was the first to espouse a policy of 'segregation'. How then is the contradiction between the reality of Philip's policies and the reality of segregation in the 1920s, and the claim on the part of Macmillan (and many others) that Philip was a segregationist, to be explained?

Macmillan, as the autobiographical passage shows ('if it was segregation they believed in . . . Philip had advocated a system of separation when it was still just possible'), made no distinction between *separation* and *segregation*[73]. It could be claimed that Philip was for separation by construing his policies as one of keeping settlers and indigene apart by an intervening space or barrier — by a policed border. But separation was never a matter of segregation — was never a matter of separating, of removing, of amputating a class of persons from the general body on the basis of some principle, dubious or otherwise. There was no question of trying to separate the yolk from an egg that had already been scrambled.

> We are living together with the Europeans and our interests are interwoven with theirs, we see no necessity for having them separated. Your scheme would work if we Natives were living in our own territory all by ourselves where no Europeans, and where nothing is in common between the Native and the European[74].

The African author, revealing a sensitivity to the divide between separation and segregation, and writing in 1927, draws a distinction that indicates what Philip was attempting and what the segregationists were intending. And since it is important to distinguish clearly between separation and segregation, it is appropriate to refer to a more recent passage where the distinction between the concepts is drawn with greater precision:

> Separation must not be confused with segregation, for the former entails a voluntary agreement between all groups resulting in separate self-governing societies which co-operate on the basis of mutual respect for one another's independence, whereas the latter, though it might be territorially based, is imposed by one group on another in order to maintain its supremacy[75].

When a settler community takes over territory (whether peacefully or violently) from an indigene community numerically superior to itself and physically, culturally and linguistically different from itself, it denies, for political purpose and, above all, for economic advantage, the dispossessed community the right to take part in the decision-making process; that is, in the governmental structure it establishes on the begotten territory[76]. This constitutes one of the fundamentals of a segregationist situation. Philip argued for a policy that prevented the dispossession which constrained and necessitated the naissance of an anti-democratic policy — a policy of segregation. This is the meaning of *his* separation; and it is probably what Macmillan meant when he claimed that Philip had 'advocated a system of separation when it was still possible'.

Macmillan regarded exclusive black territoriality as being equivalent to segregation, but when exclusiveness was compromised by white encroachment, he tended to see this as intermixture[77]. In his understanding the African tribesmen, before 1779 and the advent of the Cape frontier wars, were segregated; to Philip's understanding they were neither segregated nor separated but merely and justly sovereign. It is an elementary point but Macmillan (and many others after him) failed to realize that segregation necessarily embodies separation but separation does not necessarily embody segregation.

8

Walker, Hattersley, Clinton, Hoernlé, Pretorius, Lewin and Marquand all unhesitatingly associated the concept of segregation with Philip because Macmillan, who after all was *the* authority on Philip, had said Philip was a segregationist. Incontrovertible evidence indicates that Macmillan made up his mind about Philip's 'segregation' not after examining the Philip Papers but before. In a letter he wrote to J.X. Merriman on 20 May 1920, he stated:

> I have the prospect of being trusted with a task in which I know you will be interested. We have all known that there has been a collection of Dr. John Philip's papers in the hands of his family . . . The great-grandson has the papers and . . . is going to send them onto me, the Family apparently trusting me to tell the truth with some sort of appreciation of the fact that the missionaries may have had a point of view . . . After all even the Philips were striving in a manner after the favourite 'solution' of this moment, 'segregation' at a time when it was more possible[78].

In the light of this, it would seem that Macmillan too hastily drew straight lines of connection between the 1830s and the 1920s. As a recent study observes: Macmillan's 'working criterion was not Philip but the South Africa of the inter-war years'[79].

History is first and foremost a discipline of context. The problem and the personality have to be seen integral with time and place. A historian tries to ensure that every important statement is studied in its specific context of time, place and circumstance. Macmillan, it is fair to state, neglected this essential and elementary precaution and transferred a modern thought to an alien age; for the doctrine of segregation was a product not of the last century but of this century and, likely as not, had its origin in the decade spanning the Anglo-Boer War and the creation of the Union[80].

When Philip formulated his ideas about frontier relations in 1832[81], European colonialism was confined to the Cape and had reached no farther than the Fish River. Beyond that contested boundary (in the Eastern Cape and in what, in time, would constitute Natal, the Transvaal and the Orange Free State), land was in the possession of the various African tribes — was, in effect, exclusively black[82].

Philip himself never used either the term 'segregation' or the term 'separation'[83]. It is, of course, wholly acceptable to use a modern concept like segregation and to apply it to an age where it was unknown, so long as pains are taken to delineate and to define it patiently and properly. As C.H. Hill sagaciously observed: 'I see no objection to using a later term of analysis like *class* even if contemporaries did not use it: provided we define clearly what we mean'[84]. A failure to do so merely leads to confusion and unnecessary muddle.

9

To understand the meaning of someone's statement, advice, proposition or appeal, it is not enough to scrutinise only the spoken or written account of what he said, even though he might have written and spoken with utter sincerity and complete command of language. To fathom his meaning, it is also necessary to determine the question that his statement, spoken or written, was meant to answer[85]. Philip tried to secure the lands of the African tribesmen — lands that they effectively possessed and that they physically inhabited — and tried to stave off the settler advance into these territories because he feared that the settlers' superior military prowess would lead to tribal dispossession. Hertzog and the other segregationists tried to ensure (within the South African nation and state) the continued white monopoly of political, economic and military power by denying black South Africans the rights of co-citizenship[86]. The contrast in these opposing aims is brought out clearly in a significant passage written in 1901 an important date because it was before Union and before the 1920s when 'segregation' had become topical:

What are the rights of the natives, and by what methods should you deal with them? Can a coloured man be educated and disciplined sufficiently to be dealt with on terms of legal equality at least, or must he be treated as one whose evidence and whose engagements are worth nothing, who must be disciplined as the beast of the field is disciplined? On this question the voice of the missionaries was clear, and it found its most powerful expression in the work of Dr John Philip . . . He can be educated and disciplined, that able and energetic advocate of the black man pleaded, and therefore the sooner you begin to treat him as a human being whose rights are sacred, the better[87].

There was a great deal of imprecision concerning the term 'segregation' in the 1920s. W.H. Dawson, a British writer and academic who visited South Africa in the early 1920s and reported on its people, places and problems, observed that the adoption of the word 'segregation' was regrettable, for it was vague and invited confusion. He also observed the careless way politicians used it, and noted that Hertzog himself had formerly used the word in a very loose way[88]. Macmillan might have been led astray by that general confusion and he might also have been unduly influenced by Smuts, who deliberately used the word 'separation' when he meant 'segregation' merely to distance his official stance from that of his rival, Hertzog[89]. Macmillan also had reservations about black and white equality: he judged Philip's views as being on occasions exceptional and extreme[90]. Whatever the case, there was undoubtedly confusion in Macmillan's mind over this matter of segregation; for, some time between 1936 and 1938, he claimed that the 'doctrine of *segregation* was born almost simultaneously with the Trekker Republics'[91].

His statement, to some extent, is given credence by F.C. Scheepers, a Trekker spokesman, who told a Native Commission in 1852:

One of the reasons which led to the emigration from the Cape Colony was that black and white were subject to the same laws . . . I do not think that the same law will restrain a savage man which will restrain a white man. I think it would be just and good that if a Kafir refuses to work, the law should be that he is to leave the country . . . I am of opinion that white and black cannot live together in peace in the same country unless the black man is in a state of subjection to the white . . . In my opinion, if a line were drawn defining the country inhabited by whites, I would have all the blacks removed beyond the line except those who would remain as servants to the whites[92].

Since the Transvaal and the Orange Free State Republics came into existence in 1852 and 1854 respectively, and since Philip died in 1851, it must be concluded — if Macmillan's statement that segregation was born with the Trekker Republics be credible — that Philip had after all nothing to do with segregation.

4 WAS HINTSA KILLED OR EXECUTED?

> I have dared to trust that The Almighty has chosen me as the instrument of his divine will, as the avenger of the atrocities of savages upon His Christian people.

Colonel Harry Smith[1]

During the sixth of the nine frontier wars (1834-35), Hintsa — the king of the Xhosa — was killed. The ama-Rharhabe had established themselves in the Ciskei and were in immediate contact with the Dutch and British settlers. The ama-Gcaleka, the other branch of the Xhosa nation which was under the direct chieftainship of Hintsa, were established in the areas east of the Kei River. In theory Hintsa was the titular head of all the Xhosa, their paramount Chief, but in practice his authority over his compatriot Rharhabe Chiefs, Maqoma, Tyhali and others, was limited and largely symbolic.

When war broke out in December 1834, it was essentially between the settlers and the ama-Rharhabe. But Hintsa, so the Cape authorities believed, was consulted by the Rharhabe and had, apparently, approved their intended actions. There is no doubt that some of his councillors and sub-chiefs did express solidarity with their Rharhabe compatriots and some (about five hundred) did actually take part in the hostilities; but then, so did some of the followers of Chief Phato (the Gqunukhwebe), who had openly sided with the settlers. It is probably fair to say that Hintsa was generally anxious to keep his relations with the Colony on a sound and friendly footing. When war broke out he adopted, officially, a policy of neutrality. On the other hand, cattle seized on the colonial side were passed when the Rharhabe were forced to retreat — through Gcaleka territory, but this was hardly Hintsa's fault.

However, Colonel Harry Smith, the *Graham's Town Journal*, Governor Sir Benjamin D'Urban and the Wesleyan missionary (in Gcalekaland), John Ayliff[2] — were all convinced that Hintsa was the primary instigator and the principal culprit for both the design and the outbreak of the war. Indeed, D'Urban was convinced of this as early as January 1835. Accordingly, Gcalekaland was invaded on 14 April

1835. A few days later, a mailcoach driver who had strayed from the convoy was killed. The Governor, the Colonel and colonial opinion held Hintsa responsible. They even held the Chief responsible for the death of a trader who had been killed almost a year earlier. War against the Gcaleka was officially declared on 24 April, ten days after the invasion.

Hintsa, sensing that the meeting with D'Urban was inevitable, hesitated about venturing into the British camp and sent envoys, but D'Urban insisted on the Chief's personal appearance. On Wednesday, 29 April 1835, the ama-Gcaleka Chief — under D'Urban's personal guarantee of safety — made his way with an escort of twenty to the British camp[3]. The Chief and his men, seated on sheep and buck-skin saddles, rode in on long-tailed steeds. They were armed with assegais and wore leopard-skin garments and bull's hide mantles: they entered looking 'like figures on a Grecian frieze'[4]. Fourteen days later the Chief took leave of the British in the form of a mutilated corpse.

1

During the fateful fourteen days with the British force, Hintsa was, according to most accounts, well received, showered with gifts[5] and informed of the peace conditions which he ratified but failed (in the stipulated period) to fulfil. He excused this dereliction by arguing that he was not present to encourage the payment of the cattle and the horses, and urged Colonel Smith to allow him to personally supervise the recovery of the reparations. But this (as it turned out) was a ploy to lead the Colonel's patrol into an ambush and so escape. His faithless plan back-fired and he was — without being recognised — killed in self-defence. This version of the story, which exonerates Colonel Smith and the Colonial forces and inculpates the victim, was put down in writing for the first time on the sixth day after the killing[6]. This account of the incident is, in essentials, repeated by R. Godlonton in 1836, by J. Alexander in 1837, by Theal between 1878 and 1926, by Cory in 1919 and by Walker between 1926 and 1928[7].

This traditional version did not, for all that, go unchallenged. Dr A.G. Campbell of Grahamstown[8], in a letter to *The South African Commercial Advertiser* (19 June 1835), charged that Hintsa had been cold-bloodedly killed and cynically mutilated. The Doctor's intelligence reached London through the London Missionary Society and came, eventually, to the notice of Lord Glenelg, the Colonial Secretary[9].

When Lord Glenelg sent his despatch of December 1835 (one of the capital documents of South African history) to D'Urban, he censured the Governor's policy and raised, in passing, queries about Hintsa's death. He wondered if the chief was justly detained and if his death was necessary even if he was trying to get away from the detachment that was accompanying him. But he admitted this was a relatively minor concern, and that what worried him more was that the Chief was slain when he was incapable of resisting — when he was wounded and trying to hide from his pursuers. The Colonial Secretary further observed that evidence difficult to ignore suggested that the Chief had asked for mercy, that two Khoi soldiers heeded his plea but that a certain Southey ignored it, shot the Chief and then mutilated his dead body. He concluded:

> I express no opinion on this subject, but advert to it because the honour of the British name demands that the case should undergo a full investigation, which it is my purpose to institute[10].

A military court of inquiry (not a legal tribunal — witnesses could, if they so desired, refuse to answer questions) was duly constituted and met at Fort Willshire between 29 August and 5 September 1836. The inquiry failed to establish whether Hintsa had called for mercy or not, but it was satisfied that the Chief was in no position, after having received two gun-shot wounds, to threaten any one. It also concluded that the Chief's body had been mutilated, but by whom it could not establish. The Court's findings did, however, dispel Lord Glenelg's suspicions[11].

Historians and writers, thereafter as if doubts had never been raised stuck to the orthodox version. Reference to the incident set out by Macmillan in 1929 — and Macmillan was the pioneer re-interpreter of early nineteenth century Cape history -while rueful in expression and exemplary in comparison, nevertheless credits the traditional version. He wrote:

> Hintsa, like an ill-fated Rob Roy, made a dash for freedom, was quickly pursued and shot; unhappily, his body was also mutilated. Though the circumstances of this tragedy gained notoriety, and became the occasion of a formal inquiry which honourably absolved

all the officers immediately concerned, yet the episode remains a mystery. As early as 2 June [1838] Sir Herschel wrote in this vein to Dr Philip, who seems to have accepted the same view: 'As I now view it, Hintsa's death is a most untoward event, but a mere chance-medley affair brought about by his own conduct'[12].

Historiographically matters stood where Macmillan had left them in 1929 until Professor C.J. Uys of the University of the Orange Free State, in a series of articles in *Die Huisgenoot*, re-examined the question in 1943[13]. But his review, perhaps because it was featured in a popular magazine and perhaps because it was written in Afrikaans, had no historiographical effect: in 1957 Walker, in the revised, expanded and third edition of his *History of South Africa* (re-titled, *History of Southern Africa*), claimed that Hintsa, in an attempt to escape, was shot by George Southey 'in self-defence'[14]. Macmillan also repeated in 1963 what he had written in 1929[15]. The controversy — in a wider context, though — did solicit attention in 1977, 1980 and 1981[16]. But, astonishingly and to this day, no specific and detailed study has been made (apart from Uys's newspaper articles) of the Hintsa killing.

2

At first, Hintsa was received and treated by the British as a sovereign. But hours later he was presented with terms under which he had to deliver twenty-five thousand cattle and five hundred horses within five days, and a second equal installment within a year. He also had to surrender his firearms, find and execute the killers of the mailcoach driver and the trader, pay a fine of three hundred cattle for each of the two victims and instruct the Rharhabe Chiefs first, to cease hostilities and then, to give up their guns[17]. The Chief was, in effect, presented with an ultimatum: either he adheres to the terms or he forfeits his safety.

The traditional version claims that the Chief was given forty-eight hours to decide whether he was going to accept or reject the 'peace terms'. Less than twenty-four hours later, however — that is, on the night of 29 April — the Chief, according to Colonel Smith, 'agreed' to all the terms of the 'treaty'[18]. The next day fanfare and cannon fire accompanied the 'ratification'. Yet five days later, none of the terms agreed upon had been honoured. How is this to be explained? Did the Chief really understand the terms? Was he practising subterfuge? Or did he understand and was he sincere but ineffective because he made his call from within the British camp? Or did his subjects ignore his instructions because they loved him less than they did their cattle and horses? Or did he fatalistically go along with the Colonel's demands, knowing full well that they were unacceptable, and knowing also that whatever objections he raised would be discounted and brushed aside?

Failure to comply with the terms — the treaty made no specific reference to what would happen if the terms were not respected and the fact that the Gcaleka were attacking the Mfengu (vassals of the Gcaleka who, after the British invasion, had been granted British protection) cancelled, it was unilaterally ruled, the safety provisions governing the Chief's visit to the British camp. The Chief, a guest according to international protocol, now became a prisoner. From 6 May the Chief, his brother Bhuru and his son Sarhili were regarded as 'prisoners of war'[19]. But a year and three months later, the Court of Inquiry, curiously undecided, was unable to declare if the Chief had been at the fatal moment a guide, a hostage or a prisoner[20].

The Chief found it impossible to comply with the conditions of the 'treaty', described by Caesar Andrews, a member of the expedition, as 'hard indeed'[21]. If he had been ready to co-operate, he became reluctant to do so once the Mfengu started leaving Gcalekaland with some twenty thousand (mostly Gcaleka) cattle[22]. As for the other provisions of the 'treaty', he had denied repsonsibility for the deaths of the mailcoach driver and the trader and had, right from the start, stressed that he had no effective or real power to command or control the Rharhabe Chiefs. Colonel Smith claimed the Chief agreed to the terms of the treaty. But did he?

The powerful and the literate leave artifacts and documents for posterity; the weak and illiterate leave dust and silence. What does the partial and available evidence indicate? Fortunately the Colonel was frank and forthcoming in his letters to his sister and to his wife; for from these we learn that the Chief was always 'horrified' at seeing the 'long paper'[23] and that he preferred the devil to the paper[24]. We also know that the Chief protested: 'What have the cattle done that you want them, or why must I see my subjects deprived of them?'[25] Hintsa's fear of the 'paper' and his protest indicate that he had never accepted the treaty. The ratification ceremony on 30 April 1835 was clearly a baroque farce: the Chief's attendance was not voluntary but commandeered[26].

Colonel Smith claimed that he treated Hintsa with generosity and kindness throughout his detention in the British camp. The Chief, he boasted, 'had lived at my table for nine days, had been loaded with presents of every description, calling himself my son, and saying that he should ever remember my kindness to him with gratitude'[27]. In the light of the available evidence, this claim is odd to say the least. On the very first night, when Hintsa was supposed to have spent four hours discussing the 'treaty' with him, Smith privately noted: 'How I bullied, threatened, talked and got around the wily Chief'[28]. He further admitted (on 7 May) that he provided the Chief with a daily dose of fear[29]. In another admission he reflected: 'Poor devils! It is hardly fair so to frighten them, but without it nothing can be done with them'[30].

On the fourth day of his fourteen-day detention — on the day before the five day limit granted to fulfil the cattle and horse fine lapsed — the Chief's life and the lives of his close associates were threatened; for word reached D'Urban that the Gcaleka were attacking and killing the Mfengu. So on this day the Governor menaced that if instructions were not immediately sent by the Chief to call off these attacks, and if the attacks did not cease within three hours, he would execute two Gcaleka for every Mfengu killed, and he further threatened that, if necessary, he was prepared to execute the Chief, the Chief's brother and the Chief's son as well.

Details of the threat vary. One account claims that D'Urban said he would hang Hintsa, Sarhili and Bhuru to the tree under which they were sitting[31]. Another claims he dangled ropes with nooses over the three for three hours[32]. Yet another claims that D'Urban made his threat and then parted, after which Smith came along, seized the Chief and threatened: 'You ugly murdering son of a debased mother now I'll tuck you up, you vagabond.' He then put nooses around the necks of the Chief and his principal councillor, Mtini, and led them to a tree. D'Urban, drawn by the commotion, intervened and put a stop to the intended execution[33]. An account by the interpreter, possibly the most reliable, claimed that Smith threatened to tie up Hintsa and Bhuru and have them shot on the spot[34].

On that same day (Saturday, 2 May), Hintsa's followers were ordered to disarm. They refused. Smith ordered soldiers to level their guns at the defiant tribesmen. The Gcaleka, astonished and alarmed, dropped their assegais. This is how Smith, in a private letter, reported the incident:

> We had a great scene in camp to-night. There are about 150 follo-
> wers of these chiefs in camp . . . I recommended that all their asse-
> gais should be given up. By way of intimidation Hintsa said his
> people would throw them. So I said I was delighted. I went in
> amongst them and ordered them to lay down their assegais. They
> began to untie them and really get ready to throw. So I laughed like
> the devil, and in a voice like thunder ordered the picquet of thirty
> men . . . to wheel up to . . . their front [and] . . . my corps of Guides
> to file round their rear. The cowards were electrified, and immedi-
> ately roared out, 'Oh, we will give them up!' and in two minutes they
> were collected. I then went in amongst them with tobacco, and oh,
> such fun as I had throwing it in amongst them and making them
> scramble for it[35].

The next day, Hintsa and his close associates were left alone until four in the afternoon when they were summoned before Smith. He met them waving the 'treaty' in his hand and berating the Chief for failing to comply with the peace terms. Towards evening he softened his tone and told the Chief that if he paid the whole amount of fifty thousand cattle within five days, he would be allowed a discount of five thousand cattle and one hundred horses[36]. But when his offer brought no response, he had the Chief marched off by ten sentries and had his tent surrounded by ninety soldiers who kept up a rotating, one-minute call of 'All right! All right!' throughout the night[37].

The following day, Smith left the Chief alone. But that night D'Urban was unsettled by a rumour that the Gcaleka were going to attempt to rescue their Chief and his brother. Smith thought the rumour far-fetched, but he nevertheless instructed one of his captains that he should, if the rescue be attempted, kill Hintsa and Bhuru[38].

After the five days allowed for the cattle-horse fine had elapsed, Smith summoned Mtini and told him that Hintsa, Sarhili and Bhuru would be detained as long as the payment remained outstanding[39]. Later, he threatened to take the three hostages with him and to prolong their detention in the Colony[40]. One account, however, claims that already on the second day of detention Smith had threatened to send Hintsa, Bhuru, Sarhili and Mtini to Robben Island[41].

Edward Driver, a trader[42], told the Chief (on 6 May) that if the

Chief gave him a good horse, he would put in a word on the Chief's behalf to D'Urban. But once the horse was given, Driver let the Chief know that the only message he was interested in passing on to the Governor was one urging his execution at the end of a rope[43].

A second and more elaborate fanfare ceremony (with a twenty-one gun salute this time) was held on 10 May 1835, when D'Urban formally annexed the territory between the Fish and the Kei Rivers and renamed it the *Province of Queen Adelaide*. Hintsa, as before, was present. The effect on the Chief and his brother was astonishing[44].

Hintsa was, of course, lavishly fed and he enjoyed the heavily sugared coffee, the soup, the potatoes and the biscuits that were made available to him[45]. There is no doubt that Smith was on more than one occasion mindful of Hintsa's rudimentary comforts: on one particular evening, he scolded one of his lieutenant's for not having made coffee for the Chief[46]. Smith was also, in small ways, generous: he gave Hintsa two dogs and offered him two 'pantaloons'[47]. He also, on the day the 'treaty' was 'ratified', presented the Chief with eight saddles and bridles, four rolls of brass wire, a dozen spades, three lengths of duffle cloth, one hundred and forty pounds of beads, a lot of buttons, several blankets, a piece of red velvet cloth sufficient for a cloak, a dozen tinder boxes, six handkerchiefs and numerous other small items[48]. But these little generosities and attention, even if sincere, were disorientating pauses in an integral programme of crude threats, open bullyings and veiled torture[49].

4

Only some thirty-five cattle had been made over to the British forces by 10 May. This was a great disappointment to Smith. After the 'ratification', Smith thought he had, with a single brilliant stroke, settled the war and recouped the stock losses. He boasted: 'I am growing a conceited old rascal and somewhat *proud of myself*[50]. But the Colonel had anticipated too much. The war with the Rharhabe was far from over and the cattle and horses that were to be so easily recovered never materialised. 'It was annoying as unsatisfactory', he would later admit, 'to recross the Kei without the redemption of the colonial cattle'[51]. But Smith was not one to await upon events: he resolved to go himself and recover the cattle-horse fine. As Gilfillan, who accompanied the expedition, sceptically observed: it was the Colonel's intention to bring back fifty thousand head but this was 'easier said than done'[52].

The traditional and official version maintains that the cattle recovering expedition was Hintsa's idea[53]. The Chief, according to Smith, actually 'begged' for such an expedition[54]. In an earlier letter to his wife, however, Smith wrote: 'I am making him go with me on a bit of a tour', suggesting that the patrol was not Hintsa's idea but his own[55].

The cattle patrol, numbering some three hundred and fifty men, set out on Sunday, 10 May at ten in the morning[56]. During the course of the march, Smith introduced further changes to the 'treaty': if twenty-five thousand head of cattle were brought in, only the bullocks would be retained; the Gcaleka could keep the cows and the calves. Later, he would introduce a further change: the only cattle wanted were the colonial herds[57].

The patrol came in sight of cattle, which were numerous and spread out in large herds. Two of the Chief's men were sent ahead to order the tending herdsmen to hand over the numbers demanded by the 'treaty'. But their mission produced the opposite effect: the cattle were driven off in all directions and the messengers fled with the disappearing cattle[58]. The sight drove Smith into a smouldering rage and a reckless frustration. Hintsa, loath to go on, warned: 'Those people will fight.' Smith, unmoved, coldly told the Chief that he had better send someone to instruct them not to flee; for he would 'follow them to hell' and if it became necessary would 'shoot man, woman, and child'[59].

The expedition, sixteen kilometres west of the Bashee River, now approached the Ngquabara River. Minutes later, Hintsa — according to most accounts — made a vain dash for freedom.

5

The traditional argument that Hintsa planned his escape is supported with reference to the fact that he rode an exceptional horse which he spared (thereby hoping to preserve his animal's strength for the intended escape) and that he was seen, just before he made his abortive break, tying a grass amulet to his person. Smith described the horse Hintsa was riding as powerful and remarkably fine[60] — a horse that was given to Hintsa by Colonel Somerset[61]. But another witness, Edgar, claims that the Chief walked for most of the expedition while soldiers escorting him prodded him intermittently from behind. It was only on the third day, and a few hours before he was killed, that Smith allowed the Chief a horse[62].

The claim that the Chief spared his horse by leading it up the various hills they encountered is compromised by Lieutenant Balfour's testimony and by Captain Southey's admission that they themselves, on occasions, led their own horses up the sharp ascents[63]. A witness reported that he noticed the Chief pluck a tuft of grass, carry it with him for a while, roll it into a ring and then fasten it to his necklace of beads; and then observed that the Xhosa used the grass to solicit 'strength or success for any undertaking'[64]. Another witness claimed that he saw the Chief's medicine man tying a charm around Hintsa's neck[65]. Whatever the truth of the matter, the grass garland — according to Xhosa custom — is an amulet worn by someone ill or depressed[66].

But given that the Chief did ride an exceptional horse, that he did save the animal's strength, that he did solicit a charm and that he did (in various ways) betray his intended escape — Caeser Andrews and Lieutenant Balfour owned that they had anticipated his escape[67] why was the Chief allowed to keep his 'remarkable' horse? Why, if these charges were not mere fabrications, was not each and every arm, including Smith's pistols, examined to see if it was functioning properly? And why, if the charges were not mere concoctions invented for retrospective advantage, was the Chief not surveyed with keener diligence and greater anticipation?

6

About half an hour before the Chief was killed, the head of the patrol negotiated a rocky, hilly and narrow path that, at the top, suddenly gave over to a considerable clearing which ran ahead for about three kilometres until it was precipitously cut by the bank of the Ngquabara River. When Hintsa reached the top of the ascent, his horse broke. A chase, led by Smith, ensued. Smith closed in and ordered the Chief to stop. Hintsa understood no English and Smith spoke no Xhosa. But the Chief, almost certainly, understood what he was being commanded to do. He chose to ignore the order[68]. Smith reached for one of his two pistols, pointed it (according to one eye-witness account) at the Chief's head and squeezed the trigger. The pistol failed to go off. Using the butt end of the pistol, Smith struck Hintsa on the jaw[69]. A second pistol was drawn and fired but failed, as before, to go off. Smith then hurled the pistol and struck Hintsa under the ear. The blow unhorsed the Chief: he fell heavily and narrowly missed being trampled by Smith's steed[70].

The Chief was well aware of the destructive power of firearms, whereas he was not to know that Smith's pistols would misfire; so that his action, when the odds were so heavily weighted against him, does not accord with someone allegedly 'wily' — unless the Chief was forced to the desperate conclusion that the only way of preserving his life, once the cattle-horse fine was exposed as a pipe dream, was to dash towards the bed of the river and to use the cover there to elude his captors. The tying of the grass amulet and the break with the horse would then, make some sense.

After the fall, Hintsa instantly sprang up and (according to one eye-witness) sent an assegai whirling past Smith[71]. All writers of the traditional account refer to the 'bunch of assegais' that the Chief was allowed to carry. All the tribesmen within the British camp were (as mentioned earlier) disarmed on 2 May — all except Hintsa: he, as a symbolic gesture, was allowed to keep his assegais. How many assegais did the Chief, in fact, carry? One eye-witness claimed that Hintsa had the usual bundle of seven assegais, another that he had three[72]. The carrying of a 'bundle' of assegais was the hall mark and the arm of an ordinary tribesman: it was the custom of a Xhosa chief to carry a single, short and small assegai[73]. It is this single, ceremonial assegai that Hintsa, after he had fallen, might have hurled or, more likely, dropped[74].

Whatever the case, the blows to the jaw and the head and the heavy fall hurt and shook the Chief. He just had time to recover his feet when the crack-shooting George Southey, Captain of the Corps of Guides, came within firing range[75].

When Smith saw Southey, he thundered: 'Shoot George and be damned to you.' Southey, armed with a double-barrelled rifle, fixed his sight on the Chief and executed the Colonel's order. The shot struck the Chief on the left leg between the calf and ankle. Hintsa fell forward on his hands, recovered his feet and compulsively continued his run. Southey hesitated until he heard Smith roaring: 'Be damned to you shoot again!' Southey aimed and emptied his second barrel. Hintsa fell again. This time the ball penetrated the lower left side of the back; just above the hip and high enough to touch the bottom of the rib cage. As before, the Chief fell on his hands, got up almost at once and continued his desperate run. William Shaw had by this time also come within firing range; he fired but missed, and earned for his failure a terrible damning from Smith[76]. Southey, in the meanwhile, stopped to reload. This gave Hintsa time to reach the river, where, according to Lieutenant Balfour (who by this time had joined Southey), the Chief threw himself down the steep bank of fifteen to twenty feet[77].

Southey and Balfour followed suit. Balfour then told the Court of Inquiry what happened next:

> When we got down . . . I said to Mr George Southey, you take to the right and I will take to the left, and we must find him. The bush was thick, and I was obliged to go on my hands and knees, pushing the bushes aside with the muzzle of my gun, I could not see two yards before me — I said, Hallo, Southey, what's that? — Southey answered — Here is one of them. I asked him if it was Hintsa? — In a few seconds he answered, Yes, come and look. I joined him as quickly as possible and found it to be the body of the Chief Hintsa, who was sitting in the water, in the niche of rocks, with an assegai in his *right hand*, as if he had been in the act of throwing it when he received his death wound, and with the remaining *assegais*, in a bundle, in his left hand[78].

George Southey provided the Court with his version of how the Chief met his end:

> Lieutenant Balfour, and myself leaped down from the bank together, I went up the stream and Lieut. Balfour down, we had proceeded some little distance, too far to be seen by each other in such a thicket, and it was impossible for me to be seen by any person on the outside of the bush. Whilst going on near the edge of the stone or rock on which I stood, and looking quickly around I saw a Caffer's head, and shot a Caffer, whom afterwards I found to be Hintza[79].

Is it conceivable that a man falls heavily from a horse running at full speed, is shot, falls again, is shot again, falls again, precipitates himself down a five to seven metre river bank (falls, in effect, a fourth time) and, after all that, clings, like a tortoise to its shell, to his 'bundle of assegais'? The spontaneous action of anyone knocked off a fast-running horse would have been to free the hands in order to break the fall[80]. Logically, Hintsa, after springing to his feet, would have had to find his assegais, undo the bunch, disengage one, aim and then throw. But let it be supposed that this was indeed the case: that Hintsa stubbornly clung, throughout his Calvary, to his sheave of assegais. The question then arises what possible purpose could he have used the assegais for? To stave off his pursuers? To defend himself against innumerable firearms? The only hope he had, once he had lost his horse, was not his puny weapons (or weapon) but his legs. Carrying a bundle of assegais under the perilous conditions he braved was more liability than asset.

The first wound Hintsa received pierced the flesh but left the bone intact. The second, in the lower part of the back, was severe enough to be in the long run fatal. Robert Daniels examined the Chief's body just moments after he had been killed. He found that the ball had gone through the body, where it touched the small ribs, and had come out through the front of the hip, where it again passed through one of the wrists[81]. The trajectory of the ball was, almost certainly, from the right side of the back to the right side of the hip and then through the right wrist[82]. Abel Hoole, when testifying to the Court, realised that Lieutenant Balfour had earlier said that the Chief held an assegai in his right hand[83] and, obviously loath to compromise that statement, temporised by stating that while he knew Hintsa had a wound in one of the wrists he could not be sure which one it was; and with evident prevarication added: 'as near as I can recollect the left wrist'[84]. The testimony of Caesar Andrews, who saw Hintsa's body moments after he was killed, merits special notice:

Did you see any assegais near the body of Hintsa? No.
Did he hold an assegai in his hand, when you saw the body after his death? No.
If he had held an assegai you would have seen it? Yes, decidedly I should[85].

Hintsa, after he was wounded, had no assegai — and even if he had, the hand capable of wielding it (the right hand) was out of action.

7

After the fall down the steep embankment, the Chief must have found that his strength was about to give out. He probably, after the second wound, ran for about forty or fifty metres. The plunge down the steep bank (which made Balfour and Southey, when they first reached it, hesitate and think again before descending) must have aggravated the wounds and sapped his strength; for when he reached the bottom, the only effort he was capable of effecting was to crawl behind a rock and lie on his side, half in and half out of the water. In this position, practically motionless, alone and helpless, he was discovered — not, as the traditional version has it, by George Southey, but by Windfogel Julie and Nicholaas Africa, the two Khoi soldiers of the Cape Mounted Rifles[86].

Windfogel Julie, a bugler, raised his rifle and was on the point of firing what would have been the *coup de grace* when the Chief, in a barely audible voice, appealed: *Taru amapecati* (mercy gentlemen)[87]. Julie heeded the appeal. Nicholaas Africa, one of Smith's escorts, also advantageously positioned to fire, heeded the plea too. But at this very moment George Southey came up from the opposite end, took deliberate aim at the stricken Chief's head and literally blew his brains out[88]. Caesar Andrews corroborates the evidence of an execution in his 'Field Diary' which was not meant for publication. His entry for 12 May 1835 read:

> Hintza sought the cover of the thick wood bordering the river, but Geo Southey fortunately coming upon the exact spot where he *lay concealed*, put his gun to his head and he paid just forfeit of his life for his treacherous attempt to *escape the fulfilment of his treaty*[89].

The assistant surgeon, W.A. Ford, found, during his examination of Hintsa's body, that the ball of the fatal shot passed through the head and, the scalp was blown open athwart — that is, from ear to ear[90]. Hintsa was shot, almost certainly, from behind the left ear as he was lying in the water on his right side. Nicholaas Africa inadvertently admitted as much. This is how the exchange between Africa and the Court enquirer was recorded when Africa was asked how the final wound was administered:

Court Enquirer: Where did Hintsa receive the wound that killed him?
N. Africa: At the back of his head.
Court Enquirer: Do you mean to say that Hintsa's back was turned to Mr Southey when the shot was fired?
N. Africa: I do not know — I do not understand how he received

78

the wound[91].

After the Chief was killed (according to Julie and Africa), Southey
dragged the Chief's body out of the water and then cut off at least one
of his ears[92]. Gilfillan, who was on the spot minutes after the killing,
and whose diary is sober and straightforward, observed that Southey
came up 'bringing with him Hintsa's ears and all his ornaments'[93].

The Khoi soldiers never fully admitted how Hintsa met his end,
while Southey and Balfour (the two other soldiers down at the River
bed) never admitted that Julie and Africa reached Hintsa before they
did. Nevertheless, a careful reading of the evidence before the Court
leaves little doubt that pressure had been put on the two Khoi soldiers
to deny that Hintsa had ever pleaded for mercy; for to maintain such
was tantamount to vindicating the stricture contained in Lord Glenelg's December despatch of 1835[94].

Edward Driver, who had seen the fatal shot being fired, was asked
by the Court if he had heard the Chief pleading for mercy. His reply:
'That is a question I decline to answer', is curious — curious because
he could have answered: 'no', 'I don't know — I was too far away to
hear' or 'yes'. 'That is a question I decline to answer' suggests a desire
to hide something. The Court, however, was unable to conclude
whether a plea for mercy had been made or not. Shepstone in his diary
noted, on 17 May 1835 (five days after the killing) that the Chief died
'crying for mercy'[95].

8

The killing of Hintsa might have become ineluctable once D'Urban
and particularly Smith realised they were never going to secure the
number of cattle and horses they had hoped to obtain, for the problem
then was what to do with the Chief. Execute him formally, either by
hanging or by firing squad? Take him back to the Colony as a prisoner?
Release him and hope that he would make good, in assurance and liberty, what he had failed to do under threat and detention? Did not the
fact of hostage and the fact of the non-realisation of the cattle-horse
fine make the Chief's physical presence an embarrassment? There is
also the consideration that Smith and D'Urban might have been
tempted to provoke an immediate succession. After all, they knew that
Sarhili would become the new Gcaleka Chief once Hintsa was no more;

and they believed that he would be more pliable than his 'wily' father[96].

A formally pronounced death sentence and a frank execution would have been beyond the bounds of civilised conduct — it is possible that a death threat might have been used as a menace but it is difficult to conceive that D'Urban and Smith were prepared to deliberately execute the Chief. Whatever the thinking and the motives, an open and formal execution would have been too blatant a disregard of international law. Imprisoning the Chief in the Colony would have been more trouble than it was worth and it is unlikely that cattle or horses (in the numbers stipulated) would have been sacrificed for his sake. As T.H. Bowker (on 6 May) observed:

> Many folks afraid that the Governor will go home with Hintsa expecting that the Kaffirs will release him by bringing the cattle. This they will never do. They like the cows better than they like Hintsa; so says everyone who has any acquaintance with the Kaffir character[97].

The detention of Hintsa within the Colony would have exposed the Governor to critics of his frontier policy[98]. Releasing Hintsa would certainly not have brought in the outstanding cattle and horses. Besides, Hintsa free would have been in a position to renounce the 'peace terms' and to condemn the annexation of Rharhabe territory. An accidental killing, where the onus for the mishap was ambiguous and where the chief *himself* was to blame, was, of course, an ideal solution. But the charge that the Governor and the Colonel deliberately engineered the killing is almost inconceivable — not to say downright calumnious. Men, however, are capable of fixing circumstances — without admitting it to themselves — to tragic ends. If an accidental killing was not cynically engineered, the base and extreme threats led or perhaps goaded the Chief into the cul-de-sac of an impossible act.

There is a suggestion, not to be neglected, that the Chief might have been threatened earlier on that fateful and fatal Tuesday. An anonymous letter (5 June 1835), probably of the Rev J. Ross [99], raised the question: 'Was the Chief threatened that morning that he ran away, with being shot in the evening if he did not bring out cattle that day?'[100].

If circumstantial evidence is anything to go by, it must be concluded that Southey killed Hintsa when he was in no position to resist and then mutilated his corpse. And it must also be concluded that the traditional version of Hintsa's death disseminates and perpetuates a lie[101]. Hintsa was not in a position to influence the relations between the Rharhabe and the Colony one way or the other. But D'Urban and Smith, without any real evidence, insisted that he did have this influence and accordingly made him accountable for the war and the cattle losses, and because the Chief failed to make good this cattle loss they — by inadvertance or proxy — executed him. 'If you wish to make this deed known by its proper name', Dr John Philip wrote to T.F. Buxton in May 1835, 'you must pronounce it in the House of Commons a murder'[102].

> From a small leather pouch he [Retief] brought forth the
> precious paper, showing it to Tjaart in a kind of triumph. 'Tell
> them you saw this. Tell them the Kaffir will sign it tomorrow and
> then the land is peacefully ours.'

J.A. Michener[1]

The treaty concluded between Retief and Dingane on 4 February 1838
forms a brief but special chapter of settler and, notably, Afrikaner history. At least two monuments celebrate the occasion: the Voortrekker
Monument Museum in Pretoria has a marble bas-relief frieze (one of
twenty-seven) showing Dingane signing the treaty; while Moordplaas
(a farm in Natal off the road from Nongoma to Melmoth) has a stele
signalling the spot where Dingane — 'signed away the land of Natal'[2].
But the treaty's miraculous recovery, the eyewitness reports of its finding, the long line of historians crediting the authenticity of its recovery
and the genuineness of its contents — all, in the 1920s, abruptly and
embarrassingly came under suspicion and debate.

1

L.A. Delegorgue, the French naturalist, traveller and writer who was
with the Trekkers during some of the time between 1838 and 1840, was
probably one of the first to provide a connected published account
after the discovery of the treaty in December 1838 — of the Retief-Dingane encounter[3]. H. Cloete, who was sent by the Cape Government
as a special commissioner to negotiate with the Volksraad of Natal in
May 1843, thereafter set out a relatively full account of Retief's misad-
venture in Natal.

Cloete's account was first cast in the form of three lectures and was
initially published in 1852[4]. Four years later, the publication was expanded with two additional lectures[5]. In a still later version of the lectures, the Cape Judge referred to the discovery of Retief's remains and
the treaty:

The emigrants . . . advanced upon the town of Umkongloof, which they still found partially burning, and on the awful hillock out of the town they beheld on one vast pile the bones and remains of Retief and his one hundred companions in arms, who, ten months before had fallen victims to Dingaan's teachery, . . . Retief was recognised by a leathern pouch or bandolier, which he had suspended from his shoulders, and in which he had deposited the deed or writing formally ceding this territory to the emigrant farmers, as written out by the Rev. Mr Owen on the day previous to his massacre, and signed with the mark of Dingaan[6].

Cloete (like Delegorgue) claimed he had seen the 'deed', and stressed that he had found it still 'perfectly legible'[7]. Moreover, he claimed that the Volksraad had actually handed it over to him, and that it ought to be (in the 1850s) among the archives of the Colonial Office in Pietermaritzburg[8].

Writers and historians thereafter asked no further questions about either the discovery or the genuineness of the treaty. Rev W. Holden in 1855, Rev J. Shooter in 1857, Theal in 1871, H. Dehérain in 1905, J.Y. Gibson in 1911, G.S. Preller in 1920, G. Mackeurtan in 1930, Walker in 1938, J.D. Omer-Cooper in 1960, L.C.D. Joos in 1965, D.R. Morris in 1966, L.M. Thompson and F.C.N. Okaye in 1969, Ransford in 1972, C.F.J. Muller in 1975 and B.J. Liebenberg in 1977 — all, without exception, repeat in essentials the recovery of the treaty as set out by Delegorgue and Cloete[9].

G.E. Cory, however, in a public address to the South African Association for the Advancement of Science in Bloemfontein in 1923, cast a mature and well-established doubt on the treaty's genuineness. The announcement was as startling as it was unexpected, for Cory was by no means hostile to the settler cause nor at odds with the settler view of South Africa's past; and yet here he was challenging one of the most cherished chapters of that past. Indeed, the declaration that 'there was never a Dingaan-Retief document' was nothing less than sensational[10].

Before proceeding with Cory's exposé, it will be useful and convenient to have a more specific idea of just how the treaty was drafted, signed and witnessed.

Unkunginsloave
The 4th February
1838.

Know all men by this that Whereas
Pieter Retief Governor of the dutch Emigrant
South afriKans has retaken my Cattle which
SinKoyella had stolen which cattle
the said Retief now deliver unto me.
I Dingaan, King of the Zoolas as here
by Certify and declare that I thought
fit to Resign, unto him this said Retief
and his Countrymen (on Reward of the
Case hereabove mentioned, the Place
Called Port Natal together with all the
Land annexed, [the second 'n' is a superscript]
that is to say from Dogeela
to the Omsoboebo River westward and
from the Sea to the North[11] as far as the
Land may be Usefull and in my possession
Which I did by this and Give unto them
for their Everlasting property.

De merk [scribble] van de
Koning Dingaan
Als getuye Als getuye]
M: Oosthuijse Noena grand raads Lid]
A: C: Greijling Inliwanio [scribble]]
B: J: Liebenberg Manondo [scribble]]

The back of the treaty carried the following certification:

Cerwiseere dat deeze omschreevene Contrackt is gevonden door
ons ondergeteekende bij de gebeente van wylen den heer P. Retief
in dingaansland op den 21 dag van December 1838 in een leedere
Jager Sak in dien vereisht zyn wy beraid dat met solemn neele Eede
te Staaven.
[We certify that the annexed contract was found by us, the undersigned, with the bones of Mr P. Retief in Dingane's country, on 21
December 1838, in a leather hunting-pouch. If required, we are

prepared to uphold this by solemn oaths.]

The certificates carried the signature of E.F. Potgieter[12].

Cory, in the early 1920s, was in the process of editing Rev Francis Owen's diary for publication. It became apparent to him that the English construction ('retaken' instead of 'recaptured', 'had stolen' instead of 'stole', 'now deliver' instead of 'now delivers' or 'has now delivered', 'thought fit' instead of 'has seen fit', 'resign' instead of 'assign', 'on reward' instead of 'as reward' and 'which I did' instead of 'which I do') and, above all, the spelling in the document ('Unkungin- sloave' instead of 'Unkunkinglove', 'Dingaan' instead of 'Dingarn', 'Zoolas' instead of 'Zoolus', 'here by' instead of 'hereby', 'Dogeela' instead of 'Tugala' and 'Omsoboebo' instead of 'Umsimvubu') did not accord with the pen of the Cambridge-educated missionary who allegedly provided the English translation at the time the treaty was signed. Comparing the handwriting of Owen's with that of the document, Cory concluded that Owen had certainly *not* drawn up the treaty. This conclusion was confirmed when he found that on 6 February — just a few hours before the massacre of Retief and his followers — Owen's diary entry read:

> Two of the Boers paid me a visit this morning and breakfasted only an hour or two before they were called into Eternity . . . They said . . . He [Dingane] had promised to assign over to them the whole country between the Tugala and the Umzimvubu rivers, and this day the paper of transfer was to be signed[13].

And yet the treaty was supposedly signed two days earlier on Sunday, 4 February.

A close examination of the treaty revealed that two of the three Zulu witnesses had signed their names. But this, Cory thought, was highly improbable as hardly any Zulu were, at that time, literate. His suspicions were further aroused by the resemblances between the signatures of the three Trekker witnesses.

The accounts by the different witnesses who claimed to have discovered the treaty with Retief's remains also revealed discrepancies, and raised further doubts about the treaty's genuineness. Further examination revealed that the certification accompanying the treaty (dated 21 December 1838 — ten and a half months after Retief's death) curiously resembled, in its caligraphy, not only the text of the treaty but also the signatures of at least two of the Trekker witnesses.

Cory suspected that the treaty, at least two of the Trekker signatures and the certificate bearing E.F. Potgieter's signature were all written by the same hand. Not being a handwriting expert himself, he asked two specialists, L. Soutter, who was employed in the Surveyor-General's Office during Kruger's presidency, and M. Manger, finger-print and handwriting expert of the South African police, to examine the writings. Soutter's findings allayed his suspicions, while Manger's confirmed them. Cory concluded that the treaty was drawn up ten months after Retief's death.

Why was such a forgery necessary? The Trekkers, Cory proposed, knew from bitter experience that their every act against the Africans would be negatively construed by both the London Missionary Society and the British Government. They feared that the latter would oppose their occupation of Natal if it was based exclusively on the right of conquest. The necessity for a non-conquest instrument legitimising their occupation mothered the treaty[14].

Cory's original aim had simply been the preparation of an important but hardly controversial diary for publication. It was only in the process of collation and verification that the emerging contradictions, obvious and impossible to ignore, forced him to question the authenticity and the genuineness of the treaty[15]. His findings, however, were spurned. G.S. Preller greeted Cory's declaration, almost at once, with a sharp and stinging rebuttal[16]. Cory's case, he charged, was 'superficial', 'reckless' and a virtual indictment of some of Afrikanerdom's greatest heroes as 'forgers and perjurers'.

A no less uncompromising retort came from the pen of a certain W.S. Wood:

It has been claimed that the paper found by the side of the bones of Piet Retief was written by the avengers of his murder, after the battle of Blood River . . . One ought not to suggest the possibility of so deliberate a forgery without clear presumptive evidence at least. There is none, and, while it is the duty of historians to seek the truth, unbiased by sentiment, it is unfair to suggest of brave and God-fearing men that they were guilty of so despicable an act until all other reasonable presumptions have been examined[17].

Wood admitted there were no eyewitnesses to the signing of the treaty, that all references bearing on the actual signing postdate the discovery of the treaty and that Francis Owen's account was the only reference of 'real historical value'; but he insisted that a verbal agreement between Retief and Dingane had been contracted and concluded before the massacre and that, therefore, it was of no matter if the treaty was forged or not.

There is thus no material purpose in attempting an answer to the question whether the historical document was actually attested by the parties named therein or not. The subject is merely one of interest to students of South African history and our historical records[18].

A third response was provided by J. du Plessis (1868-1934, author of *A history of Christian missions in South Africa*, 1911). Du Plessis' article, written in Dutch, was more elaborate, less emotional and more balanced than Preller and Wood's but it did, for all that, reject Cory's case[19].

Two and a half months after Cory's initial statement, a debate on the theme of the 'Retief-Dingaan ooreenkoms' (agreement), with Cory, Preller and Dr W. Blommaert (1886-1934) present as speakers, was held at the University of Stellenbosch (24 September 1923)[20]. Blommaert and Preller set out to refute Cory's charge.

Cory's case fixed, essentially, on five areas of contention:

(1) Owen's reputed authorship of the treaty

(2) The date on the treaty

(3) The signatures and names of the Zulu witnesses on the treaty

(4) The testimony of those who discovered the treaty

(5) The handwriting on the treaty: first in the text; then — in the signatures of the three Trekker witnesses and finally in the certificate signed by E.F. Potgieter.

2

Between Cloete in 1843 and Preller in 1920 South African historical writing took it for granted that Francis Owen was the author of the treaty. Theal, for instance, in 1871 wrote:

On February 4th Dingaan had fixed for signing a formal cession of the whole of the Natal district to Pieter Retief, for himself and the emigrant farmers for ever; and the Revd Mr Owen, then residing with Dingaan, was requested to draw — out and witness the instrument, which he accordingly did in English; and to this document Dingaan and some of his principal councillors affixed their marks, after the tenor thereof had been fully interpreted to them by the Revd Mr Owen[21].

Cory's statement in July 1923 made it absolutely clear that Owen was not, and could not have been, the author of the treaty[22]. Blommaert and Preller readily conceded this point. It is, for all that, an unflattering reflection on the state of South African historiography that it was necessary to wait for Cory's pronouncement in 1923 when Henri Dehérain, the French historian, had already in 1905 (eighteen years earlier) dismissed Owen's authorship of the treaty[23].

3

The agreement that was found on 21 December 1838 was signed according to the date it bears — on 4 February 1838. Yet Owen's diary entry (a reliable source for what happened when Retief visited Dingane on the second occasion, and which no one contests) made it quite clear that the agreement could not have been signed on Sunday, 4 February 1838[24].

Neither Preller nor Blommaert contested this particular piece of evidence[25]. They did, however, suggest that the anomaly arose either because Retief had drawn up the treaty before (and had anticipated that it would be signed on the fourth when, as it turned out, it was signed on the sixth), or because he mistook his calendar and dated it the fourth when he should have dated it the sixth. Preller suggested that the latter case was plausible because Jane Williams, Owen's servant at the time of the massacre, also made a date error in her testimony of the events of that period[26]. This argument fails to consider that Jane William's account was recorded almost thirty years after Retief's death[27]. But, assuming that Retief did make a mistake (Preller refers to a letter the Trek leader misdated when he reached Dingane's capital)[28] and that he did become confused about the dates, would not one or all of the three witnesses (Oosthuijse, Greijling and Liebenberg) have reminded him that the day the treaty was being signed was not the *fourth* but the *sixth*?

The former argument — that the treaty was drawn up and dated in advance — is also plausible, but is it plausible that the date of the signing should have been put down in advance and then neither altered nor corrected when it no longer accorded with reality? Especially since the spelling of *annexed* — written at first with a single 'n', *was* altered on the treaty? Furthermore, is it possible that Retief would wilfully have pre-dated the treaty to coincide with a Sunday — the day of the Sabbath?

4

The names of the three Zulu witnesses on the treaty are: Noena (who is described as a great councillor), Inliwanio and Manondo. Inliwanio and Manondo appear to have signed their names. Since there is no evidence that any Zulu in Umgungundhlovu, at that time, could write, Cory was, understandably, sceptical of this part of the treaty[29]. Blommaert, however, dismissed Cory's scepticism and judged it naive. The Belgian-born historian pointed out that if Cory had been sufficiently acquainted with medieval records, he would have known that the person drawing up the treaty simply wrote down the names of the witnesses without either their signatures or their marks. The signs on the treaty, after the Zulu names whether they be scribbles or crosses — have no signatory import and therefore have no intrinsic bearing on the value or otherwise of the treaty[30].

Whatever the case, a more serious point of controversy arose out of the identity of these Zulu witnesses. The treaty drawn up with Captain Gardiner in May 1835 bore the names of Dingane's principal councillors: Nzobo (or Dambuza) and Ndhlela (or Umthlella). George Champion, the American missionary, described Ndhlela (on 2 August 1837) as 'the greatest man in the country next to the king'[31]. Dingane told both Gardiner and Owen that it was the custom in his country not to do anything important without the knowledge of his Councillors. Indeed, Gardiner even referred to a 'truimvirate'[32]. Yet in the treaty, found in December 1838, the names of these councillors were (as Cory was to put it) 'conspicuous by their absence'[33].

J.Y. Gibson, twelve years before Cory's controversial statement, found that the names of the Zulu witnesses were 'not elsewhere to be met with amongst those of the prominent men of the time'[34]. On investigation, he was able to track down two of the three names. They turned out to be attendants of Dingane: one a private servant, the other a medicine man[35].

Preller's response to this puzzle was to suggest that their not being councillors did not make their status any the less worthy, and the fact that Gibson (some seventy years later) was able to trace at least two of the witnesses, argues not against but for the treaty's genuineness[36].

These arguments merit consideration but Preller himself, before 1923, had recognised that a treaty without the witness of Ndhlela and Nzobo was irregular, for in his 1920 study of Retief he claimed that when the treaty was signed, Ndhlela and Nzobo *were present*[37].

The belief that the two principal Councillors were present at the signing of the treaty was not exclusive to Preller: Dick Uys (a contemporary of Retief) also shared the conviction[38]. A fairly recent specialist study insists that Ndhlela and Nzobo did not want to sign the treaty because Retief had not been the first claimant to the coveted land. This, again, is an argument of sorts but Dingane had told Gardiner (and it seems clear he had the two Councillors in mind): 'I will not overrule the decision of my Indoonas'[39]. Whatever the case, these separate references to Ndhlela and Nzobo confirm the importance of the two Councillors and compound the mystery of the absence of their signatures. It is hardly likely that Dingane would have allowed a medicine man and a servant to participate in an important matter of state. It was not in keeping with Zulu tradition and, by all accounts, not in keeping with Dingane's manner — servants were never present when he received white delegations; besides, his head servant was called 'Masipula'[40].

The presence of at least one councillor — one just below the rank, according to Zulu protocol, of Nzobo — would have been imperative at the signing if for some reason Ndhlela and Nzobo would not or could not attend. This indispensable dignitary should have been either Mpande (the King's half-brother) or Mapita ka Soyiyisa (the King's cousin)[41], yet the treaty, curiously, shows him to be *Noeana* — and Zulu oral history make no reference to *Noeana*, councillor or otherwise.

5

There are several eyewitness accounts of the discovery of the remains of Retief and his companions in arms and the all-important treaty. The discrepancies among these first hand, primary accounts impressed Cory. Two of these, in particular, attracted his attention: the certificate (signed on 9 January 1839 by A.W.J. Pretorius, C.P. Landman, H. Pretorius, P.D. du Preez and E.T. Potgieter) upholding the treaty's recovery and authenticity[42], and the certificate of E.D. Ward Parker which made a similar though not identical claim[43].

In the first document, Hercules Pretorius and Du Preez vowed that they found the treaty and then handed it over to Commandant Andries Pretorius; and they also vowed that Evert Potgieter *was present* when their find was handed over. In the second document, Parker swore he was present when Potgieter found the 'treaty' or 'Grant'. In other words, Evert Potgieter, passive and observant in document one, becomes active and involved in document two.

Cory made no reference to any other discrepancies but there were others. In document one, the two discoverers of the treaty claim they found it 'by the bones' of Retief. In document two, Ward Parker claimed it was discovered 'on the murdered Body' of Retief. In document one, the treaty is found on 21 December; in document two, it is found 'on or about' 23 December.

An examination of two further eyewitness accounts reveals more contradictions. Charl Celliers' testimony of the discovery of Retief's remains and the treaty reads:

> We found the corpses about 1 200 yards from Dingaan's dwelling ... They lay with their clothes still on their bodies. No beast of prey or bird had disturbed them. Those who had know him recognized Mr Retief. A glossy waitcoat was part of his apparel; and he had a leather bag on his shoulder containing his papers, amongst them the treaty concluded by him with Dingaan, ... It was a matter of wonder to us all that the bodies had lain there so long, and that the papers had remained free from corruption, and were as little soiled as if they had been kept in a closed box[44].

The second testimony is that of J.G. Bantjes, secretary to Commandant Pretorius. Bantjes kept a journal of the campaign that culminated in the battle of Blood River. In his entry referring to the discovery of the slain Trekkers and the treaty, he noted:

> Mr Retief we recognised by his clothes, which, although nearly consumed, yet small rags were still attached to his bones, added to which

91

there were other tokens, such as his portmanteau, which was almost all consumed, in which there were several papers, of which some were damaged and rained to pieces; but some were found therein, in as perfect a state as if they had never been exposed to the air; amongst which was all the contract between him and Dingaan, respecting the cession of the land, so clean and uninjured, *as if it had been written today* [emphasis added], besides a couple of sheets of clean paper, on one of which the chief commandant wrote a letter to Mr J. Boshoff, the following day[45].

Discrepancy in these testimonies is evident in the description of the state of the clothes, the bodies and the papers. According to Celliers the clothes were still on the dead; according to Bantjes the clothes were 'nearly consumed'. According to Celliers no beast or bird of prey disturbed the dead (and he seems to imply the dead were whole and not reduced to a pile of bones)[46]; according to Bantjes bones and skeletons, with bits of rags still attached to them, were discovered. According to Celliers the papers in the leather container (and he seemed to imply all the papers) 'remained free from corruption'; according to Bantjes some of the papers were perfect while others were 'damaged and rained to pieces'.

Commandant Pretorius' account of the discovery of the treaty (contained in a despatch dated 22 December 1838, and addressed from Dingane's 'capital') was cast as follows:

We are now encamped in Dingaan's capital. Here we found the bones of our unfortunate countrymen, Retief and his men and which we interred . . . The Zoolas took nothing from them except their arms and horses. We found among their bones, independent of several other things, Mr Retief's Portmanteau containing his papers, some of them very much defaced, but his treaty with Dingaan is still legible[47].

Pretorius' claim that the treaty was 'still legible' contrasted with Bantjes' claim that it was 'so clean and uninjured, as if it had been written today'. But there is a more important and puzzling aspect to this despatch because the same Pretorius sent a letter, dated 31 December 1838, to *Sooilaer*, the camp where Erasmus Smit was the minister. From Smit's diary it is evident that this was the first written report to reach the camp. Its contents — Pretorius described in detail the engagement

92

that had taken place at Blood River — confirmed that this was so[48]. Referring to the discovery of the remains on Kwamatiwane, the letter noted: 'We have had the good fortune to be able to take up and bury *the bones* of the unfortunate martyrs of our Brothers together with those of the late His Honour the former Governor Mr P. Retief'[49]. Nothing is said of the treaty.

Judging from this letter dated 31 December 1838 — ten days after it was claimed the treaty had been found — there was no such thing as the discovery of the treaty. It is possible, of course, that Pretorius did not think the discovery warranted written announcement or, at the moment of writing, it might have slipped his mind, or, it might also be argued, he had mentioned it in the earlier letter that had gone astray and did not bother to repeat the information in the (hypothetical) second letter. Whatever the case, on 4 January 1839 (thirteen days after the discovery of the treaty) a further letter from Commandant Pretorius, dated 3 January 1839, reached Smit's camp. But this, as before, made no reference to any treaty — recovered or otherwise[50].

The first mention in Smit's diary of the ten and a half month old treaty appeared in the entry for 9 January 1839:

Today I received a return visit in my hut from the Commander General Pretorius. His excellency allowed me to see the agreement that had been found in the pouch of the martyred and lifeless Governor, by Dingaan. I asked for an authentic copy in order to enter it here [in his diary], but (that) could not obtain it today. I have however seen and read it[51].

Smit, according to this testimony, saw and read the 'authentic copy' of the treaty that was discovered at Kwamatiwane. It must have been evident to him, as a man of deep religious conviction, that the document was not only a significant affadavit but also, because of its singular survival, an almost mystical manifestation; and yet he did not see fit to copy it out there and then.

Finally, there is the testimony of William Jurgens Pretorius, who served with Commandant Pretorius' forces and was present when the expedition reached Dingane's capital on 19 December 1838[52]. His testimony read:

We found the bodies of the men who had been murdered with Retief on the 3rd February [they were, of course, killed on 6th February,

93

and the treaty was supposedly signed on 4th February]. Superstition had probably withheld the natives from meddling with anything on the persons of those whom they had murdered. Their clothes even their money — had not been touched[53].

Pretorius went on to state that they remained on the height in the neighbourhood of Dingaan's city for 'more than a week'[54], but he made no reference to any treaty. Is it likely that an eyewitness would have referred to the remains on Kwamatiwane without mentioning the treaty? Was the treaty discovered by a handful of men independent of the rest of the force of some 450 men? Was the rest of force not even aware that such a treaty had been found? Even if this was the case, it remains curious that a member of the expedition, one of the discoverers of the slain Trekkers, is utterly silent about what was, after all, *the* event the extraordinary, miraculous and incredible recovery of the all-important grant and deed.

6

Could the paper on which the treaty was written have weathered the elements, as well as the curiosity of individual Zulu, for not one hundred but three hundred and sixteen days? The point made by W.J. Pretorius that the Zulu did not meddle with the bodies of the dead Trekkers is certainly correct. R.B. Hulley (Francis Owen's interpreter) noted that Kwamatiwane was, except for those authorized by Dingane, out of bounds to all Zulu[55]. So no human being, at least among the Zulu, could have taken away or meddled with the container holding the treaty. What effects the fauna had is uncertain, but the roaming hyenas and the vultures hovering over the hillock devoured human flesh at an astonishing rate[56].

Could the elements have disintegrated or irreparably damaged the container? The day after the massacre, and all the succeeding days of February 1838, the heat in Zululand was intense and exceptional[57]. The rainfall season in Natal lasts from October to February or March, and the rainfall in 1838 was particularly abundant[58]. In that year parts of Kwazulu had heavy rains in February, 'abnormally heavy rains' in May and June, severe thunderstorms in April and December, and violent wind storms in September and November[59]. The elements therefore did not spare the objects exposed on Kwamatiwane. The precise effects of this corrosion on the leather container with its pieces of papers is, of course, difficult to establish, but Bantjes had claimed the 'portmanteau' was 'almost all consumed'.

7

The descriptions of the leather container holding the treaty are extraordinarily varied, with the inconsistencies of the eyewitnesses matched only by the inconsistencies of the historians. Celliers referred to a 'leather bag', Bantjes and Commandant Pretorius to a 'portmanteau', Bezuidenhout to a 'pocketbook' and the *We* of the certificate to both a 'leathern bag' and a 'leathern shooting bag'; while Cloete said it was a 'pouch or bandolier', Voigt and Theal a 'leather despatch bag', Walker a 'knapsack' and Liebenberg a 'bag'[60]. But according to Preller, the treaty was within a leather pouch which was in another knapsack or game bag[61]. Preller based this new description on Delegorgue and on a declaration made by a certain A. Schmidt in a *Die Volkstem* article dated 14 July 1923. The French traveller was certainly in Natal at the time, but he was — as far as the recovery of the treaty was concerned — no eyewitness; he merely reported what others had told him. He did not refer (which is also the view of Du Plessis)[62] to a leather container within a leather container, but rather to a *portefeuille en cuir*, a tanned leather wallet[63].

8

Another problem connected with the leather container dating back to the day Retief was killed concerns the manner in which the leather container reached the top of Kwamatiwane. According to Celliers, the distance between where the Trekkers were captured and where they were actually executed was some 1 200 yards (over a kilometer) away. The victims were seized and dragged to their place of death. In his journal Bantjes claimed that the sticks and spokes with which they had been beaten littered the road between Umgungundhlovu and Kwamatiwane[64]. Yet Retief's leather container, throughout the brutal seizure, the repeated beatings and the long violent dragging remained on his person, undisturbed and intact — and, if Celliers's testimony is to be credited, remained undisturbed and intact 'on his shoulder'.

After Retief was killed, his heart and liver were removed for an undoubtedly ritualistic purpose[65]. This operation, performed at a moment when blood and death were freely flowing, must have been done brutally and hastily. And yet the leather container, so Celliers claimed, remained intact on the shoulder of the unfortunate Trekker leader.

9

Some sort of leather bag or container must have been associated with the person of Retief for it to be featured so prominently in the matter of the treaty. Indeed, there is pre-December 1838 evidence that such a bag did exist. Erasmus Smit on one occasion referred to Retief's 'attractive leather bag'. But this, according to Smith, was used as a sort of envelope to deliver letters to an African chief named 'Limoen'[66]. Did Retief recover the bag? There is no way of knowing. But, more crucially, could the bag have survived more than ten months of extreme exposure? And if it did, what happened to it after it was discovered?

Those who claimed to have seen the treaty after it was removed from Kwamatiwane — Smit, Delegorgue and Cloete — did not claim that they had seen (contrary to expectation) *the* or *a* leather container.

It is also notable that none of those who shared Retief's fate (and they numbered about a hundred) seemed to have carried or shouldered a leather container — or, if they did, theirs seemed to have weathered the elements less fortunately than Retief's.

Leo Weinthal[67] claimed that in 1891 he saw the 'old parchment' treaty 'in a leather satchel' in the basement of the government buildings in Pretoria[68]. It is surprising to discover that in 1891 — more than half a century later — the treaty was still not separated from its incubator, the leather container. Why, it might legitimately be queried, was 'one of the most sacred State-documents of the Transvaal' (in Weinthal's words) not reverentially preserved with other vital state documents; and why was the leather container — the surviving personal property of hero and martyr Piet Retief — not assigned to the safe keeping of some or other museum[69].

Where is the leather container today? Preller claimed the leather bag was destroyed in 1886, which compromises Weinthal's assertion that he had seen it and actually handled it five years later[70]. An article by Dr Moerdyk (the architect of the Voortrekker Monument), entitled 'The Historical Frieze', which appeared in the official guide *The*

Voortrekker Monument, features the twenty-seven panels covering the four walls of the Hall of Heros inside the Monument. The twelfth panel, titled 'The signing of the Treaty Between Retief and Dingaan' shows Retief with a leather bag strapped to his shoulder; and Dr Moerdyk in the accompanying caption indicates that 'The leather wallet worn over Retief's shoulder was *modelled from the original* which was found on his skeleton and which contained the signed treaty'[71]. This suggests that when work started on the frieze in the 1940s the original 'wallet' was still extant and in the possession of some museum.

Information from the Voortrekker Monument Museum in Pretoria encouraged hopes that the 'wallet' could still be traced. But investigation in this direction proved fruitless[72].

10

Who was the author of the treaty? Preller wondered if it was Retief or Gert Maritz or Mrs Erasmus Smit or Daniel Lindley — he even wondered if it might not have been J.J. Burgers, Secretary of the short-lived Natal Volksraad. But a close examination of Burger's writing convinced him otherwise; he therefore tentatively suggested it must have been Retief who dictated and Thomas Halstead who wrote[73].

Blommaert did not venture to commit himself, even tentatively, to any specific name. He thought it unimportant since the authorship did not in itself affect the treaty's authenticity[74]. In the end neither Preller nor Blommaert could reach any finality about the treaty's author except to conclude that the style and spelling suggested that he must have been Dutch-speaking.

Two years later, a certain Mr Kacholhoffer, the Pretoria representative of the *Rand Daily Mail*, who had a habit of visiting the State Archives in the Union Buildings regularly, learnt that the archive's latest acquisition was the Soutter collection. While looking through the collection he discovered two handwritten copies of the treaty: an old one in English and a more recent one in Dutch[75]. Since he had already seen reproductions of the treaty, he concluded that the original treaty and the copies he had found were written by the same hand[76].

The way these copies found their way to the State Archives (in this story already rich in coincidences) is singularly coincidental. Mr J. Lyall Soutter, who was employed in the Surveyor-General's office during Kruger's presidency and who was one of the two handwriting

97

experts Cory consulted — the expert who did not sustain Cory's suspicions — claimed that he was preparing an official paper sometime before 1902. He had used official documents and had taken some files home with him. In February 1924, while moving house (some twenty years later), he discovered an official file among his newspaper cuttings. He concluded that the file was, as he put it, 'inadvertently not returned on completion of the work'[77]. In any case, he returned the file 'without bothering to examine it' to the State Archives. Two years, later an article in *The Star* notified him of his serendipity. Thus he had no idea of its contents prior to the period when he, in his own words, gave all the assistance in his power to help Preller prove that the treaty was authentic[78].

Mr Soutter was a loyal and responsible state servant, a government official for more than thirty years: there is, therefore, no reason to doubt his testimony. But it is for all that curious that a February 1924 letter addressed to him from the Archives and informing him of the file's contents went astray[79]. But if it be accepted that this, too, was mere coincidence, why then did the archivists not inform either Preller or Cory, or both, of their finding? Why did they leave it for a prying *Rand Daily Mail* reporter to discover, some two years later, the importance of Mr Soutter's long neglected file?

The copy of the treaty in the file indicated that the author of the original treaty was Jan Gerritze Bantjes[80]. Comparison of the writing with the original journal that Bantjes kept of the Pretorius campaign against Dingane and with a family letter that was in the possession of Bantjes' daughter, and the fact that a daughter of Bantjes had herself vouched that her father had indeed written the treaty all conclusively identified Bantjes as the author of the treaty[81]. This, of course, was the Bantjes who served as Commandant Pretorius' secre-tary; the Bantjes whom Erasmus Smit — in January 1837 — described as a young, talented 'Coloured man'[82]; the Bantjes who, along with others, discovered the treaty on Kwamatiwane; the Bantjes who had claimed that the treaty, on its recovery, looked as clean and as uninjured as the day it had been written; the Bantjes who was engaged as a clerk with the Natal Volksraad; and the Bantjes who, shy of appearing as a defendant in a civil case involving a considerable amount of money, fled Natal in January 1840[83].

Preller's finding was a revelation. But confined to some newspaper articles — the Afrikaans ones were unsigned — to an introduction (to Bantje's journal) and to a footnote, it has been largely ignored or overlooked[84]. A dozen years after Preller's disclosure, an article 'Die Groot Trek' still claimed that the author of the treaty remained unknown[85]. Twenty-three years after the disclosure, a reference work in which the treaty was reproduced asserted: 'It is not known who wrote the English text'[86].

Does this incontrovertibly prove that Cory was correct and that the treaty was, in effect, a forgery? Not necessarily. Bantjes could have been with Retief at some point between 11 January 1838 (when Retief returned from his expedition against Sekonyela) and 25 January 1838 (when Retief set out for Dingane's capital) and he could, during this period, have drawn up the treaty for Retief. Bantjes did, after all, have the reputation of being the amanuensis of a number of different Trekkers. It was he who wrote the report for Uys after Uys had spied out Natal as a possible area of settlement[87]; and Delegorgue did believe that Retief came with a treaty already drawn up and ready to be signed[88].

Even so, Preller's revelation raises a whole crop of new problems and still leaves some outstanding questions unanswered. First, where was Bantjes between 11 and 25 January 1838? If he was in the camp with Retief, and if he did draw up the treaty some time between 11 and 25 January, why did Erasmus Smit, who was in the camp, not know that such an important and eminently legitimate event had taken place? If a treaty had been drawn up, Smit would have known about it and probably have witnessed it or, at least, recorded that it had been drawn up. Yet his diary makes no reference to such an occurrence[89].

Secondly, is the date '4th February, 1838' on the treaty written by a different hand? Or was Retief so sure that Dingane was going to sign it on the *fourth* that when he putatively asked Bantjes to draw up the document, he instructed him to date it such?

Thirdly, on discovering the treaty, why did Bantjes (on 21 December 1838) not admit and even boast that it was *he* who had drafted the historic document? Bantjes was twenty-one when the treaty was discovered and sixty when he died. In the interval of nearly four decades, he took no opportunity to correct Cloete's well publicised statements (of 1843, 1852 and 1856) that it was Owen who had been the author of the treaty. Why did he hold his tongue about the fact that he had drawn up the treaty for Retief before the Trekker leader set out for Dingane's capital?

Fourthly, when Pretorius showed the treaty to Erasmus Smit in January 1839, why did he not also inform him that Bantjes had written it out for Retief more than ten months previously?

Fifthly, Bantjes remained in Natal until January 1840. During much of that time he served as a clerk in the Natal Volksraad; he therefore had ample opportunity to inform many people in leading positions that it was he who had been the author of the historic treaty. And yet until Cory raised doubts in 1923 and Preller established the fact in 1926, no one and nothing had connected the authorship of the treaty with Bantjes. How is this curiosity to be explained?

11

Cory first suspected and then, after due consideration, concluded that the certificate written on the back of the treaty (addressed from 'Dingaansland', dated 21 December 1838 and signed by E.F. Potgieter) was written by the same hand that wrote the treaty. Blommaert, whose method of verifying evidence relied principally on handwriting comparison, sought and found, in the Cape Archives, a document written and signed by E.F. Potgieter. He also sought and found authentic signatures of the three Trekker witnesses. From this, two direct conclusions were drawn: Potgieter's signature on the back of the treaty was genuine and the text of the certificate was not in the hand of Potgieter. That is, Potgieter did not write out the certificate but he did sign it.

These handwriting comparisons, it is important to note, start with an initial handicap: original handwriting specimens (primary archival documents) are compared with what in all likelihood was a photo reproduction of a document, which — according to at least one eyewitness — was (in 1838) only legible. It is not known when the surviving 'copy' was made. The original (in the words of Cory) 'mysteriously disappeared in the early nineties' when it must have been in a fairly precarious state[90]. There is also the additional problem that the surviving copy is not (so it is claimed) a photo reproduction but a 'tracing'[91]. This compounds the existing difficulty, for as one of the two handwriting experts Cory consulted observed:

> From the photo it is almost impossible to find out how and when a letter begins or ends. There are no pen marks to guide one and much must be left to the individual intelligence and knowledge of how letters are usually formed[92].

Under such conditions *signature comparisons* cannot count for much, but where several lines of text are concerned the matter is different. The frequency of letters, the beginning and ending of words (especially capitals) allow for some legitimate comparison; so only one of the two conclusions: the handwriting of the text was not Potgieter's, is credible. The other conclusion: Potgieter's signature is authentic, is neither here nor there.

Who then drew up and wrote the certificate? Preller, after examining several possibilities, came to the firm conclusion that it was J.J. Burger, the well-known Secretary of the Natal Volksraad. The snag is that Burger was not there when the treaty was discovered. How then is the date 21 December 1838 and the lieu 'in Dingaansland' to be explained? Preller, with reason, concluded that the certificate was written neither on the date specified nor in the place designated, but was written in the 1840s and probably (although this is suggested more than stated) in Pietermaritzburg[93].

Preller then argued that Burger wanted to certify the treaty (in anticipation that its genuineness would be contested) by soliciting the various discoverers to sign the declaration he had written at the back of the treaty. He had made a start with Potgieter's signature and was going to obtain the signatures of the rest of the 'we' of the certificate (recall the words: 'If required, we are prepared to uphold this by solemn oaths') when the British intervened in Natal and cut short his initiative[94]. Whatever its merits, this argument does not account for the date and the place preceding the text of the certificate.

Preller advanced this argument as an explanation for the anomalous character of Potgieter's certificate both before and after he discovered that Bantjes had drawn up the treaty. An alternative explanation (for what it is worth) is provided by the second of the two handwriting experts consulted by Cory:

> I am of the opinion that the writing of the treaty is merely a modification or the unhabitual way of writing of the person who wrote the Certificate ... After close examination I am of opinion that the treaty is written in disguised handwriting, and that it was written by the person who wrote the certificate and the signature E.F. Potgieter at the back of the treaty. The style of handwriting is precisely the same in the treaty as it is in the certificate, the size is relatively the same, the slope is the same to the horizontal, the method and angle of formation corresponds, and in many instances letters and portions of

words when compared from both documents agree to such an extent that they are practically replicas of each other. The disguise is principally confined to the capitals of the treaty, no two of which are exactly alike in construction or formation. Smaller letters are to some extent disguised but not to such a degree as the capitals[95].

12

A discerning observer remarked that Dingane was 'thoroughly acquainted with human nature'[96]. The Chief may have been cruel, but he was no simpleton[97]. He might not have understood the legal niceties of a land cession but he had a good idea of what Retief was after: he therefore had a practical and an intelligent appreciation of what the treaty signified[98]. When Gardiner reminded him in 1837 of the grant of land he had made over to the missionary in 1835, Dingane requested written proof and when Gardiner could not produce it, he accused the missionary of lying[99]. Owen's diary reveals on several occasion Dingane's fascination with the written word[100]. When two travellers, A. Cowie and B. Green, died of fever on their way back to Zululand from Delegoa Bay, their Khoi servant left their notes with the Zulu Chief. Dingane ensured that they were safely delivered to H.F. Fynn, demonstrating he appreciated the value of the documents[101]. If Dingane did understand the concession as such, why did he not, after killing Retief, ensure that the treaty was either recovered or destroyed? This point did not escape Dehérain, for he noted that if Dingane had attached any importance to the document he had signed he would have, after the massacre, hastened to have it recovered or destroyed[102]. It could, of course, be argued that the Chief allowed the treaty to remain in Retief's possession because, in the end, he neither appreciated nor understood what he had signed. If the argument be granted, then it would not matter if the treaty was a fake or not, since Dingane, under the circumstances, had clearly not intended it to be what the Trek leaders assumed it was.

13

Leo Weinthal made the last claim (in 1891) to have seen the treaty[103]. He said the original treaty was written on *blue* woven foolscap paper, that it was folded in four, that the watermark — representing Brittania was distinct and that it bore, on the reverse side, an 1830 manufacturing date. He also claimed that the writing was absolutely legible and that the paper was spotted with dark stains which (he assumed) must have been caused by Retief's blood[104]. Yet when the treaty was found one of the eyewitnesses, D.P. Bezuidenhout, claimed the paper on which the treaty was written was white.

The one possibility of verifying the colour (and by the same token the quality) of the paper on which the treaty was written was to trace the original letter that Commandant Pretorius wrote to Boshoff on 22 December 1838, on one of the sheets found in Retief's 'wallet' (recall that Bantjes had claimed Retief's 'portmanteau' had contained 'a couple of sheets of clean paper, on one of which the chief commandant wrote a letter to Mr. J. Boshoff'). But, unfortunately, the original of this letter could not be traced[105].

One point in Weinthal's description of the treaty merits brief comment. The dark stains or bloodstains were not mentioned by any of the previous witnesses claiming to have seen the original treaty. If the sheet was bloodstained, the leather container could not have been as weatherproof as its original finders claimed — indeed, as Preller himself claimed — it was.

As far as is known, the original treaty disappeared sometime in 1900 and has never been seen since[106].

14

How did Cory, to whom the honour is due for the first critical look at the treaty's genuineness, react to the charge that his findings were superficial and reckless? He had not, as pointed out earlier, anticipated the total and vehement defense of the traditional view of the treaty. The emotional storm it brewed up drove him to seek sanctuary, first in discretion and then in silence.

In the last sentence in the essay version of his contribution at the University of Stellenbosch, Preller announced that on 15 December 1924 (actually 1923), that is, on the eve of 'Dingaan's Day' (now the 'Day of Vow'), Cory had taken the opportunity to declare that he had been mistaken and that the treaty was indeed genuine.

The occasion was the opening of Piet Retief's old Cape home as a museum. It was, as was to be expected, a highly emotional event. Cory addressed the meeting (at Mooimeisjefontein, Riebeeck East) and at the end of his address he made his apology. His aim all along, he emphasized, had been for the truth. With the information he had at hand the previous July, he could do nothing but come to the honest conclusion that the treaty was a fake. But since then many students, especially those from the University of Stellenbosch, had made a thorough search through the archives of the Houses of Parliament.

The Grahamstown paper *Grocott's Mail* reported the rest of the speech in this manner:

> There were three Dutch signatures on the Treaty which struck him as having been written by the same hand — two of them least. *Now these three signatures had been found on three separate documents in the archives which showed that those on the Treaty must have been genuine; therefore the document must have been signed at Umkungunlovu* [emphasis added]. Sir George went on to explain that when he was working at the matter he worked at what was called a 'facsimile' of the original ... He understood it to be an actual copy of the original. After this discussion had been going on for some time Mr. Leo Weinthal ... wrote out to South Africa saying that he was the one who in 1893 made *a tracing of the original* [emphasis added] and a lithograph of that tracing was ... taken to be a facsimile of the original[107]. Mr Weinthal having traced the two documents, the Treaty and the certificate, it was obvious that the same handwriting which he (Sir George) thought he detected in both of these documents actually was *the handwriting of Mr. Leo Weithal* [emphasis added] and not of the people who made the original Treaty. With these two points, the bottom had been knocked out of his argument. (Applause).

These were slight and fragile, indeed, even contradictory, arguments. If the tracing revealed the handwriting of Leo Weinthal and not the handwriting of those who wrote on the original treaty, how is it possible to authenticate their real signatures (found in the archives of Cape Town) with the *traced* signatures of Leo Weithal? And, anyway, Cory was aware of these arguments when he took part in the Stellenbosch debates in September and he did not think they were convincing then. What was it that caused him to change his mind? Was he just being 'diplomatic'[108]?

In the preface to his contribution at Stellenbosch University, Cory noted the accusations of self advertisement and sensation made against him, denied these and declared his real purpose: 'My sole and only wish is to see cleared up the difficulties which confront the investigator in the study of this document'[109]. Three years later (when the fourth volume of his *The rise of South Africa* appeared), he had ample opportunity to clear up the difficulties in a less charged atmosphere; for the first chapter of the volume dealt with 'The Boer Trek' and, of course, the Retief-Dingane encounter. Surprisingly, he made no reference to the controversy that he had started and which had willy nilly engulfed him in 1923. The passage, however, where he refers to the actual discovery of the treaty, reveals — by tenor and tone — his non-diplomatic and true conviction:

On the 21st [December 1838] they [the Trekkers] formed their camp on the place where Retief and his men had been murdered and then performed the sad task of collecting the bones of their kinsmen and reverently burying them. The skeleton of Retief was found amongst the remaining rags of his clothing which had been exposed to ten months' variety of weather, there was a wallet which contained, so the diarist tells us, the contract between Retief and Dingaan respecting the cession of Natal 'so clean and uninjured as if it had been written today'[110].

6 WAS RETIEF REALLY AN INNOCENT VICTIM?

'This is a beautiful district', exclaimed Hans, as he examined the various attractive features of the scene; 'it is too good for a black savage to own'.

Captain A.W. Drayson[1]

In the story of the Retief-Dingane clash, Retief, in the authorised view, is portrayed as the hero: upright, responsible and statesmanlike[2]. Dingane, in sharp contrast, is painted as the villain: monstrous, murderous and mendacious[3]. When white South African students (in a 1930s questionnaire) were requested to cite three episodes of early contacts between black and white that impressed them at school or elsewhere, the most mentioned was the 'murder massacre of Piet Retief and his company'[4].

1

In the received account of the Retief-Dingane encounter, the incursion and the purpose of Retief's entry into the Zulu territory, with whatever nuance they may be expressed, are consistently projected as if they were predestined and ineluctable. Thus, it is claimed, the determination of some Trekker leaders and their respective clans 'to shape their course towards Natal seems to have induced Retief also to follow their track'[5].

The trekkers 'in good faith', it is suggested, 'entered Natal *believing that Dingaan was prepared to permit it*; they were prepared to settle down without the slightest intention of molesting anyone and undoubtedly would have done so, had they been permitted'[6]. It is further suggested that conflict had been none of the Trekkers' doing[7].

What is proposed is that the leader of one community enters — on his own volition — the territorial domain of another, seeks out its chief executive and requests — without, ostensibly, offering anything in return — nothing less than a sizeable portion of property in land. Retief, by going to Dingane, acknowledged the Chief's sovereignty over

Zululand and the adjoining territories. Under normal circumstances for the sake of protocol, if for nothing else — he should have come bearing a gift; in the event, he came conspicuously empty-handed[8]. Where, in this request, if Retief was to avoid the charge of disguised extortion, was the element of reciprocity, of fair exchange, of equity?

2

Retief reached the Zulu capital on 5 November 1837. Three days later he met Dingane, stated his business, made his solicitation and Dingane (so most accounts have it) complied. There was, it is admitted, a single proviso: Retief had to restore some cattle which appeared to have been stolen by a group of Trekkers. Retief denied the charge and accused the Batlokoa Chief, Sekonyela. He also vouched that he would recover the stolen herd and by so doing prove the Trekkers' innocence.

This understanding, the traditional versions imply, introduced the missing element of reciprocity. Retief would recover the cattle, bring in (if possible) the culprit, Sekonyela, and would as a result earn the right to a portion of Zulu territory.

It is difficult to credit the idea that the recovery of some stolen cattle — the loss of 300 hundred or so cattle was, after all, 'a fleabite' to Dingane was payment in kind for a sizeable parcel of real estate[9]. H. Rider Haggard has a fictionalised Retief recover and return to Dingane not 300 but more than 5 000 head of cattle[10]. This tends to some credibility, but the concept of bartering away territory for cattle was alien to the Zulu[11]. Besides, without missile weapons or the mobility of carriage, the vacant stretch of territory was their indispensable safety perimeter, their dry moat; just as it was for the Germans when they were tribally organised[12].

Retief insisted that Francis Owen (who at the Chief's insistence was present) put the understanding down in writing, which the missionary did as follows:

To go on now with the request you have made for the land. I am quite willing to grant it. But first I wish to explain that a great many cattle have been stolen from the outskirts of my country by people with *clothing, horses and guns*. These people told the Zulus that they were Boers, . . . It is my wish now that you should show that you are not guilty of the charge which has been laid against you, as I now

107

believe you to be. It is my request that you should retake my cattle and bring them to me, and if possible send me the thief, and that will take all suspicion away from me, and I will cause you to know that I am your friend. I will then grant your request[13].

Retief's visit and understanding with Dingane (in a fairly recent work of history) is set down in this manner:

Apparently Retief paid a successful visit to the Zulu king at the beginning of November, 1837. Dingaan declared that he was prepared to grant Retief an extensive area between the Tugela and the Umzimvubu, on condition that Retief restored to Dingaan the cattle stolen from him by Sikonyela; this would prove that the cattle had not been stolen by the Trekkers[14].

This account of the understanding, as indicated by Owen's letter and as suggested by the quote of a historian, begs commentary. The text of the understanding was formulated in Dutch, translated into English for Owen and then explained (by Owen) through an interpreter (probably Richard Hulley) to the Chief. Translations vary from good to bad, but whatever the standard, they always imply a change of some sort[15].

Owen was at pains to stress the incongruity of the understanding. He told Retief that Dingane could hardly consent to give to the Dutch what he had already given (by signing a treaty in May 1835) to the British[16]. The objection was received in silence. But when Owen asked Retief why then was he going after Sekonyela, the Trekker leader answered that he was doing so to vindicate their reputations. Owen tried to prevent him confronting Sekonyela, urged him to verify Dingane's information and to confront Dingane's informers in the presence of the Chief himself. But Retief had already made up his mind. After this exchange (which took place in Owen's quarters), Owen and Retief returned to Dingane's royal hut to attend the Chief's signature. Owen noted in his diary that he had asked Dingane, in front of the Trekkers, if he had not already given the land Retief was requesting to the British government. Dingane responded by saying that he would speak to Retief about this once the cattle were recovered. It was then stressed, either by Dingane or by one of his councillors, that no statement had been made as to which or what country would be given to the Trekkers. None present made any objection to this clarification[17].

Dingane did not promise to transfer that part of Zululand that Retief and his followers coveted[18]. This is also the opinion of Gibson, for in 1923 he observed that there was no evidence indicating that terms were either proposed or agreed upon concerning a concession. The only terms that were agreed upon were for certain conditions to be satisfied before actual negotiations could begin[19]. The element of reciprocity, in this case, falls away. The reference Dingane made about territory for the Trekkers — the only one he made was for them to repair to the lands they had seized from the Ndebele[20].

3

Retief had concluded alliances of friendship with several African chiefs, including Sekonyela, before meeting Dingane[21]. But after the meeting with the Zulu leader, Retief did not hesitate to turn against his ally. He lured Sekonyela to Mphrane, the Wesleyan missionary station run by James Allison[22], and there ensnared the Batloko Chief. D.P. Bezuidenhout described how the actual arrest was carried out:

I had a pair of handcuffs in my bag; and, as Sikonyela was sitting on the ground, I ran up to him and said, 'Look at these beautiful rings'; and thereupon I closed the handcuffs on his arms, saying, 'That is the way in which we secure rogues in our country'[23].

Sekonyela was then ransomed for cattle well in excess of the numbers claimed by the Zulu — seven hundred instead of three hundred. One recent critic noted: 'If Sikonyela was a thief because he took cattle belonging to Dingaan, then by the same token Retief was a thief when he took cattle that belonged to Sekonyela'[24]. Retief also ransomed Sekonyela for fifty-three horses and thirty-three guns[25]. The Batlokoa Chief was held captive for three days. The ransom came in slowly. The Chief's followers even entertained the idea of burning down the mission house over the heads of some forty Trekkers who (during a spell of bad weather) had taken refuge there. It was only the intervention of James Allison that resolved the impasse and prevented the prolongation of Sekonyela's detention[26].

Retief's action against Sekonyela, it is sometimes suggested, was legitimate because Sekonyela had, after all, stolen cattle from Dingane. Besides, the Trekkers (it is also suggested) had proof of this: the 4 October 1837 diary entry of minister Erasmus Smit provides the evidence[27]. Yet an inspection of that entry reveals the following:

> I heard . . . that the supreme Kaffir chief, Sekonyela, on the 3rd of this month passed by this vicinity with 50 men, 200 head of cattle, sheep and horses, and that they here recovered the booty stolen from them by Dingaan[28].

Sekonyela (according to Smit) was only recovering property that he evidently thought belonged to him. There was, therefore — at least to his mind, no question of theft.

Further evidence casting a critical shadow over Retief's action after the killings of 6 February — comes from Sekonyela: he sent a letter to the remaining members of Retief's camp (on 28 February 1838) demanding the restitution of 'his cattle'[29].

Retief (as most accounts have it) did, true enough, accomplish his mission against Sekonyela without bloodshed, yet he did it in a way that was more foul than fair or (as one observer put it) 'not unlike those [ways] sometimes employed by Dingane'[30].

4

The problem for Retief, after his campaign against Sekonyela, was how to approach Dingane: should he go to Umgungundhlovu as an ambassador (as he had done, though ambiguously, on the first occasion) or should he go as a leader of a powerful army. The debate within his camp, before he set out, is usually contrasted between those who, like Gert Maritz, suspected the Zulu Chief's motives and therefore favoured a visit with a small party, and those who, like Retief, favoured an over-trusting course and therefore advocated a visit with a large number of men[31].

The question was not an apolitical one between prudence and recklessness — but one of how to obtain the right to remain and reside in Zulu territory: was it to be by supplication or by threat?

Retief set out not with five men, as he had done on the previous occasion, but with five score men and ten score horses and even this large force was less than that which he initially envisaged[32]. When the party reached Umgungundhlovu, they immediately put on an ostentatious display of power. Without waiting for the Chief's solicitation or per-

110

mission, they made 'the air resound with their guns' and the earth re-
verberate with their horses[33] — it was a forewarning: the menace was
formidable, for it was not only the presence of an experienced and
hardened cavalry come in considerable numbers, but also the twin de-
feats of Mzilikazi and Sekonyela that loomed as a threat and fluttered
as an invisible banner. Retief and the Trekkers may have overestimated
the intimidation of their menace or misjudged its consequence by
underestimating the Chief's resolve to save his kingdom, but they had
a clear appreciation of the stakes: they knew they were going to the
Zulu capital not as a solicitous embassy, but as a potential and cock-
sure war party.

5

Whether Retief's second visit to Dingane was too trusting or too pro-
vocative matters little, for the Nguni Chief according to the conventional view — was already premeditating treachery. Before the
Trekkers reached Umgungundhlovu, Dingane had called in his regiments in preparation for the attack. 'He brought in reinforcements,'
Walker wrote, 'till fully 3000 warriors lay hidden in the rings of huts
that lined his great palisade'[34]. Sustaining the charge of premeditation (and, therefore, treachery), the conventional view also refers to
Isuguabana (Sigwebana, Dingane's half-brother and Chief of Khangela), who — reportedly — was ordered by Dingane to attack Retief and,
when he refused, was condcmncd (along with his tribe) to death[35].
It is further argued that Dingane betrayed his intentions by asking
Owen to write to Retief informing him that he should summon all his
people and bring them to the capital 'without their horses'[36].

The charge that Dingane brought in three thousand reinforcements
and 'hid' them in huts is disputable for two reasons. Umgungundhlovu
was designed to house at least three thousand warriors[37]. On every
major occasion a large influx of people, as well as warriors, proceeded
to the Capital. Owen, for instance, on 19 December 1837, noted that
the Umgungundhlovu regiment was collecting to celebrate the feast of
first fruits and that the town was filling up with men[38]. But of greater
significance, Dingane told Owen to inform Retief that 'he promised to
gather all his army to sing and dance in the presence of the Dutch'[39].
Dingane's intention of having a large body of men at Umgungundhlovu was no secret — there was no question of him *hiding* his men.

111

Did Dingane order Sigwebana to attack and kill Retief? The evidence on this matter is far from conclusive. The Reverand George Champion, who had many of Sigwebana's tribesmen living near his station, inquired into the affair. The accusation by Sigwebana against Dingane, he concluded, was both a 'forgery' and a 'fabrication'[40]. The American missionary, nevertheless, did inform Retief of the rumour[41]; so Retief was at least forewarned.

Of greater importance was Dingane's own reaction to the rumour. He told Owen: 'As if I was dependent on Isiguabana, as if I could not have called out other Captains to execute such a scheme'[42]. Indeed, if Dingane was determined to annihilate Retief, at that moment, he could have used greater resolve and better appointment.

When Owen asked Dingane how the Trekkers could come to Umgungundhlovu without horses the Chief replied, without hesitation and as if it was anything but a major consideration: 'Tell them then that they must bring their horses and dance upon their horses in the middle of the town, that it may be known who can dance best, the Zooloos or the Abalongo'[43]. The charge of premeditation was obviously hasty and, likely as not, false.

6

After Retief and his men were killed, Dingane's warriors attacked the Trekker settlements which were dispersed over a sixty kilometer front stretching from (what is today) Colenso to Willow Grange[44]. The Zulu regiments killed five hundred and thirty-one men, women and children; which included two hundred and fifty (mainly Coloured) servants[45]. These were great and disastrous losses — the more so because they involved so many women and children[46]. And yet the American missionary, Daniel Lindley (no enemy of the Trekkers), noted in a letter dated 27 February 1838 that the Zulu army, given the opportunity it had, had accomplished 'very little indeed'[47]. The fighting force of the Trekkers had been, it is true, grievously attained one hundred and sixteen of the seven hundred and twenty men capable of bearing arms were dead[48]. But this, though severe, constituted a loss of just over sixteen per cent; the Trekkers still retained eighty-four percent of their fighting strength: Daniel Lindley's observation was not quixotic.

All this suggests that either the Zulu military command was incompetent or, which is more probable, inadequately prepared. Why was this so? The principle reason is because the decision to attack was made on Monday-Tuesday 5-6 February 1838 — not in advance, not with forethought but in precipitation. Indeed, the Zulu regiments were surprised by the scale and size of the settlements at the foot of the Quathlamba Mountains[49]. Dingane and his councillors had intelligence of the Trekker settlements but it was a general intelligence not one associated with a military campaign, or with premeditation. All this suggests that Dingane, far from taking the initiative, was reacting to events.

7

The agreement which Retief had Owen draw up was, in spite of translation, clear on one point: If possible, Sekonyela had to be sent to Dingane[50]. When the Chief heard that Retief had had the Batlokoa under his power, and had then released him, he was vexed. But of greater import, Dingane was persuaded that Retief had reneged on their October agreement. He told Owen that Retief 'had told a lie' when he had made the promise to send Sekonyela[51].

Retief, in Dingane's eyes, was acting as his emissary of war[52]. Leaving aside the questionable ethics of the agreement, *physically* it would have been possible for Retief to make over his captive to Dingane; *morally*, it was — with the interdictory presence of missionary Allison — quite impossible. But this moral dimension of Sekonyela's capture was not one that preoccupied Dingane. Besides, the Chief had a full report of how Sekonyela had been tricked and treated — the missionary James Backhouse, who received his information from Allison, characterized the act as being both wicked and mendacious[53]. Owen, while noting Dingane's obvious disappointment, prevailed upon him not to include in his letter to Retief the charge of lying. Whereupon the Chief maintained (as Owen reported):

He did not say that they had told a lie, but he could not stop his people's mouths, who would be sure to say so, therefore in order to satisfy them it was necessary that Mr Retief should send him the guns and horses with the cattle[54].

In Dingane's mind Retief had failed to live up to their understanding.

113

Yet he was willing to waive the infringement, provided Retief handed over, with the recovered cattle, the confiscated guns and horses. This demand was not farfetched or unwarranted. Retief was acting as his agent against someone who was reputed to have committed a crime against Zulu property, within Zulu territory and under Zulu jurisdiction. Retief, in setting out to prove that the Trekkers were innocent of theft, undertook the role of Dingane's law enforcement officer. He had therefore no independent authority to punish Senkonyela. The only authority he had came out of the agreement concluded at Umgungundhlovu. Dingane's demand for the guns and horses had, at least, legal justification. At any rate, it seems Retief did inform the Chief's messengers that if their Chief so desired, he could have the guns and horses[55]. But when Retief reached the Zulu capital, he informed Dingane that he had no intention of handing over the guns and horses. Whereupon the Chief must have concluded that the Trekker leader had indeed lied and was not being 'one with him'[56].

8

No record of what was said or what happened during the meeting that Retief had with Dingane on 4 February 1838 was ever made. The assertion by the two Trekkers that Dingane was going to give them or (as Owen recorded it) 'assign' to them the land between the Thunkela and the Mzimvubu Rivers is puzzling. Dingane indicated on more than one occasion that he wished the Trekkers to settle the territory they had conquered from Mzilikazi[57]. The selling, bargaining away or assignment of land was (as already stated) entirely foreign to the custom and alien to the thinking of both the Nguni and the Bantu[58].

The area between the Thunkela and the Mzimvubu Rivers was, more than once, put under the charge of white authorities[59]; and these appointments were confirmed in written documents in so-called 'treaties'. But in the minds of Dingane (and before him Shaka) these 'treaties' were no more than written records or attestations of authority granted to different persons to rule over the designated area: they were, in sum, written but revocable appointments[60]. If the assertion of the Trekkers was credible; that is, that Dingane did promise to give them the land, then Dingane was, on this occasion, wilfully deceiving and misleading them. On the other hand, and perhaps more credibly, this assertion was just an extreme manifestation of the Trekkers' whim to mistake the fiction of their desires for the fact of their frustrations: they might have received what was never accorded.

During the vital meeting something was said by Retief to Dingane that made Halstead (the nineteen-year old interpreter) visibly hesitate and falter in his task. Dingane, sensing insincerity, wanted another interpreter not one linguistically more competent but one less connected or tied to the Trekkers. (Halstead, recall, also accompanied Retief on the first visit to Umgungundhlovu.) Dingane, in effect, accused Halstead of lying[61].

That evening Dingane ordered four messengers to cover the seventy-five kilometres to Umhlatusi, the American missionary station. Their assignment was to find and bring back the seventeen-year old Zulu-speaking Charles Brownlee[62]. When the messengers reached the youth, they told him (on Monday morning, 5 February 1838) that Dingane 'could not understand the Boers'[63].

The words which Halstead hesitated to translate or fudged must have been *the* words of the meeting. But what were they? What were these grave and fateful words that Dingane was so anxious to understand and that Halstead was so loath to translate? There — is, of course, no definite way of knowing, but Dingane's various disclosures after the death of Retief provide a lead.

Dingane told Owen that he did not mind having white people come to his country, provided they came as visitors and not as settlers; he did not want them building houses in Zululand. He also admitted that he did not mind the missionaries who came by 'fews and fews', but he could not suffer the Trekkers who came like an 'army'[64]. Dingane said he had made it clear to the Trekkers during the meeting that he objected to their making homes in Zulu territory but 'they would not take his No'[65].

This, it would seem, is a fairly unambiguous index of what happened during a tense and strained moment of that meeting. Retief insisted on having the land between the Thunkela and the Mzimvubu assigned to the Trekkers; Dingane, just as insistently, refused — and it was not the handing over of the land in itself that he objected to but the idea of giving to a powerful 'tribe' the authority to inhabit the indispensable defence space of the Chiefdom.

Dingane undoubtedly invited the Trekker leader to settle the territory conquered from the Ndebele, advice which eventually led Retief to reply (perhaps in these terms): If you do not want us to inhabit the Thunkela-Mzimvubu area you will have to make good all the Trekker cattle you took from Mzilikazi. (Dingane, recall, said the Trekkers wanted him to hand back the cattle his warriors had captured from the Ndebele)[66]. A contemporary Zulu witness indicated that this was, indeed, a crucial element in the contention between the Zulu and the Trekkers. He observed:

> I remember the Boers coming to Ngungundhlovu after their cattle; they said these cattle were *their fruits*. They said the Zulus had taken what were their cattle. 'Did not the Zulus who seized them see dry corpses lying not eaten by vultures?' — for there were no vultures at the place of Mzilikazi, and therefore the cattle which were in Mzilikazi's possession became theirs. The Zulus replied, 'You say these are your cattle? No cattle ever left Zululand after once getting here', thus refusing to give them up[67].

The amount of cattle demanded must have been considerable. It is probably this demand, most likely coupled with a veiled threat, that made Halstead falter in his task as interpreter.

In the end Dingane was almost certainly presented with the stark choice of either making over to the Trekkers either a vast number of cattle or a vast stretch of territory. Faced with Hobson's choice, the Chief must have in part sought clarification and in part played for time: he requested leave to consult his councillors and he sent messengers for Charles Brownlee[68].

9

Retief and his party arrived at Umgungundhlovu on Saturday, 3 February 1838. They met Owen early that afternoon and promised that they would attend his Sunday service the next day. The promise was not kept. Owen, in his diary entry, commented:

> I felt grieved because it would have had an amazing influence on Dingane's mind, if they had not only resisted on this occasion his desires to entertain (saying it was Sunday) but had also come in a body to the station. Nevertheless, it is one of those things which, much to be regretted, it is not our part rashly to censure, as I am persuaded there was no wilful or predetermined contempt of the Day of the Divine word[69].

This is enigmatic, for the Trekkers were by habit and custom strict observers of the Sabbath. Years later, a Boer general would observe the Sabbath during the Anglo-Boer War siege of Mafeking[70]. If the initiative for the meeting came from Dingane, the Trekkers could have asked him to postpone the meeting until the following day. Dingane would probably have been accommodating, since he was aware of the Sabbath and had some idea of its significance[71] — and so had (according to Gardiner) Nzobo and Ndhlela[72]. Why did Retief not, therefore, have the meeting postponed, especially since he only proposed to leave (or so it would seem) on the following Tuesday? Did he agree to meet Dingane on the Sabbath because he realized that he would then be unencumbered by a missionary witness and untrammelled by the missionary's embarrasing reminder that the land in question had already been made over to the British[73]? Retief had, it is well known, no particular love for certain missionaries, whom he judged 'interested and dishonest'[74]. Besides, his recent experience with both Owen and Allison must have evoked old images of past grievances and made him wary of their participation in Trekker affairs. This consideration (if the argument be granted) must have convinced him that meeting Dingane on the Sabbath had its advantage. He could, if it was necessary, 'fall into a passion' with the Chief, without having to bother about the niceties of legal and moral restraint[75].

Retief, there can be little doubt, uttered a threat against Dingane that Sunday and, if the matter be carefully considered, he could hardly have done otherwise — unless, of course, he was prepared to recognise that the Zulu were entitled to their land and was, therefore, willing to return from whence he came. But this, given the nature of the Trek, was hardly possible.

10

On the historic Tuesday, 6 February 1838, Owen noted: 'My mind has always been filled with the notion however friendly the two powers have heretofore seemed to be, war in the nature of things was inevitable'[76]. This is a key observation, for Retief's entry into Natal — contrary to prevailing opinion — was no anodyne or fortuitous act but a calculated though risky wager. By infringing the spatial domain of the Zulu, Retief had unilaterally harnessed Zulu politics to Trekker politics and had, in effect, given notice to the Zulu that the Trekkers were intent on challenging their sovereignty. Before reaching Dingane's headquarters, Retief wrote in a letter to the Chief:

> Our anxious wish is to live with the Zulu nation. You will, doubtless, have heard of our last rapture with Umsilikazi resulting from the frequent and ruinous robberies committed habitually by his tribe; in consequence of which it had become absolutely necessary to declare war against him, *after having in the first instance failed in every attempt to arrange our differences*. I shall set out in a few days for the country of the Zulus *in order to settle with you our future relations* [77].

He was literally warning Dingane to accept Trekker hegemony or brave the terror of Trekker guns and horses. Later, in a reference to the nemesis of wicked kings, he would venture to be even more explicit:

> The great book of God teaches us that kings who conduct themselves as Umsilikazi does are severely punished, and that it is not granted to them to live or reign long; and if you desire to learn at greater length how God deals with such kings, you may enquire concerning it from the missionaries who are in your country[78].

What would Retief have done if Dingane had told him politely but firmly that he was not in the philanthropic business and that the answer to his 'request' was a resolute and irrevocable *no*? Would Retief have expressed regret, bid the Chief adieu and set his wagons rolling in some other direction? Of course not. Indeed, when Retief visited Dingane on the first occasion and *before* any sort of meeting or point of negotiation could be fixed, the owners of a thousand trek wagons had already started occupying and settling Zulu territory[79]. Retief's entry into Zululand constituted a resolution to reduce the Zulu to underlings either peacefully or violently[80]. – Dingane had the unenviable choice of submitting quietly to a species of territorial mugging or of foolhardily and desperately resisting a force greater than his own. He decided, for better or worse and as a true patriot, the latter course. But when Mpande replaced him as chief in February 1940, and when the new chief, as vassal, made over to the Trekkers a vast amount of land and a dizzying number of cattle, Retief's incursion into Zululand was brought to its logical conclusion: Trekker might triumphed over Zulu right.

Was Retief an innocent victim? Certainly not. While it would be rash to claim that he got what he deserved, it is, nevertheless, true that his end, if dishonourable, was only as dishonorable as his intent.

7 WAS THE MAKAPAN CAVE SIEGE A MASSACRE AND A TREKKER VICTORY?

An eye for an eye and a tooth for a tooth is not Christian dealing, but it is the dealing with which fair unbiased history proves to have been in the end most productive of good and least productive of evil, when communities of white men have conterminous frontiers with tribes of blacks.

C.P. Lucas[1]

1

A particularly violent clash between Dutch farmers and Ndebele tribesmen took place in the Waterberg district of the Transvaal in November 1854. The result was a spiral of killings that ultimately led to the massacre of an entire tribe. A summary of the standard account, by Theal[2], claims that Hermanus Potgieter, a man of 'violent temper and rough demeanour', entered Makapan's capital with a party of men with the intention of trading some ivory. This Makapan was of a 'ferocious disposition' and had the reputation, among the surrounding tribes, of being 'a man of blood'. Unfriendly newspaper correspondents charged Hermanus Potgieter and his men with having made demands, without payment, for sheep and oxen. These same correspondents also alleged that Hermanus Potgieter demanded gifts of African children. These charges, Theal objected, were improbable, for white men would hardly have ventured thus. Tribesmen are easily vexed and it is possible that some banal act had excited them 'to frenzy'.

Potgieter was 'flayed alive' and his skin was prepared in the same way as that of a wild animal. Makapan's forces then attacked neighboring settlements. The Trekkers in Zoutpansberg and Rustenberg abandoned their homes and formed laagers. P.G. Potgieter led a commando to the troubled area, discovered that the tribesmen had found refuge in a nearby cave and came across the scattered remains of their white victims. Punishment, Potgieter decided, should be total. The strength of his force was augmented by the arrival of a second commando under

120

M.W. Pretorius.

An African sniper aimed his rifle at Potgieter and found his mark. Paul Kruger, then a fieldcornet, sought to aid the wounded leader but on reaching him found that he was already dead. The farmers tried unsuccessfully to smoke out the Africans. Later they tried to stop up the entry of the Cave with 'brushwood and stone'. Some days later the refugees began to feel the want of water. Many of them tried to slip out of the cave at night but the attempts proved fatal. It was cruel, but the Trekkers were determined 'to make a terrible example of Makapan's people'. After twenty-five days a party, meeting little resistance (four men were slightly wounded), entered the cave. They discovered passages leading from the great hall but the stench of putrefaction and the want of lighting prevented them from venturing any farther.

Something like two thousand seven hundred Africans, according to Commander Pretorius, were killed: nine hundred outside the Cave and double that number within. 'Makapan's clan was almost annihilated'. Horse sickness finally called the campaign to a halt. Makapan's allies were not subjugated but it was thought that the nasty fate of the Chief's followers would deter any further resistance. The camps were disbanded on 30 November. This, then, is the traditional account.

An African who had been present when some of the events took place and who had taken an active part in some of them was found and questioned[3]. Contrary to Theal, he claimed that Hermanus Potgieter had been preying on the tribe by making extravagant demands for stock and labour and by repeated acts of cruelty, and that matters came to a head when Hermanus Potgieter killed the chief's brother.

Makapan's younger brother, while out hunting one day, killed a buffalo calf. While he and others were standing over it, fieldcornet Hermanus Potgieter arrived, flew into a temper and said that only fullgrown animals must be killed, and not a cow in calf; and then, without warning, he turned upon the chief's brother and fired a fatal shot.

When Makapan was informed of his brother's death, he resolved, with the aid of a confederate, Mapela, to retaliate. Mapela was given the task of avenging the death of Makapan's brother. Hermanus Potgieter and his party were lured to Mapela's capital (the story of a roaming heard of elephants was sufficient to bait the ivory-hungry Potgieter), where they outspanned and then proceeded on foot to where they thought the elephants were located. Presently they were met by some of Mapela's warriors. Some had broken-off assagais concealed under their clothes, others, by portering a piece of ivory, posed

121

as a decoy. The latter group placed the exceptionally large tusk they were carrying on the ground some distance from the wagons. They then enjoined the Trekkers to come and examine it. Excited and delighted, they left their rifles and hurried towards the rich seam of ivory. While thus engaged they were attacked and killed -all except Hermanus Potgieter who, gravely wounded, managed a successful dash to his wagon. Kheresa, a man of great strength, gave chase and (with his broken-off assegai) repeatedly assailed the stricken Potgieter. Potgieter reached his wagon, secured his rifle but then collapsed and, with blood oozing from his mouth and nostrils, died.

Mapela then informed Makapan that vengeance, as far as Hermanus Potgieter was concerned, had been done. The Makapan's warriors immediately proceeded to carry out a second set of mass killings. The African witness emphasized that Makapan survived the cave siege.

Which of these conflicting accounts, if either, is to be credited? Or is the truth somewhere between Theal's version and that of the African participant?

In Theal's version, there is an unmistakable impression that the misdeed on the part of the Africans was sanctioned by a single chief. Three other historians (E.A. Walker, J.A.I. Agar-Hamilton and L.M. Thompson) support Theal's view of the event, and agree that only one chief, 'Makapan', was the instigator of the mass killing[4], but Paul Kruger (who was, of course, a participant) claimed that the killings were the work of both 'Makapan' and 'Mapela'[5]. These chiefs are identified with more precision by A.O. Jackson[6]. Mankopane, chief of the Langa, was variously known as 'Magopane', 'Mapela' and even (occasionally) as 'Makapan'. The early settlers in the northern Transvaal formed the habit of calling him 'Mapela' and sometimes, incorrectly, 'Makapaan'[7]. To add to the confusion, Mankopane's confederate, the chief of the Kekana, was called *Mokopane*.

2

Theal suggested that Hermanus Potgieter was killed because Mokopane ('Makapan') was 'ferocious' and 'a man of blood'[8]. Mokopane, it is true, did acquire the nickname 'Setswamadi' or 'Setsuamadi', which literally means 'he who bleeds'[9]. The name came to him because he and his tribe suffered severe losses during three attacks by the Pedi[10]. To confuse 'he who bleeds' (one who suffers) with 'a man of blood' (one who makes others suffer) is equivalent to confusing victim with aggressor. At any rate, it was *Mankopane* (and not Mokopane) who killed Potgieter.

It is possible (as Theal has indicated) that the Africans were irritated by some banal, unintended offence[11]. But if the African participant's evidence is credible, then Hermanus Potgieter was hardly the victim of quick irritation or gratuitous frenzy. Walker stressed that the tribesmen had 'just cause of complaint'[12], and even Theal admitted that Hermanus Potgieter was violent in temper and rough in demeanour[13]. The deaths of Hermanus Potgieter and his followers are not too difficult to fathom. There is considerable evidence testifying to Potgieter's unlawful and cruel behaviour towards the Langa, the Kekana and the other neighbouring tribes[14].

The most eloquent testimony of his dastardly deeds was offered by Khosilintse, a neighbouring chief, to the missionary Robert Moffat on 22 November 1854:

> The Boers have for a long time been robbing and oppressing Mangkopane [Mankopane] and his people. When the Boers re-turned from Moselekatse a long time since, when they went to try to take his cattle did Moselekatse not tell you? — they returned by the Bamapela tribe, fired on them; and took many wagon loads of their children on the day. Mangkopane, their chief, got a present from another chief of a few guns and horses. As soon as the Boers heard this, they took them from them, because a kaffir must not have a gun or a horse. Ask Mangkopane how many of his own children . . . have been taken and made slaves, how many of his people have been murdered! The Boers went again to demand tribute and to take what they liked. His heart was full of anguish for the loss of his eight children. His heart was in anguish for his people, who came mourning over their own losses[15].

The records of the Trekkers (although Kruger's *Memoirs* is silent about this) also indict the misdemeanor of Hermanus Potgieter. Fieldcornet H.J. van Staden, from Magaliesberg, informed Pretorius (on 4 May 1854) that Hermanus Potgieter and nineteen other whites attacked a chief named 'Ramaglabootla' and his people, robbed them of their cattle and seized some of the women and children[16]. The war council of the Trekker Government condemned this misconduct and even instructed A. van der Walt (another fieldcornet) to order Potgieter to restore the stolen cattle and return the abducted women and children. Potgieter, however, was unresponsive and unrepentant, no police action was ever taken to remedy the crime[17].

Immediately after the killing of Potgieter and his followers, six other clans began to attack neighbouring settlements[18]. But both Kruger and the African witness were explicit; a party of travellers, independent of Potgieter's group, was set upon and killed. During this brief period of unrest and violence three different parties were killed by two different chiefs.

3

Communications between Schoemansdal (and Soutpansberg) and Pretoria followed a route which crossed the Nyl River about ten kilometres south of Potgietersrus. Mahalakwena, the ford at this spot (renamed 'Moorddrif' after 1854), was the usual outspan point for white travellers, traders and hunters. Mahalakwena was just over a kilometre from Mokopane's capital[19]. Some time in September 1854, a group of twelve travellers, journeying in two wagons from Soutpansberg to Pretoria, stopped at the ford. Mokopane's warriors attacked them and killed every member of the party[20]. According to M.W. Pretorius (from his Magaliesberg report of 6 December 1854), the victims were dismembered, and one of them (a man) was decapitated and his severed head was cast into the river[21].

While the killings at Mahalakwena ford were taking place, M.A. Venter and his son entered Mokopane's village (now Pruissen), probably to trade or barter corn. Once inside, the two men were set upon and killed. M.W. Pretorius — three months after the killing — claimed that he had seen their dismembered limbs, their fat and their grilled hands[22]. The implication, obviously, was that the Venters had fallen victim not only to homicide but also to anthropophagy[23].

Fothane was the residence of Mankopane. Here, on the same day, Hermanus Potgieter and seven or eight of his followers, were also, without warning, set upon and killed[24].

4

Theal wondered (without concluding) whether it was the settlers' disregard of African beliefs, unwitting offence or violent language which resulted in retribution. A careful consideration of the available documentation indicates that the grievances against the settlers were both general and specific. The Kekana and the Langa, offshoots of the Natal Ndebele, established themselves in the Transvaal some time during the seventeenth century. The Kekana had their territorial base about thirteen kilometres south of Potgietersrus, on the present-day farms of 'Pruissen' and 'Vier-En-Twintig Riviere'. Mokopane became their leader in 1835 or 1836. The Langa had their first base twenty-five kilometers north of Potgietersrus, but later they shifted farther west to what is today the 'Suid-Holland' farm. Mankopane became their chief some time in 1836[25].

The two groups' first contact with white settlers was probably in 1837 when Louis Trigardt entered their territory. Therafter, a steady trickle of Trekkers encroached on their domains. At first, relations between the tribesmen and the settlers were cordial[26]. But the settlers' growing incursions in greater numbers told on the tribesmen. The settlers, careless of the Kekana's and Langa's needs, had an unappeasable appetite for tribal stock, land and labour. Friction between the two communities was inevitable[27]. The turning point for Mokopane came some time between 1847 and 1848 when some Trekkers attacked his people and made off with a number of livestock and some women and children[28]. Mankopane suffered similar losses[29]. The two Chiefs, with no one but themselves to rely on for redress and protection, gradually started arming themselves[30].

In the meanwhile the Trekkers, with the accord of the British government, established their republican state in March 1852. They believed (on the presumption that they had conquered the territory from Mzilikazi) that all the African groups in the Transvaal now owed them allegiance. They were mistaken in this, for neither of the two chiefs had ever been a vassal of Mzilikazi[31]. Mokopane and Manko- pane rejected Trekker overlordship not only because they wanted to maintain their independence for its own sake, but also because they felt the oppression of a system which assumed that every adult African, on the simple demand of a farmer was liable to a labour tribute. They were also reluctant to accept the Trekker 'apprenticeship' or *'inge-boekt'* system which, in their eyes, was a species of slavery. Finally, they found unacceptable the interdicts against procuring and bearing firearms and against obtaining, rearing and riding horses.

To the Trekkers, however, the conduct of the two chiefs was mere brazenness. Piet Potgieter knew that they were busy acquiring arms and he solicited the Volksraad to ensure that arms smuggling by whites to blacks be declared a capital offence[32]. He also sought sanction to disarm forcibly all Africans bearing firearms[33]. A War Council meeting at Olifantsrivier had, as far back as September — 1852, declared Mokopane and his followers outlaws and enemies of the republic. The chief could bring hostilities to an end, the declaration maintained, if he agreed to sign a peace treaty and if he subjected himself to Republican decree[34].

5

The killings were appalling and gruesome, but they were not a manifestation of inherent cruelty or a natural taste for blood — nor yet of cannibalism but of disproportionate power. The two Chiefs hoped that their actions would be sufficient to dissuade the whites from encroaching on territory they regarded as belonging to them.

With the exception of Hermanus Potgieter, the choice of victims seems to have been quite arbitrary. The twelve travellers at Mahalakwena ford were probably unknown to Mokopane, but (as indicated already) the track joining Schoemansdal to Pretoria cut a swathe through Mokopane's territory. Moreover, traffic on it had been increasing and was threatening to become permanent. In using it, it never occurred to the settlers that they were trespassing on Mokopane's territory. The choice of killing the settlers on that particular spot was probably Mokopane's way of protesting and dissuading other settlers from using the road.

But in examining the action of the Kekana (if not the Langa), it is necessary to bear in mind the experience of J.J. Engelbrecht who went to Mokopane's capital to trade. When he had successfully concluded his business, he made ready to leave but some of the Kekana warriors detained his oxen and barred his departure. Three days later, without any explanation, he was allowed to go. A day or two later Engelbrecht learnt of the killings[35]. Why was his life, at that particular moment of high tension, spared? Perhaps it was because he had always dealt fairly with the Kekana. At any rate his survival suggests that the killings did not signal an indiscriminate and wanton onslaught on all whites.

The gloom inside the Cave was so intense that the Trekkers could hardly see. This obscurity precluded a direct attack and made a prolonged siege inevitable, but this does not in itself explain why a siege was undertaken. The Kekana had anticipated their defence and this is the principle reason why a long, drawn-out siege became necessary. The dolomite cave had two openings that led to two enormous and imposing chambers. Each of these in turn had gorges leading to a series of pasages, some of which led to points which, even today, have not been fully explored[36]. In front of each opening the Kekana built outer defence walls of rock piles. The actual entrance of each opening was also protected with a built-up stone emplacement. The construction of these two walls created a kind of inner court. The mouth of the cave was near the summit, while the approach was at the foot. The sanctuary was thus naturally fortified. Most of the Kekana had spears. Many had guns, were well provided with powder and lead, and were capable of using their firearms with effect[37]. Having used the cave before, they had some appreciation of what to expect and had provisioned themselves with food, and were adequately supplied (by a stream passing under the cave) with water.

On the morning of 25 October 1854, the Trekkers stormed the cave[38]. They broke through the first stone barrier emplacement, probably using their two field pieces to blow the walls apart. Between the stone redoubts, the Trekkers found and recovered four wagons. The Kekana, meanwhile, fell back behind the second defence perimeter[39]. Fumes from the firing within the cave were so intense that a virtual smoke screen was created. According to their own accounts, the Trekkers killed one man and lightly wounded two; the attack was called off in the afternoon.

New attacks began on the following two days, but these too were unsuccessful. The Trekkers discovered that beyond the second stone emplacement, the chambers had also been criss-crossed with stone-walled redoubts. Because of the firing, trying to storm the cave proved daunting and hazardous.

On 28 October the Commando held a council to discuss strategy. A plan was adopted to collapse the top of the cave by setting off explosive charges. Holes were made just above the chambers of the cave and on the following Monday the charges were set off. The explosion, instead of causing a general collapse, merely produced cracks and seams on the hardy limestone surface of the cave[40]. The failed experiment was costly. Powder was expensive and — though the commando was initially well supplied — limited. No second attempt was made.

A new tactic was now adopted. An attempt was made to smoke out the Kekana. The Trekkers had their African levied servants bring up to the brow of the mountain hundreds of wagon loads of wood and scrub. The loads were then tumbled down to the foot of the cliffs so that a tinder pile built up in front of the mouth of the cave. Then torches were hurled down to set the whole alight[41]. But this too proved ineffective.

The Trekkers then decided to increase the attacks. The water supply was cut off by diverting the stream outside the cave[42]. Stone redoubts were set up within range of the cave, and from the cover afforded by these the Trekkers trained their guns on the cave's openings and kept up a twenty-four hour watch. The tight vigil was aimed at stopping further stocking of food and drink which they estimated must be running low by this time. But the surrounding area outside the cave was covered with trees and shrubs, and clandestine movement into and out of the cave, especially under the cover of darkness, was still possible; so the three-hundred-strong contingent of black labourers serving the Trekkers was ordered to clear the area around the entrance.

On the fifteenth day of the siege (8 November) it was resolved to block up the openings of the cave, which implied that movement out and into the cave by the Kekana and their confederates was still going on — or was suspected of still going on. For the next five days the black labour force gathered and dumped fifteen hundred loads of trees, shrubs and stones in front of the cave's opening[43]. The Kekana reportedly tried to slip out of the cave under the cover of darkness, but the attempt (according to one account) was dearly paid for. More than seven hundred fell victim to the gunfire of the night patrol[44]. Women and children thereafter gave themselves up in greater numbers; the Trekkers claimed that by 12 November, they had captured, some four hundred women and children.

In a letter addressed to S. Schoeman on the nineteenth day of the siege, Commander Pretorius reported that he had no need of reinforcements — he did, however, state that he would welcome more gunpowder as he did not know how long the Kekana could hold out[45]. Gunpowder (the only item the Trekkers did not themselves have to supply) was expensive; the administration of the Trekker government (as it then was) often admitted that gunpowder was the one item it could ill afford[46]. So it is not surprising to learn that the surplus powder requested was never supplied.

The Trekkers claimed that on 17 November a further three hundred and sixty-four women and children gave themselves up. On the same day, a company of Trekkers entered the cave. Inside they discovered (according to their own report) many dead and decomposing bodies, and they recovered thirty-four guns, some lead and powder, and some other items[47]. Small patrols entered the cave again the next day. Casualties were suffered, but these were (reportedly) light: four men were slightly wounded. These patrols came to the conclusion that resistance was over[48].

Was the siege called off because there were no more tribesmen to fight or were other considerations involved? Theal did state that horse sickness was the main reason for the abandonment of the siege without horses the Trekkers were, of course, vulnerable. But the siege was abandoned also because the rainy season had begun, which, apart from the general inconvenience of inclement weather, meant that the water supply — if this had effectively been cut off — stood a greater chance of being renewed. Twenty-eight days in one spot and thirty-nine days away from home and family was a long time for the Trekkers to endure. Gunpowder, despite the recovery of some in the cave, was running low; and the anticipated booty in livestock, women and children, which promised to be so bountiful, tarnished as the siege dragged on.

7

How many Kekana succumbed and how many survived the siege will never really be known[49]. To begin with, it is not known how many Kekana entered the cave in the first place. The claim that 'the want of water'[50] took its toll of the besieged has to be set against the knowledge that there was an underground passage which did contain water; and against the fact that the inner walls of the cave, about seven hundred and fifty meters from the entrance, did provide water, albeit, in trickles[51]. Perhaps many of the old, the young, the sick, the wounded and the frail did perish in the cave, but it is also likely that many — possibly the great majority — survived the blockade by quitting the cave through the main openings or through secret exits that were known or discovered during the siege; or through the mouth of the cave when the siege was over[52].

If two thousand were killed inside the cave, such a large number of dead human beings would have left an equally impressive number of skeletons. No one, however, took the trouble to tally these remains. The figure of two thousand was therefore neither objectively determined nor independently confirmed[53]. The adage that the first casualty of war is truth is particularly relevant to casualty figures: belligerents play down their own and exaggerate those of their enemy. In this case the African voice is silent. The figure of two thousand must be pitted against circumstances: exact computation must have been hampered by the obscurity within the cave, the reported stench of the decomposing bodies, the fear of snipers' bullets and the convenient but not always accurate habit of tallying in round numbers.

Whatever their actual losses during the siege of Makapansgat, there is little doubt that the Kekana were 'decimated tribally' or 'almost annihilated'[54]. Their former coherence was made impossible by the state of enmity with the Trekkers. To have maintained that coherence, after the survival of the siege, would merely have invited new attacks and fresh retaliation. Instead they broke up and joined remnants of other groups, and there must be a strong suspicion that many of the survivors joined the Langa tribe under Mankopane.

8

After the report of the patrols on 18 and 19 November, the siege was called off on the grounds that resistance was over, yet, significantly, Commander Pretorius did not himself venture into or near the cave. One report claimed that because of the suffering his people had endured, Mokopane, the Kekana chief, committed suicide out of noble remorse; but another attests that he was alive and well in 1909[55].

The livestock captured during the siege was meagre and in fact just after the siege was lifted, a cattle-gathering expedition under Kruger was sent northwards to the capital of chief Maraba. As Kruger explained:

Commandant General Pretorius sent me with a small commando to Maraba's town, where we had heard that a large number of Makapaan's cattle had been stored. I was to look into this matter and attack Maraba's town if it offered any resistance. But I met with none. Some of the Kaffirs fled, and the remainder surrendered. The latter declared that they had never shared in his crimes, and that they were quite willing to restore such of his stolen cattle as were in their possession. This was done, but only a thousand head were discovered. So soon as I had possession of the cattle, I returned, leaving Maraba's kaffirs unharmed[56].

From the point of view of booty the campaign against Mokopane was not much of a success. Some thirty-four guns, one thousand two hundred calves and three thousand three hundred cattle (it is not certain if this included the thousand taken from Maraba), and — for the Trekkers shared them like they did the livestock — seven hundred and sixty-four (or perhaps slightly more) women and children. The Trekkers lost two men, including one of their two Commanders, and had several of their men wounded. Most of the captured livestock was sold and the proceeds went either to cover the cost of the gunpowder or to serve as compensation for the survivors of the dead[57].

When a few years later calls were made to the same Trekkers to volunteer against Mankopane who had not yet been chastised the cave besiegers refused, complaining that as a result of their campaign against Mokopane they had grown considerably poorer. And they lamented that the cattle they had brought out from the Kekana country had been depleted by lung sickness[58].

9

After providing an account of the Trekkers' campaign against the Kekana, C.L. Norris-Newman, English journalist and author, reflected:

Sad as it is, yet I think the above description teaches a lesson, and shows us that savages must be fought, to a great extent, with their own weapons. It was only by so doing that the few Boers in the Transvaal were then enabled to maintain their position amid hordes of savages: whereas, in later years it has required a large army to effect, with much greater loss of time and material, that which a few mounted Boers, fighting on a different system, used to do in a comparatively short but summary way[59].

E.A. Walker echoed the same view when he noted that 'it was a stern

131

lesson and until they began to fight among themselves the Transvaalers had little further trouble with the tribesmen'[60]. Was this, in fact, the case?

Five separate expeditions were launched against Mankopane: the first in December 1855, the second in July 1856, the third in April 1858, the fourth in March 1868 and the fifth in July 1868. He defied and survived each until the Trekkers, wearied with the effort of fighting him, acquiesced in the independence he had always claimed. They concluded peace and displayed, in their private correspondence, a more than healthy regard in wanting to maintain that peace[61].

Mankopane, cast as the chief villain of the piece — the man putatively responsible for 'skinning Hermanus Potgieter alive'[62] — emerges from the story of the cave siege as a fierce but exemplary African patriot[63]. He lived to the ripe old age of seventy-two and never, between the twenty-three years spanning the attacks and his death, was he ever subjugated.

Was the Siege of Makapansgat a massacre? Perhaps. Was it a Trekker victory? Hardly.

8 WAS GANDHI'S SOUTH AFRICAN STRUGGLE INSPIRED BY RACE, CLASS OR NATION?

As he himself said, he grafted *Snell on Equity* to the *Bhagavadgita*.

R.A. Huttenback[1]

Gandhi came to South Africa in 1893 and left in 1914. He led, during most of the twenty-one year span, struggles against the Natal Government, the Transvaal Government and the Union Government. What was the guiding principle, the driving force behind this fight? Was it a civil rights struggle, a case of championing the cause of the Indians, Coloureds and Africans against the racist politics of an all-white administration? Was it a class strugggle in the interests of the Indian trading class or, alternatively, of the Indian labouring class? Or was it a nationalist struggle in the cause of India and the Indian nation?

1

During his South African sojourn, Gandhi never questioned the right of the whites to rule and regulate the destiny of South Africa. In July 1909 he acknowledged that the Indians recognized that the white population 'should remain predominant in South Africa'[2]. He also, perhaps in a naive way, endorsed non-miscegenation when he noted, in a political retort, that he too was committed to race purity, but protested that purity of race should not be the privilege of only one sector of the community[3].

He accepted white superiority but rejected black equality. In February 1904 he complained to the Johannesburg medical health officer: 'Why, of all places in Johannesburg, the Indian Location should be chosen for dumping down all the Kaffirs of the town passes my comprehension'. He urged that the Town Council 'withdraw the Kaffirs' and lamented that the 'mixing' was unfair and an undue tax on the Indians' patience[4]. He complained when he and fellow passive resisters were classed, while in prison, with the Africans[5]. He was critical of the whites' ignorant and — careless use of the term 'Coolie', yet his own use of the term *Kaffir* was no less ignorant and no less careless.

When in March 1906 the Coloured community circulated a petition, addressed to the King, in which they complained of not having the franchise in the Transvaal and in the Orange River Colony, he wrote, justifying the Indians non-identity with the petition: 'We consider that it was a wise policy, on the part of the British Indians throughout South Africa, to have kept themselves apart and distinct from the other Coloured communities in this country'. He admitted that the Coloureds and the Indians had common grievances but their respective claims, he insisted, had very little in common[6]. He also protested when the Natal Government wanted to open Durban's Higher Grade Indian School to Coloured children[7].

In 1906 some Zulu under a minor chief, Bambatta, smarting under an increased poll tax, protested. The white Natalians designated and then treated their discontent as a 'rebellion'. The Colonial forces were mobilized and sent out to chastise the malcontented Zulu. Gandhi, considering he was a British subject and a Natal citizen, was moved to demonstrate his loyalty in a practical way: he offered to organise a stretcher-bearer corps, as he had done during the Anglo-Boer War. But during the voluntary service the cold-steel spite of the colonial forces, their relentless tracking down of their foe and their trigger-happy readiness to kill turned his stomach. Loyalty to the Empire, however, made him hold his tongue. He admitted later that he bore the Zulu no grudge; that they had not, after all, harmed the Indians. He also admitted that he had doubts about the 'rebellion' itself. But he upheld his conviction that the British Empire was there to serve mankind and that loyalty prevented him from wishing it ill. His decision was therefore not influenced by the legitimacy or otherwise of the 'rebellion'[8]. This statement, however, was made in 1927 — two decades and more after the event. In 1906 his choice was less ambiguous:

What is our duty during these calamitous times in the colony? It is not for us to say whether the revolt of the Kaffirs is justified or not. We are in Natal by virtue of British power. Our very existence depends upon it. It is therefore our duty to render whatever help we can[9].

The division between Indian and African was, in his eyes, not antagonistic yet both precise and proper. In a 1906 letter he referred to

134

'the evident and sharp distinctions that undoubtedly exist between British Indians and the Kaffir races'[10]. In 1909 he expressed his opinion on this question clearly and succinctly: 'We may entertain no aversion to Kaffirs, but we cannot ignore the fact that there is no common ground between them and us in the daily affairs of life'[11].

Gandhi, of course, was no racist. Writing of his prison experience, he reflected that not being classed with the whites was to a certain extent acceptable, but being classed with the Africans was not. On the other hand, being with the Africans provided an opportunity of witnessing their treatment, of experiencing their conditions and of observing their habits. In this light, he concluded, 'it did not seem right to feel bad about being bracketed with them'[12].

The Chinese — a small, recently arrived community of about a thousand — accepted imprisonment, burnt their certificates and were generally present at crucial moments of the Gandhi-led struggle in the Transvaal (at least, between 1906 and 1908); yet Gandhi always looked upon them as being incidental to the fight. He never allowed their participation to become completely and truly part of the passive resistance movement[13].

In the consequence of these various positions, it would be patently false to maintain that Gandhi was the champion of the underprivileged and unrepresented 'non-whites'. His fight was, beyond doubt, exclusively on behalf of the Indians; but which Indians: the traders or the labourers?

2

The Indians Gandhi found in Natal were a divided, heterogeneous community. An attempt has been made recently to describe them sociologically as a mish-mash of 'merchants, migrants, commercial elite, new elite and underclasses'[14]. The description, although helpful, is unsatisfactory — who, for instance, made up the 'non-commercial elite', the 'old elite' and the 'overclasses'? What is essential for the purpose at hand is to note that:

Most of the Indians came to Natal as indentured labourers as new or temporary slaves[15]; whereas a minority came as fee-paying passengers. This difference of origins, though affected by time and change, remained crucial.

Most of the passenger Indians were traders. They came with capital and many had businesses, or were linked with businesses, in Mauritius and India.

Most of the indentured Indians came from Madras, spoke Tamil and were Hindus; most of the passenger Indians came from Gujarat, spoke Gujarati and were Muslims.

The ex-indentured labourers, who did not re-indenture and who did not return to India, took up small-scale cultivation, became fishermen, hawkers, waiters, small traders and − if they were educated −policemen, teachers, court interpreters and (exceptionally) lawyers. But whatever trading success they attained, commerce always remained marginal and was, distinctly and clearly, the preserve of the passenger Indians.

The passenger Indians came to trade and not to settle. They had no identification crisis; they looked upon India as their country and did not, during the whole of Gandhi's stay in South Africa, cease to regard it as such. The ex-indentured Indians, in their majority, came to South Africa in the hope of starting out again − came, in brief, as settlers. By 1908 one of their spokesmen could claim that he was colonial-born and by implication not an 'Indian'[16].

Gandhi always insisted that the Indians in South Africa, though divided by caste, language, region and religion (not to mention class and history), were united in their common bond to India. Being an Indian himself he could hardly help being aware of the many divisions and the few but fundamental distinctions which made one Indian differ from the other, but he insisted, over and over again, that the Indians were one:

This campaign knows no distinctions of Hindus, Muslims, Parsis, Christians, Bengalis, Madrasis, Gujaratis, Punjabis and others. All of us are Indians, and are fighting for India. Those who do not realize this are not servants but enemies of the motherland[17].

Yet he drew a line between the indentured labourers and the other Indians. The indentured Indians were not, he believed, 'free men'. And even when they were free they came under the provision of special laws[18]. He therefore accepted that there was a certain logic in checking their movements, and that a curfew law could, in their case, be justified.

His bias by upbringing, tradition and culture was with the trader class. He naturally identified with those who were clean, educated and civilized; and just as naturally endorsed Cecil John Rhodes' anti-democratic formula of equal rights for all civilized men. In 1895 he wrote: 'I am confident that the Indians [and he was, of course, referring to the passenger Indians] have no wish to see ignorant Indians who cannot possibly be expected to understand the value of a vote being placed on the Voters' List'[19].

In 1908 he wrote that the Asiatic question was primarily a trade question[20]. Earlier, when a handful of colonial-born Indians (the so-called 'New Elite') dared to question the unrepresentative nature of the Natal Indian Congress, he would scold them, charge them with being ungrateful and admonish them for ignoring everything that Congress had done for them. Emphases in Congress, he conceded, were on trader interests (the dissidents thought traders and trader interests too evidently monopolised the proceedings of Congress) but this he considered inevitable and just:

If the Indian traders today loom large at the Congress meetings, it is because they are the most in danger; and if they were neglected or allowed themselves to be neglected, who will suffer? Certainly the whole Indian community; for throughout the world it is the commercial class that supplies the sinews of war and even common sense to the community or nation to which it belongs[21].

Two years later, in 1909, during the Passive Resistance Campaign, he emphasized once again that it was the businessmen who shouldered the burden of the struggle. It was their stake which was most at risk because they enjoyed 'a higher status'; it was they who most acutely felt the disgrace of discrimination[22].

When the Anglo-Boer War broke out in October 1899, Gandhi seized the opportunity to demonstrate the loyalty of the Natal Indians by organising an ambulance corps. The Indians, he declared, were ignorant of arms but there were other battle-field duties, no less vital, that they could and were willing to perform[23].

To demonstrate loyalty to the British Empire was clearly one of the reasons why Gandhi wanted the Indians to participate in the War. A second, perhaps subordinate, but certainly revealing reason — was to rebut white sneers and accusations that the Indians were mere money-gatherers and rank opportunists; that they would not in the event of an invasion render the slightest aid and that it would be up to the whites to defend them. He therefore felt it was 'a golden opportunity' for the

Indians to prove that the charges were groundless[24].

Gandhi evidently had in mind the passenger-traders. The white Natalians did not hold the same opinion of the indentured labourers; the planter class, at least, recognised their importance and acknowledged the beneficial effect their coming had had on Natal's economy. Gandhi himself was aware of this, for he had declared that Natal owed 'its present prosperity to the indentured Indians'[25]. The stigma of opportunism was never levelled at the indentured or ex-indentured labourers; on the contrary, their presence was regarded as a military asset against the threat of a possible Zulu attack[26].

The Ambulance Corps was formed with about three to four hundred ex-indentured and about seven hundred indentured Indians. From the former group came the thirty-seven that served as Gandhi's lieutenants. According to Gandhi, they were made up of barristers, accountants, masons, carpenters and ordinary labourers. All sections of the Indian community were represented — all except the passenger-traders[27].

At Spionkop, at Vaalkranz and at Colenso the Indian Ambulance Corps, risking life and limb, worked under heavy fire. A British general is reported to have said: 'These Indian fellow-subjects of ours are doing in Natal a work which requires even more courage than that of the soldier'[28].

The aim of physical participation in the War was to rebut the charge that the trading class Indians in Natal were cowardly and avaricious. Participation was to demonstrate that the traders were not only loyal British subjects but also staunch defenders of home and able resisters of invasion. Yet none of the passenger-traders assisted under battle conditions — none of them actually participated in the Ambulance Corps.

They did, it is true, contribute the £65 to the Durban Women's Patriotic League, entertain the wounded who were under the charge of the Ambulance Corps (with scarce cigarettes, cigars, pipes and tobacco), and provide the cloth that Indian women volunteers handmade into pillow cases and handkerchiefs for the wounded soldiers[29]. The traders thus gave money and goods, but an ex- indentured woman who made a living from the daily sale of fresh fruit is reported to have emptied the contents of her basket into a lorry transporting soldiers from the Durban wharf, saying that it was all she could give that day[30]. In the light of the humble woman's gesture, the traders' contribution to the War effort was modest indeed.

The anticipated goodwill and political reward which was supposedly to accrue from the sacrifice made, in the main, by the labourers, was destined not for the vindication of all the Indians but for the exclusive vindication of the traders. In this respect Gandhi championed the rights of the Natal traders.

All commentators, Gandhi included, agree that the meeting which took place at the Empire Theatre, Fordsburg, Johannesburg on Tuesday, 11 September 1906 marked the beginning of the Passive Resistance movement[31]. Gandhi recorded that 'the business of the meeting was conducted in Hindi or Gujarati', and that 'credit' for organizing it was due to the Hamidia Islamic Society, a Johannesburg Muslim benevolent society that was established in July 1906. The Hamidia Islamic Society and the British Indian Association (a body formed in 1903) were dominated by the Transvaal traders. The leaders of both organisations were often one and the same people[32]. The moving spirit of the meeting was not Gandhi but Hajee Habib (or Sheth Haji Habib), whom Gandhi described as 'a very old experienced resident of South Africa'[33]. Habib, more significantly, was also the brother of Dada Abdulla. Dada Abdulla's extensive Natal-based business was one of the biggest Indian commercial enterprises in South Africa[34]. Habib led; Gandhi, with some hesitation, followed. This is evident from the English translation of Habib's contribution:

I solemnly declare that I will never get myself registered again and will be the first to go to goal. (Applause) I recommend the same course to you all. Are you all prepared to take the oath? (The Assembly stood up to a man and said, 'Yes, we will go to gaol!') Only by so doing shall we succeed. We tried this method in the days of the Boer Government also. Some 40 of our men were once arrested for trading without licenses. I advised them to go to gaol and not seek release on bail. Accordingly, they all remained there without offering bail. I immediately approached the British Agent, who approved our action and ultimately secured justice for us. Now that a British Government is in power the time has come for us to go to gaol, and go we will[35].

Gandhi might have suggested the tactic of gaol-going[36], and he did, at least, help draft the all-important gaol-going resolution, but the tactic of defiance, and of going to prison was — as Habib's address testifies — a manner of protest native to the Transvaal traders long before

139

Gandhi ever thought of the idea. So at this stage Gandhi did not lead the Transvaal traders; the Transvaal traders led him.

The Passive Resistance Campaign 'fed on jail sentences'[37]. By January 1908 one hundred and fifty-five were incarcerated and by March 1909, one hundred and eleven[38]. But jail sentences, though on occasion harsh, could not compare with deportations and withholding of trading licenses. Once the Transvaal Government started applying these, the movement lost its momentum, slid into a stalemate and reached the doldrums by early 1909[39]. But whether the movement was at a crest or in a trough, the volunteers were nearly always from the ex-indentured community a community that in the Transvaal was in a minority[40].

A few traders, notably Ahmed Mohammed Cachalia, a Surti Memon, 'one of the rarest among the Mahomedans' (as Gandhi described him), understood and met the sacrifices that had been demanded[41]. But the vast majority of Transvaal traders supported the movement on the understanding that it would protect them against legislation seeking to destroy their businesses. By October 1907 it dawned on them that they stood a better chance of preserving their businesses with Smuts's Acts than with Gandhi's protests[42]. Hajee Habib, the moving spirit, the firebrand of the all-important meeting at the Empire Theatre, temporarily and conveniently left the Transvaal in December 1907[43].

As early as November 1907, Gandhi was condemning the Memons - the spearhead of the Indian trading class in the country districts of the Transvaal for having given up the fight[44]. By March 1909 he admitted that with the exception of the Tamils and a handful of Parsis, all the other sections of the community had abandoned the struggle[45]. By June 1909 the leaders of the Transvaal traders, anxious to terminate the crisis, forced his hand and persuaded him, in spite of his reluctance he was convinced his time would be better spent in jail — to lead a deputation to the British Government in London[46]. He and Hajee Habib — a recent adherent to the actual struggle, for he had not himself been to prison[47], and the initiator of the deputation idea — sailed for England on 21 June 1909.

The two-men deputation failed to obtain a meeting with Generals Botha and Smuts, who were there finalising the impending Union of South Africa. But they did meet with Lord Ampthill (the former Governor of Madras), who volunteered service as a kind of shuttle diplomat. From his intelligence it was clear that General Botha was unwilling

to budge; and it was also clear that even if he were, his white electorate would persuade him to think again. General Botha, Lord Ampthill
assured them, was prepared to concede unspecified reforms but these
categorically excluded the repeal of the Asiatic Act and the amendment of the Immigration Restriction Act. Stubbornness on the part of
the Indians, the General had added, would only invite trouble and increase hardship for themselves.

Habib's response, which was brief and a far cry from the uncompromising and moving September 1906 Empire Theatre address, was
revealing and unedifying:

> I accept General Botha's offer on behalf of the *conciliation party*. If
> he makes these *concessions*, we will be satisfied for the present and
> *later on struggle for principle*. I do not like the community to suffer
> any more. The party I represent constitutes the majority of the com-
> munity, and it also holds the major portion of the community's
> wealth[48].

Gandhi endorsed Habib's representative claim and admitted that he
himself spoke on behalf of the smaller and poorer section of the community, but emphasized that they were fighting not only for practical
relief but also for principle, and that between the two he would prefer
to give up practical relief rather than concede principle. He asked Lord
Ampthill to convey their respective responses to Botha[49].

It is apparent that the two delegates entertained, as Gandhi himself
put it, 'divergent views'[50]. The meaning of this divergence is clear:
the traders had abandoned faith in passive resistance. They left Gandhi to struggle on with his band of faithful followers — left him, as they
saw it, to bang his head against a wall[51].

It is true that the traders had accepted Gandhi's leadership — and
even his quixotism — as long as it did not touch their pockets, but when
he began to equate poverty with saintliness, they demurred. They told
him repeatedly that truth and business were incompatible. Religion,
they had stressed, was a spiritual matter; separate and distinct from the
practical affairs of business. How were they to react, how could they
react when Gandhi (who obviously had them in mind) preached — like
a prophet and advised (to their minds) like a madman:

> It is not enough to live by the laws of supply and demand . . . Bigger
> fish prey on smaller ones . . . they know not better. But God has en-

dowed man with understanding, with a sense of justice. He must follow these and not think of growing rich by devouring others — by cheating others ... where Mammon [an obvious thrust at his fellow Gujaratis] is God, no one worships the true God. Wealth cannot be reconciled with God. God lives only in the homes of the poor ... To teach the people to get rich at any cost is to teach them an evil lesson[52].

Gandhi has been described as 'the chief representative of the Transvaal merchants' and as 'their strategist and tactician'[53]. This was so initially but even then only superficially; for the Transvaal traders were out to protect their businesses while Gandhi was out to protect a principle. For a time, between 1906 and 1908, their respective interests coincided but once these began to diverge the gulf between them became unbreachable.

Gandhi's struggle was obviously not inspired by merchant or trader interests. Could it then have been inspired by the interests of the labouring class and by the educated class of colonial-borns could it have been, in brief, inspired by the interests of the indentured and ex-indentured Indians?

3

Gandhi, as has been seen, was impatient with the educated, mainly colonial-born Indians — the spokesmen of the labouring class Indians, who protested about the Natal Indian Congress being too preoccupied with trader grievances. As for the labourers themselves, Gandhi did protest about the coercive £3 tax, an impossibly onerous measure designed to force the labourers either into re-indenture or into repatriation; but there is no indication that he ever visited a sugar plantation, a tea or coffee estate, a coal mine or any of the other places that housed and employed Indians in large numbers[54].

His attitude is perhaps not difficult to understand, for he believed that while they were an asset to Natal's economy, they nevertheless by their status, their appearance, their ignorance and their poverty gave an unflattering and disparaging impression of Indian; and he had implied as much when (in 1902) he observed that in a sense, the Indians themselves were to blame for the feeling of hatred they engendered among the colonials; for had they been followed or represented 'by better-class Indians', who could be the equals of the whites in every sphere, the bad blood apparent then would not have arisen, would not have been present[55].

His attitude towards the labourers, however, underwent a gradual change: first, when Balasundaram, an indentured labourer called at his home in 1894 and complained that he had been beaten and maltreated by his white employer — the wretched labourer still bore the traces of his injury: two of his front teeth were broken and his mouth was bleeding[56]; and secondly, when he later came to know the descendants of these labourers in the Transvaal. His faithful band of followers were nearly all Tamil. Some were or had been petty traders, hawkers, peddlers, waiters or factory workers but most, even so, had links — whether recent or remote — with the indentured experience[57].

The turning point, however, came with the arrival in October 1912 of G.K. Gokhale — 'the most revered Indian political leader of his day'[58]. Gokhale met Botha and Smuts and assured Gandhi that the contentious, restrictive measures would be repealed — along with the iniquitous £3 tax.

The coupling of the grievances of the labouring Indians of Natal with the grievances of the trading Indians of the Transvaal was a feat exclusively and uniquely of Gokhale's. Gandhi admitted as much: 'If Gokhale had not come over to South Africa, if he had not seen the Union ministers, the abolition of the £3 tax could not have been made a plank in our platform'[59].

Why was this so? Why had Gandhi not independently thought of the £3 tax grievance before 1912? He did, after all, protest against it when it was first mooted in 1894, and he continued to protest against it when it was made law in 1896. In the Transvaal his concern and his attention were, excusably, engaged elsewhere; although — even then he did refer to a case involving the tax in April 1906, and wrote an article for *Indian Opinion* (as late as 1910) titled, 'The £3 tax again'[60]. Yet in his *Satyagraha in South Africa*, first published in 1928, he lamely considered why the tax had not formed part of the struggle before Gokhale's arrival:

When a wrong, no matter how flagrant, has continued for a long period of time, people get habituated to it, and it becomes difficult to rouse them to a sense of their duty to resist and no less difficult to convince the world that it is wrong at all[61].

143

However, in 1905 he stated that there was 'no remedy' and that the only solution was reconciliation with the fact of the law[62]. Later, upon his return from the first deputation to England (in 1906), he made a stop at Verulam, an ex-indenture stronghold. The welcome committee wanted to know if there was any prospect of the tax being repealed. Gandhi replied that they had put up a stiff fight when the tax was imposed but that at present it was very difficult to obtain any redress in the matter[63]. Familiarity, habit and *fait accompli* were not the real reasons why the tax was not 'a plank in the platform' of the passive resistance campaign before 1913. Gandhi, with his lawyer's mind and with his conviction that law was religion and religion was law, had persuaded himself that the distinction between an indentured and an immigrant Indian was clear and sharp: free Indian immigration was a matter of Imperial policy; indentured labour was a matter of 'contract and bargain'[64].

The £3 tax had no place in the struggle before 1913 because the problems of the indentured labourers, the ex-indentured labourers and the tax were, as far as principle was concerned, peripheral to India's relations with Britain. To Gandhi's way of thinking, the tax was not an Empire issue. It only became one when it was not repealed — non-repeal was a breach of faith with Gokhale and, therefore, an insult to India. He appealed to the Indian miners of Newcastle to come out on strike not because they had been abused and exploited (he had admitted that he had no quarrel with the mine-owners) but because India's honour had been put at stake. He told a group of strikers, during one stage of the march, that they had come out 'not as indentured labourers but as servants of India'[65].

Pay and conditions were not Gandhi's concern; the inspiration behind his struggle, whatever it might have been, was not a pro-labour one.

4

A proposed law (the Draft Asiatic Law Amendment Ordinance) in August 1906 set out to control the residence of Indian men, women and children by enforced registration on the assumption that every Transvaal Indian was guilty of having entered the Province illegally. To Gandhi's mind, such procedure and practice were totally alien to British justice, for instead of working on the assumption of innocence before guilt, it acted on the opposite principle: the innocent many were made to suffer for the guilty few[66]. Besides, the Act was tantamount to a pass law; it carried a proviso for finger prints.

The registration issue came to be embodied in the Immigration Restriction Act of 1907. Opposition to this law was the generator of Gandhi's Passive Resistance or, as he preferred to call it, 'Satyagraha' (literally, soul force) movement. From 1906 to 1914 Gandhi contested a number of different laws; but whether the law coerced the Indians into finger-print registrations, prevented them from entering the Transvaal or denied them trading rights, he doggedly and consistently opposed these laws because they violated the principle of equality between white and brown *British*.

In the aftermath of the Indian Sepoy Revolt of 1857 (the 'Indian Mutiny' of British history), Queen Victoria made a policy statement that came to constitute the Proclamation of 1858; where, in part, she declared:

> We hold ourselves bound to the natives of our Indian territories by the same obligations of duty which bind us to all our other subjects, and these obligations, by the blessing of Almighty God, we shall faithfully and conscientiously fulfil.
> And it is our further will that, so far as may be, our subjects, of whatever race or creed, be freely and impartially admitted to offices in our service, the duties of which they may be qualified by their education, ability, and integrity, duly to discharge.
> In their prosperity will be our strength; in their contentment our security; and in their gratitude, our best reward[67].

Gandhi's trust in this declaration, which he called 'the Magna Charta of the Indians', and his faith in the British Empire ('Hardly ever have I known anybody to cherish such loyalty as I did to the British Consti-tution') remained fast and fixed until 1919; that is, a full four years after he had left South Africa[68]. In a 1908 speech he declared, 'The British Constitution taught us, it taught me when yet a child that every British subject was to be treated on a footing of equality in the eye of the law'[69].

His years of study in England (1887-1891) reinforced his childhood convictions. England was to him the centre of civilisation, the land of poets, philosophers, intellectuals and statesmen — the land whose Empire was benevolent, altruistic, impartial and colour-blind. These convictions, firmly held and sincerely cherished, came under an unexpected and severe buffeting in Natal; for here he was thrown out of a train and forced to spend a night shivering in the waiting room of a forlorn and forsaken station. The experience, he once admitted, was the most creative in his life[70]. The physical attack on his person, the rank disregard for his constitutuion so unexpected, jolted his convictions. To appreciate why this was so, one must understand that to his mind British justice, British beneficence and British altruism were axiomatic truths that put India's relations with Britain beyond contention[71]. Now, for the first time, the connection between India and Britain was brutally spurned and ridiculed. The dim realization that the presence of the British in India was a matter more of might than of right unbalanced him, scattered his convictions and sent him reeling morally.

The befriending of whites: J.J. Doke, H.S.L. Polak, A. Cartwright, H. Kitchin and A. West (English-born for the most part) reassured him and restored his faith. His belief in the Empire held. The Natal whites were ignorant, he would inform them what 'true imperialism' meant; he would make them realize that 'coloured British subjects' were entitled 'to be treated the same as the other British subjects'[72]. Thus when in Durban he organised a wreath-laying ceremony to mark the death of Queen Victoria (February 1901), he mentioned the Proclamation of 1858[73]. Later, he issued a souvenir brochure that had a picture of the late Empress and, alongside it, a caption bearing the all-important section of the Proclamation[74].

An editorial of *The Natal Mercury* (18 January 1897), notwithstanding its recognition of the Proclamation's authenticity, dismissed it as a futile attempt to get the Indians accepted in South Africa. It stressed that there was a strong and deeply-rooted prejudice against the Indians, a hostility to their entry into the country and a repugnance against their customs and way of life. It concluded: 'They may be British subjects by law, but they are aliens by what is stronger than law, viz., racial traditions and instincts'[75].

Gandhi was fully aware of this argument. In his first-ever publication, a pamphlet entitled *The Indian franchise: An appeal to every Briton in South Africa* (1895), he pleaded:

Although the 'British subject' idea has been rejected by the Press as a craze and fad, I have to fall back upon that idea. Without it . . . the Indian would have been an impossibility in Natal . . . I, therefore, appeal to every Briton in South Africa not to lightly dismiss the

'British subject' idea from his mind. The Proclamation of 1858 was Her Majesty's act ... done, not arbitrarily, but according to the advice of Her then advisers, in whom the voters, by their votes, had reposed their full trust. India belongs to England and England does not wish to lose her hold of India. Every act done by a Briton towards an Indian cannot but have some effect in moulding the final relations between Britons and Indians[76].

In time he abandoned reference to the Proclamation, realising that not only ordinary white South Africans but also responsible politicians shared the view of *The Natal Mercury* editorial. Later, when Natal and the Transvaal became part of the Union of South Africa, he would do battle not for the recognition of the Proclamation but for the ideal and the spirit it embodied — for what he called 'the beautiful vision' of the British Constitution[77]. And it is because of this attachment to the ideal of a colour-blind Empire that he chose to contest the Immigration Act of 1907. He wanted Act 2 of 1907 to be repealed and the Immigration Act to be amended. And he appealed: let the amendment allow any cultured Asiatic immigrant to enter the Colony on equal terms with Europeans, and allow (by way of an education test) no more than six a year to enter the Colony and the 'British Indians will be satisfied'[78].

The statutory six cultured Indians he sought admission for mystified friend and foe alike. Gokhale thought it was 'largely theoretical'[79]. Lord Ampthill thought it 'quixotic'[80]. W.P. Schreiner, who lent Gandhi a patient ear, thought that providing for the entry of six educated Indians, as a special favour, ought not to be an obstacle — an opinion with which Smuts concurred[81]. A recent historian, in conformity with many of Gandhi's contemporaries, also judged his demand in this respect 'politically foolish'[82].

Patrick Duncan, the first Governor-General of South Africa, was, however, more perspicacious:

The position of the Indian leaders is that they will tolerate no law which does not put them on an equality with Europeans in regard to restriction on immigration ... They insist on equality in the terms of law itself. It is true that this claim is not always put forward in so many words. It generally appears in the demand for admission of a small number of educated Indians. It is agreed — and the argument deserves consideration that a community such as the Asiatic community of the Transvaal requires the services and the moral influence of a certain number of educated men. It is on this argument that Mr. Gandhi appeals for sympathy to the European community here and to the people of England. But behind it is the claim which he has never given up nor abated that *there must be nothing in the law which imposes on the immigration of Asiatics restrictions which are not imposed on Europeans*[83].

Gandhi was aware of Duncan's views and he acknowledged, while specifically referring to the article that contained the passage just cited, that Duncan had 'truly analysed the struggle'[84]. Gandhi, of course, had no intention of 'flooding' the white-dominated parts of the British Empire with British Asiatics, what he wanted to safeguard was not the principle of Indian immigration as such, but the principle of Empire equality. This to him was neither quixotic nor foolish but quintessential; for he made an important, though subtle, distinction between theory and practice: 'theory should be sound, though one may fail to carry it out in practice'. Safeguarding theory was obeying the law of higher nature; departing from it in practice was giving in to the temptation of base human nature[85]. However negative a practice may be, it should never, he protested, be enshrined in law.

To Gandhi, allowing in theory an educated brown Briton to enter South Africa like a white Briton put India's relations with Britain on a par, ensured reciprocity and engendered mutual respect[86]. It is with this ideal in mind that he wrote: 'We are not fighting on behalf of the educated or the highly educated but for India's honour'[87].

Preserving 'India's honour' meant, in one sense, that his view of the Empire and the status of India's part in that Empire stood fast; and this preservation was paramount because he sincerely and ardently believed that the meeting of Englishmen and Indians was providential: an advantage not only for themselves but also for mankind[88].

It is difficult to understand the motives of Gandhi's actions in South Africa without taking into account the development of Indian nationalism in India. To cover the subject adequately would, of course, be inappropriate here, but it suffices to note that some of the principal events between 1885, when the Indian National Congress held its first meeting, and 1914, when the First World War broke out, coincide remarkably with the rise of Gandhi in South Africa. In 1891 Tilak, a 'left nationalist' in opposition to the more moderate 'liberal nationalists' like Gokhale, openly opposed the British authorities and accused them of attacking Hinduism because they tried to interfere with the custom of child marriages; in 1892 Congress, for the first time, criticised representation through nomination; in 1895 Tilak revived the festival of Shivaji, the hero and liberator of Maharashtra from the Moguls; in 1897 a British health officer was assassinated; in 1905 the partition of Bengal sparked off country-wide revolts, set in train the nation-wide singing of *Bande Mataram* (Hail Mother) — the Indian *Marseillaise* — and transformed a sedate, elitist nationalist movement into a fiery, popular and country-wide unrest; in 1906 the Swadeshi (boycott) movement was launched; in 1907 the Seditious Meeting Act was passed, and there was an open split between the 'left' and 'liberal' wings of the nationalist movement; in 1908 Tilak (the most important nationalist leader since 1906) was arrested and sent to prison for six years, workers in a Bombay textile mill went on strike in protest and a bomb was thrown at a British District judge; in 1909 Curzon Wyllie, a member of India House, was assassinated in London; in 1910 the Indian Press Act, which gagged the nationalist newspapers, was passed; and in 1911 the Morley-Minto Reforms overturned the Bengal partition[89].

Gandhi's thoughts and writings, while he was involved in South Africa, were never divorced from India; so that in 1909, while he was still enmeshed in the politics of the Transvaal and still weighed down by the dwindling passive resistance campaign, he wrote (on his return voyage from England) a pamphlet titled *Hind Swaraj*, which was later to constitute his credo, setting forth how and why Indian independence must eschew violence and embrace 'satyagraha'[90]. The Transvaal struggle, India and the British Empire were separate entities but never, to Gandhi's heart and mind, autonomous. As he said: 'The struggle was not on behalf of a handful of Indian residents in the Transvaal. It was on behalf of the whole of India. Indeed on behalf of the whole Empire'[91].

Transvaal anti-Indian legislation drew a sharp distinction between brown and white British subjects. The Acts denied the moral contract of India's association with Britain; a denial that undermined the very basis of Gandhi's perception of that partnership. This explains the high-toned and impassioned way he opposed these Acts:

The doctrine laid down by the Transvaal Government, and assented to by the Imperial Government cuts at the foundation of the Empire ... If the doctrine ... be true, the people of India cease to be partners in the Empire, and it is in order to resist this dangerous, immoral and pestilent doctrine that we in the Transvaal are fighting[92].

Here was the true inspiration and the real spur of the struggle as Gandhi saw it in November 1909. And true and real it remained until the very end. The report of his farewell speech in July 1914 (the month he left South Africa for the fifth and last time) noted:

> Behind that struggle for concrete rights lay the great spirit which asked for an abstract principle, and the fight which was undertaken in 1906, although it was a fight against a particular law, was a fight undertaken in order to combat the spirit that . . . was about . . . to undermine the glorious British Constitution.

The choice, it went on to point out, was between 'two courses': either he and his compatriots break with the British Empire or they fight to preserve the ideal of the Constitution[93].

Gandhi's attachment to India was pious, his adherence to its nationalism was mystical and his commitment to its image as 'motherland' was devout. 'I think of my love for the Motherland', he admitted, 'as an aspect of my religion'[94]. To him, serving India was equivalent to serving God. And since, as he often said, 'truth is God, or God is nothing but truth'[95], fighting the good fight for India was equivalent to fighting the good fight for 'truth'. The fight that Gandhi led in South Africa was not a race or class struggle (nor even an individual or personal struggle) but a national struggle — a struggle on behalf of truth, God and India.

Abbreviations

CHBE E.A. Walker (ed.), *Cambridge history of the British Empire*, vol VIII, South Africa (2nd ed. Cambridge, 1963).

Cory *The rise of South Africa* (London, 1910-1930, repr. Cape Town, 1965), 5 vols.

DSAB, I *Dictionary of South African biography*, vol I, ed. by W.J. de Kock (Cape Town, 1968).

DSAB, II *Dictionary of South African biography*, vol II, ed. by W.J. de Kock and D.W. Kruger (Cape Town, 1972).

DSAB, III *Dictionary of South African biography*, vol III, ed. by D.W. Kruger and C.J. Beyers (Cape Town, 1977).

DSAB, IV *Dictionary of South African biography*, vol IV, ed. by C.J. Beyers (Cape Town, 1981).

500 Years C.F.J. Muller (ed.), *Five hundred years: A history of South Africa* (2nd rev. ed. Pretoria, 1975).

History G.M. Theal, *History of South Africa*, 11 vols (London, 1888-1919, repr. Cape Town, 1964).

NOTES

INTRODUCTION

1. *The Black problem* (Lovedale, 1920), 73.

2. *Debates with historians* (London, 1967), 278; *The political mythology of apartheid* (New Haven and London, 1985), 12.

3. *The political mythology of apartheid*, 231; see also 54-68.

4. See his chapter, 'The strange career of Slagtersnek' in *ibid*, 105-143.

5. Lionel Forman, *Black and white in S.A. history* (n.p., n.d.), 5.

6. On 8 August 1938, in order to celebrate the centenary of the Great Trek, the ox wagon *Piet Retief* set out from Cape Town on its long trek to Pretoria. The precise starting point of the journey (in Cape Town) was from the foot of the statue of Van Riebeeck. See Thompson, *The political mythology of Apartheid*, 184.

7. H.B. Thom (ed.), *The journal of Jan van Riebeeck*, 3 vols. (Cape Town and Amsterdam, 1952), 'Introduction', I, xxvi.

8. 'Khoisan resistance to the Dutch in the seventeenth and eighteenth centuries', *Journal of African history*, XIII, I (1972), 62.

9. B. Willan, *Sol Plaatje South African Nationalist 1876-1932* (London, 1984).

10. See M. Ferro, *Petain* (Paris, 1987); G. Duby, *Guillaume: Le Maréchal ou le meilleur chevalier du monde* (Paris, 1984).

11. C. Saunders, *The making of the South African past* (Cape Town, 1988), 137.

12. (Johannesburg, 1952).

13. In M. Kooy (ed.), *Studies in economics and economic history* (London, 1972).

14. 'The labour market of the Cape Colony, 1807-28', in Shula Marks and A. Atmore (eds.), *Economy and society in pre-industrial South Africa* (London, 1980).

15. *Ibid*. 196.

16. *The fire next time* (Harmondsworth, 1964), 18.

17. 2 vols. (London, 1828, repr. New York, 1969).

18. (London, 1957, 1965 imp.), 185.

19. (Edinburgh, 1920, repr. Cape Town, 1963), 103. It is fair to point out that Molema did stress that 'it is said' that Hintsa was killed while trying to escape.

20. *Bantu, Boer and Briton* (London, 1929), 111-12.

21. (University of the Witwatersrand, 1971).

22. *Sir Harry Smith Bungling hero* (Cape Town, 1980); and *The House of Phalo* (Johannesburg, 1981).

23. 'Fiction in history' in Essays in English history (Harmondsworth, 1976), 11.

24. *DSAB*, II, 142-45.

25. This chapter, by a happy coincidence, has much in common with Thompson's 'The Covenant' (the fifth chapter of his *The political mythology of apartheid*, 144-188).

26. By F.N.C. Okaye, in the *Journal of African history*, X, 2 (1969). The French historian, Marianne Cornevin relies on Okaye's article to refute the pro-settler and pro-apartheid charge that Dingane was nothing but a bloody despot. See *L'apartheid: Pouvoir et falsification historique* (Paris, 1979), 101.

27. See J. Kruuse, *Madness at Oradour* (London, 1969); and R. Mackness, *Oradour: Massacre and aftermath* (London, 1988).

28. See D. Brown, *Bury my heart at Wounded Knee: An Indian history of the American West* (London, 1972), 347-52.

29. (London, 1961), 311.

30. *General Smuts*, 2 vols. (London, 1936), II, 107.

31. S. Bhana and B. Pachai (eds.), *A documentary history of Indian South Africans* (Cape Town, 1984), 111.

32. Maureen Swan, *Gandhi: The South African experience* (Johannesburg, 1985), 109.

33. *Ibid*, 225 and 271.

CHAPTER ONE

1. 'Cape Colony, 1806-1822', *CHBE*, 218.

2. (1813-1873) missionary of the London Missionary Society, and celebrated African explorer.

3. I. Schapera (ed.), *David Livingstone South African papers 1849-1853* (Cape Town, 1974), 73. Livingstone's essay, as far as it is known, was never published in his own life time. W.G. Blaikie, however, featured it as an appendix in the 2nd ed. of his, *The Personal life of David Livingstone* (London, 1881).

4. See note 3 above.

5. See 70-95, especially 73.

6. D. Moodie (1794-1861) civil servant, author and Natal politician. He was the first to have material from official sources printed. Between 1838 and 1841 he published, in three unbound parts, *The Record, or A series of official papers relative to the condition and treatment of the native tribes of South Africa*, which he himself had assembled, translated and edited. *The Record*, (reprinted in Amsterdam and Cape Town, 1960), has rightly been described as 'a monumental source book' (*DSAB*, II, 489).

7. *Livingstone's South African papers*, 178-9.

8. *Jan van Riebeeck: A biographical study* (London, 1936), 197.

9. *Compendium of the history and geography of South Africa* (Lovedale, 3rd rev. ed. 1878), 66.

10. *Kraal and castle: Khoikhoi and the founding of White South Africa* (New Haven, 1977), 116.

11. *De stichter van Hollands Zuid-Afrika: Jan van Riebeeck, 1618-1677* (Amsterdam, 1912),93.

12. See Chapter II, 'The fort and the garden', in *Race attitudes in South Africa* (London, 1937), 15-38, especially 20-1.

13. 'Jan van Riebeeck and his settlement', *South African Journal of economics*, 20(4), December 1952, 324.

14. *South Africa in the making, 1652-1806* (Cape Town, 1966), 8.

15. *Three lectures on the Cape of Good Hope under the government of the Dutch East India Company* (Cape Town, 1857). The pamphlet was reproduced in *Selections from the writings of the late E.B. Watermeyer with a brief sketch of his life* (Cape Town, 1877), 26-95, especially 42-5.

16. 'Jan van Riebeeck and the Hottentots', *South African Archaeological Bulletin*, VII(25), March 1952, 10.

17. Godée-Molsbergen published (in 1937), *Jan van Riebeeck en zijn tijd*. This was a condensed version of his earlier work of 1912. A second edition followed in 1943. An Afrikaans edition (*Jan van Riebeeck en sy tyd*, Pretoria, 1968, 63-4) was translated and edited by Professor B.J. Liebenberg of the University of South Africa.

18. She claims that the Dutch herd-boy, who was killed by one of the Khoi clans, and whose death precipitated the crisis between Dutch and Khoi, took place in 1657 when it actually took place (four years earlier) in 1653. 'Khoisan resistance to the Dutch in the seventeenth and eighteenth centuries', 62-3.

153

19. H. Dehérain, the French historian, can also be included in this list. He made (in *Le Cap de Bonne-Espérance au XVII siècle*, Paris, 1909, 36-7) no reference to Van Riebeeck's harsh proposals but referred instead (as Dr Böeseken had done) to Van Riebeeck's 'peace' proclamation, and to a 1660 Van Riebeeck statement: 'Notre objet principal est de vivre en amitié avec les habitants du pays et de commercer avec eux' (Our principal object is to live in friendship with the inhabitants of the country and to trade with them). See also, *Journal of Jan van Riebeeck*, III, 277.

20. 'The Khoisan to c. 1770', in R. Elphick and H. Giliomee (eds.), *The shaping of South African society, 1652-1820* (Cape Town, 1979), 11 (emphasis added).

21. H.C.V. Leibbrandt, *Précis of the Archives of the Cape of Good Hope: Letters and documents received, 1649-1662*, 2 vols. (Cape Town, 1898-9), II, 60. See also Moodie, *The Record*, 140; and also the letter Van Riebeeck addressed to the Batavian authorities (18 April 1657) where he stated that the Company's chief object at the Cape was 'the raising of wheat and the obtaining of cattle in great abundance'. H.C.V. Leibbrandt, *Précis of the Archives of the Cape of Good Hope: Letters despatched from the Cape, 1652-1662*, 2 vols. (Cape Town, 1900), II, 304.

22. Private trading was a VOC plague. See C.R. Boxer, *The Dutch seaborne empire* (London, 1965, 1977) 203-5; and Thom, 'Introduction', *Journal*, I, xxiii-xxiv.

23. *Journal*, I, xxiv.

24. See *The Record*, 1-4 for the report of Proot and Jansz.

25. *The Record*, 7.

26. Leipoldt pointed out that this request of Van Riebeeck's (on 28 May 1652) 'shows that he regarded the founding of the supply station at the Cape as a temporary commission which could be successfully carried out in a few months' (*Jan van Riebeeck*, 118). See also *DSAB*, II, 800.

27. *The Record*, 32.

28. As Theal (in *History of South Africa*, II, 129) noted: 'A more dutiful servant no government ever had'.

29. The journal entry for 10 January 1654 recorded: 'The worst is that the men from the ships can hardly be kept away from these people - indeed, some skippers, discreet in other ways, dared to say that if they did not get from us as many cattle as they wanted, they would go inland with hundreds of men to shoot cattle, and if the Hottentots did not want to exchange them, they would seize them'. *Journal*, I, 203.

30. Quoted by Boxer, *The Dutch seaborne empire*, 95.

31. 'By 1648 the Dutch were indisputably the greatest trading nation in the world'. *Ibid*, 27.

32. See Margaret Spilhaus, *South Africa in the making*, 8.

33. Goodwin, 'Jan van Riebeeck and the Hottentots', 6.

34. MacCrone, *Race attitudes in South Africa*, 21.

35. See respectively notes 6 and 21 (above), and note 7 (of the 'Introduction').

36. The Dutch first met the Goringhaicona, whom they called 'Strandlopers' and 'Vismans'. This Khoi clan had no cattle and lived on seafood and eatable flora. The Dutch then met the Goringhaiqua, whom they called variously: 'Saldanhaman', 'Saldanhars', 'Saldaniers' and 'Kaapmans'.

37. *Journal*, I, 111-12.

38. Autshumao or Herry (1600-1663), chief of the small tribe of Goringhaicona (Strandlopers). Accompanied an English ship to Java sometime between 1631 and 1632. On 7 April 1652 he dined with Van Riebeeck aboard the *Drommedaris*. He was employed first by the Dutch as an interpreter (pidgin English serving as medium), and then as an intermediary or agent in bartering deals with the stock-holding Khoi tribes.

See *DSAB*, II, 296.

39. *The Record*, (9 April 1652) 10.

40. *The Record*, 37.

41. *Ibid*. 44; and *Journal*, I, 208.

42. *Ibid*. *Journal*, I, 208-9.

43. *The Record*, (22 April 1654) 49-50.

44. *Ibid*. (6 October 1654) 54. See also Leibbrandt, *Letters received*, I. 144.

45. *The Record*, 60; Leibbrandt, *Letters despatched*, II, 84-6.

46. *The Record*, 75.

47. (1619-1682) soldier and high-ranking official of the VOC. Visited the Cape twice. Privately, he judged Van Riebeeck 'too ambitious, too impetuous and too impulsive' (Leipoldt, 245). For more details on Van Goens, see *DSAB*, I, 825-6.

48. *The Record*, 95.

49. *Ibid*, 99.

50. *Ibid*.

51. *Ibid*, 105-6.

52. Leibbrandt, *Letters despatched*, II, 310.

53. For further details on Cunaeus, see *Journal*, II, 230.

54. *The Record*, 120.

55. Had experience of Batavia, foresaw the consequences of European settlement, tried to forge an anti-settler coalition and led, for a brief period, resistance against the Dutch. He died in 1663, unlamented and unrecognised as one of the early resisters to Dutch colonisation. See R. Elphick's article in *DSAB*, III, 233-4.

56. R. Elphick (in 'the Khoisan to c. 1770', 7) makes the useful distinction between the Khoi tribes near Table Bay and those beyond. The tribes near the Bay (the Goringhaicona, the Goringhaiqua and the Gorachouqua) he refers to as the 'Peninsulars'. The tribes mentioned here: the Chariguriqua and the Chorachouqua were obviously the traditional rivals of the 'Peninsulars'.

57. *The Record*, 123.

58. *Ibid*.

59. This obviously meant that the XVII did not think the killing of the herd-boy or the theft of forty-two cattle merited Van Riebeeck's drastic proposals.

60. *The Record*, 140.

61. *Ibid*, 152.

62. *Ibid*, (7 May 1659) 160.

63. *The Record*, 162.

64. *Ibid*, 169.

65. *Ibid*, 213. On 23 December 1658 some free colonists had complained, officially, against restricted trading and unfair pricing.

66. F. Fouché, for instance, wrote (in 'Foundations of the Cape Colony, 1652-1708', *CHBE*, 125) that in April 1662 Van Riebeeck 'relinquished his command on promotion to a post in the East, which he had long been soliciting'.

67. Van Riebeeck was posted to Batavia. Ambitious as he was, he certainly hoped that one day he would secure the post of Councillor of India (Theal, *History*, III, 129 and Leipoldt, 238). In Batavia there was no post for him to fill, but, after a two month wait, he was temporarily appointed to the Court of Justice. Later he headed the VOC's establishment at Malacca (Malaysia). He held this post until 1665. The former head of Malacca had been a Councillor of India but when Van Riebeeck took over the establishment, Malacca had lost its importance for the Company (Theal, *ibid*, 130) and had become by that time the Company's 'refractory child' (Leipoldt, 241). But even in Malac-

ca Van Riebeeck exercised a variant of his 'principle', which called forth this rebuke from the XVII: 'God's blessing is not to be expected on unjust measures to ensure our profit, and such have never been our intention or desire' (Leipoldt, 242). Later, however, Van Riebeeck became secretary of the Council of India or as Thom (more edifyingly) put it, 'secretary to the High Government of India' (*Journal*, I, xxvi); and remained secretary, without a voice in the debates or the proceedings, until his demise in 1667.

Truth is, Van Riebeeck would have been one among many Dutch merchants in the East had it not been for the *subsequent* history of the Cape settlement.

68. 'Van Riebeeck was a buyer. He was the servant of a trading company, and his preoccupation, from the day he landed in South Africa until the day he left, was with the cattle trade, to provide food for his men and fresh supplies for scurvy-ridden ships'. Monica Wilson, 'The hunters and herders', in *The Oxford history of South Africa*, edited by Monica Wilson and L. Thompson, 2 vols. (Oxford, 1969 and 1971), I, 64.

CHAPTER TWO

1. *The Covenant* (London, 1980, paperback ed., 1983), 518.

2. See H. Dehérain, *Le Cap de Bonne-Espérance au VII siècle*, 39-40; and Shula Marks, 'Khoisan resistance to the Dutch', 55-80.

3. Small-pox, measles and other infectious diseases ravaged the various Khoi communities in 1663, 1666, 1674, 1713 and 1767 (see J.C. Chase, *The Cape of Good Hope and the Eastern Province of Algoa Bay*, London, 1843, repr. Cape Town, 1967, 8).

Van Riebeeck (see his journal entry for 12 October 1652) quickly became aware of the inveigling influence arrack could have on the Khoi. Eva, who served as Van Riebeeck's interpreter, was the first Khoi convert to Christianity - she was also the first Khoi alcoholic (see R. Elphick and R. Shell, 'Intergroup relations: Khoikhoi, settlers, slaves and free blacks, 1652-1795' in *The shaping of South African society*, 118).

By the beginning of the eighteenth century alcohol had become a well-established part of the wage structure for Khoi farm workers. Collins (in his report) recommended its abolition *in 1809* (see Moodie, *The Record*, part V, 22).

4. See J. Philip, *Researches in South Africa*, II, 373-8 for the text of the Proclamation.

5. T. Pringle (in *Narrative of a residence in South Africa*, Cape Town, 1966, 241) referred to 'the protective clauses of Lord Caledon's well-meant proclamation'.

6. W.M. Macmillan, *The Cape colour question* (London, 1927), 281 (hereafter cited as *CCQ*).

7. See Philip, *Researches*, II, 378-80 for the text of the proclamation.

8. This eighteen-year provision, however, was rarely respected. See *ibid*, I, 180-1.

9. See H.A. Gailey, 'John Philip's role in Hottentot emancipation', *Journal of African history*, III, 3 (1962).

10. See Pringle, *Narrative of a residence*, 249; and J. Rose Innes's preface (x) in J. Read, junior, *The Kat River Settlement in 1851* (Cape Town, 1852). For the text of the Ordinance, see *British Parliamentary papers, 50 of 1835*, 217-18.

11. *History*, V, 236 and 499; and *The story of nations: South Africa* (6th ed. London, 1899), 178.

12. Cory, I, 199-202 and II, 366-75; J.C. Voigt, *Fifty years of the history of the Republic in South Africa, 1795-1845*, 2 vols. (London, 1899, repr. Cape Town, 1969), I, 109-10 and 163; and C.P. Lucas, *The history of South Africa* (Oxford, 1899), 148-9.

13. See F.E. Auerbach, *The power of prejudice in South African education* (Cape Town, 1965), 56-62.

14. See G.E.F. Schutte, 'Dr John Philip's observation regarding the Hottentots of South Africa', *Archives year book of South African history*, part 1 (Cape Town, 1940), 109, 235 and 238; P.H. Kapp, 'Dr John Philip se opvattinge en sy werksaamhede in Suid-Afrika' (Unp. D. Phil. thesis, University of Stellenbosch, 1974), 36-169 and, especially, 104 and 150; and C.F. Kotzé, 'A new regime, 1806-1834', in *500 Years*, 132-38.

15. *CCQ*, 222.

16. *The Cape Coloured people 1652-1937* (London, 1939), 121-31, 160-1 and 183-6.

17. *The role of the missionaries in conquest*, 16-17.

18. See 'The labour market of the Cape Colony', 171-207, especially 197. See also the editors' 'Introduction' in the same volume, 21; and H. Giliomee's essay, 'Processes in development of the Southern African frontier', in H. Lamar and L. Thompson (eds.), *The frontier in history* (New Haven, 1981), 105.

19. A. Ross, *John Philip (1775-1851): Missionaries, race and politics in South Africa* (Aberdeen, 1986), 115.

20. *CCQ*, 256-7.

21. 'The problem of the Coloured people 1792-1842', *CHBE*, 294 and 299.

22. See *Researches in South Africa*, I, 263-4; and *CCQ*, 216.

23. See Ross, *John Philip*, 97, where this aspect of Philip's outlook is set down in greater detail.

24. Quoted by Jane Sales, *Missions stations and the Coloured communities of the Eastern Cape 1800-1852* (Cape Town, 1975), 110.

25. *Great Britain, Parliamentary papers, 1836, Report of the Select Committee on Aborigines (British Settlements)*, 747 (hereafter cited as *Report on Aborigines*).

26. *Ibid*, 740.

27. Duly, 'A revisit with the Cape's Hottentot Ordinance of 1828', 35.

28. Quoted by Duly, 38. W.B. Boyce (in *Notes on South Africa*, London, 1838, repr. Cape Town, 1971, 119-20) also observed: 'In a country so thinly peopled, and with such large farms; it is difficult at once to detect the loss of a cow or a few sheep, and yet more difficult to obtain evidence sufficient for legal conviction, even in cases otherwise morally certain. But even if the evidence be sufficient, the Magistrate may be so far removed, that the farmer finds it prudent to put up quietly with the loss, rather than throw away his time and money for a mere nominal punishment of the criminal'. Chase (in *The Cape of Good Hope*, 134) made the same point in 1843, when he stressed: 'The great complaint is, that from the widely scattered state of the inhabitants the laws are inoperative'.

29. *Report on Aborigines*, 744; and *CCQ*, 244.

30. *Report on Aborigines*, 743.

31. See Marais, *The Cape Coloured people*, 110-12; and P.R. Kirby (ed.), *Sir Andrew Smith 1795-1850* (Cape Town, 1965), 144-5.

32. The text of the draft act is reproduced in *Report on Aborigines*, 749-57.

33. See Jane Sales, *Mission stations*, 110.

34. Duly, 'A revisit with the Cape's Hottentot Ordinance', 43.

35. 'The Vagrant Law was a commonplace attempt of reactionary, or merely ignorant, employers to get state sanction for a policy that would secure a plentiful supply of cheap, subservient, and exploitable labour' (*CCQ*, 243).

36. Sheila T. van der Horst, *Native labour in South Africa* (London, 1942), 37-8.

37. The classic later example of such legislation was the Natal Governfment's Section 2 of Franchise Law Amendment Act of 1896, which discriminated against Natal-born Indians without specifically mentioning the term *Indian*.

38. See Marks and Atmore, *Economy and society in pre-industrial South Africa*, 21.

39. See Read, *The Kat River Settlement*, 112-13.

40. J.M. Bowker, *Speeches, letters and selections* (London, 1867, repr. Cape Town, 1962), 129.

41. *Report on Aborigines*, 747.

42. *Ibid.*

43. Quoted by Read, *The Kat River Settlement*, 33.

44. Cory, II, 341; and A. Wilmot and J.C. Chase, *History of the Colony of the Cape of Good Hope* (Cape Town, 1869) 292-3.

45. For a brief and revealing history of the Ordinance, see Macmillan, *Bantu, Boer, and Briton* (London, 1929), 66-7; and the revised (1963) ed. 87-88. See also Monica Wilson, 'Co-operation and conflict: The Eastern Cape Frontier', *Oxford history*, I, 241.

46. See Margaret Donaldson, 'The Council of Advice at the Cape of Good Hope, 1825-1834' (Ph. D. dissertation, Rhodes University, 1974), 370-3.

47. See Susan Newton-King, 'The labour market of the Cape Colony', 196.

48. Marais, *The Cape Coloured people*, 183.

49. See *CCQ*, 254.

50. As Jane Sales (in *Mission stations*, 50) observed: 'One of the clearly stated goals of the early missionaries was to help the people change their way of life from a nomadic pastoral type to a settled peasant type, which was considered to be a higher stage of *civilization*'.

51. Voigt, *Fifty years of the history of the Republic in South Africa*, I, 111-12.

52. Chase (in *The Cape of Good Hope*, 238) drew attention in 1843 to the presence of these Bechuana, as well as some 'Mantatees', when he noted: 'The northern districts have been from time to time further supplied with labourers from the Sichuana country, or the country north of the Orange River, known by the name of Bechuanas, a mild, quiet, but restless race; and the Mantatees, the remnants of tribes broken up and dispersed by the Zoolah conquests . . . They are chiefly employed as herdsmen, but they also visit farms in small parties, and undertake piece-work, such as the construction of dams, cattle and sheep pens, which labour they perform in an efficient manner'.

53. Jane Sales, *Mission stations*, 101.

54. See chapter four below.

55. *Narrative of a voyage of observation among the colonies of Western Africa . . . and of a campaign in Kaffirland . . . in 1835*, 2 vols. (London, 1837), II, 47.

56. Sheila T. van der Horst, *Native labour in South Africa*, 15.

57. Macmillan, *Bantu, Boer, and Briton* (Oxford, 1963), 149.

58. Jane Sales, *Mission stations*, 136.

59. *Ibid*, 118.

60. *CCQ*, 253.

61. See D.H. Varley and H.M. Matthew (eds.), *The Cape journals of Archdeacon N.J. Merriman, 1848-1855* (Cape Town, 1957), 31-2. Chase (in *The Cape of Good Hope*, 238) described them in 1843 as being 'a very intelligent people, extraordinarily attached to money, and temperate or rather sober in their habits'. He also stressed that they converted their wages into cattle, and that when they had accumulated a sufficient amount of stock, they left their employment and then led an independent existence.

62. Dock work at Algoa Bay, once exclusive to the Khoi, became in 1843 the preserve of the Mfengu. See Chase, *The Cape of Good Hope*, 238; and Jane Sales, *Mission stations*, 118.

63. Moyer, 'The Mfengu, self-defence and the Cape frontier wars', in C. Saunders and R. Derricourt (eds.), *Beyond the Cape frontier* (London, 1974), 101. See also Monica Wilson, 'Co-operation and conflict: The Eastern Cape Frontier', *Oxford history*, I, 249.

64. Peires, *The House of Phalo*, 168.

65. Act No. 27 of 1857. See T.R.H. Davenport, 'The consolidation of a new society: The

Cape Colony', in the *Oxford history of South Africa*, I, 310.

66. Sheila T. van der Horst, *Native labour*, 28.
67. See Jane Sales, *Mission stations*, 102.
68. *Notes on South African affairs*, 126-7.
69. See Ross, *John Philip*, 184.
70. Jane Sales, *Mission stations*, 134.
71. See Ross, *John Philip*, 186.
72. Pringle (in *Narrative of a residence*, 254) noted that among the Khoi it was generally observable that they had 'an earnest desire to procure for their children the benefits of education'.
73. Marais, *The Cape Coloured people*, 270.
74. Jane Sales, *Mission stations*, 154.
75. Marais, *The Cape Coloured people*, 270.
76. Jane Sales, *Mission stations*, 117.
77. *Ibid*, 116.
78. See Philip to Tidman, 11 March 1845; quoted, in part, by Ross, *John Philip*, 185.
79. See Ross, *John Philip*, 185.
80. T. Kirk, 'The Cape economy and the expropriation of the Kat River Settlement, 1846-53', in *Economy and society in pre-industrial South Africa*, 241.
81. *Ibid*.
82. Elliot to the Directors of the LMS, 2 February 1848. Quoted by Ross, 204.
83. Cory, V, 326.
84. T. Kirk, 'Progress and decline in the Kat River Settlement, 1829-1854', *Journal of African history*, 14, 3 (1973), 415.
85. Jane Sales, *Mission stations*, 104.
86. Kirk, 'Progress and decline', 417.
87. See Ross, *John Philip*, 202-3.
88. Kirk, 'Progress and decline', 422.
89. See Ross, *John Philip*, 207.
90. Quoted by Read, *The Kat River Settlement*, 47.
91. *Ibid*, 79-80.
92. *Ibid*, 88.
93. *Ibid*, 'Appendix', 4.
94. Kirk, 'Progress and decline', 419-22.
95. Kirk, 'The Cape economy and expropriation of the Kat River Settlement', 242.
96. See Ross, *John Philip*, 225.
97. *Ibid*, 210.
98. See Read, *The Kat River Settlement*, 26-7.

CHAPTER THREE

1. *Smuts: The fields of force 1919-1950* (Cambridge, 1968), 476 (the 'He' in the quote refers to Smuts).
2. (1775-1851) Scottish-born, superintendent of the London Missionary Society; arrived in South Africa in 1819 and, apart from two visits to Britain (1826-9 and 1836-89), remained in South Africa for the rest of his life.
3. Macmillan, *CCQ*, 171.
4. Quoted by MacCrone, *Race attitudes in South Africa*, 129.
5. Quoted by C.F.J. Muller, 'The period of the Great Trek, 1834-1854', in *500 Years*, 154.

6. See M. Legassick, 'The frontier tradition in South African historiography', in *Economy and society in pre-industrial South Africa*, 48; and J.W. Cell, *The highest stage of white supremacy: The origins of segregation in South Africa and the American South (Cambridge, 1982), 3-4.*

7. MacCrone, *Race attitudes in South Africa*, 131-6; Sheila Patterson, *Colour and culture in South Africa*, 175-6; L.M. Thompson, *Politics in the Republic of South Africa* (Boston, 1966), 24; P. van den Berghe, *South Africa: A study in conflict* (Berkeley, 1967), 14-15; and S. Dubow, 'Race, civilisation and culture: The elaboration of the segregationist discourse in the inter-war years', in Shula Marks and S. Trapido (eds.), *The politics of race, class and nationalism in twentieth century South Africa* (London, 1987), 71-94.

8. M.W. Swanson, 'The Durban system: Roots of urban apartheid in Colonial Natal', *African Studies*, 35, 3-4, 1976, 169.

9. *The South African problem: A suggested solution* (n.p., 1909), 15.

10. 'Problems in South Africa', *Journal of the African Society*, XVI, No. LXIV, July 1917, 297.

11. Quoted by C. Tatz, *Shadow and substance in South Africa: A study in land and franchise policies affecting Africans 1910-1960* (Pietermaritzburg, 1962), 62.

12. See E.P. Dvorin, *Racial separation in South Africa* (Chicago, 1952); the quote appears opposite the title page. Sheep, cattle, lions and elephants are respectively distinct species. Interbreeding among these different species is normally impossible. Within each species, there might be non-fundamental differences like colour - nothing, for instance, prevents a white Charolait bull from mating with a black or brown Frissian cow or vice versa. Colour distinction among cattle is equivalent to that which operates between various races and nations. The difference between white and black in South Africa, or elsewhere, is social and cultural but not biological. To place that social and cultural difference on a par with the biological difference that separates a lion from an elephant is to slip from science to superstition.

13. *History*, V, 505.

14. 'Dr John Philip's observation regarding the Hottentots of South Africa', 239.

15. *500 Years*, 137.

16. *Researches in South Africa*, I, 233-4 (hereafter cited as *Researches*).

17. *Report on Aborigines* (15 June 1836), 554.

A. Ross quotes a passage, in *John Philip*, 95, which clearly reveals Philip's non or anti-racialism: 'It may seem invidious to compare the Hottentots with the Farmers of South Africa, but without attempting to lesson my Country, I have no hesitation in affirming, that you will find as rational ideas, as large a quantum of intelligence, and as much religion and morality, as much appearance of civilisation as in many villages of the same population in Great Britain'. Thompson (in *The political myth of apartheid*, 163) stresses that Philip was a 'formidable critic of Afrikaner racism'; it would be more accurate to say that he was a formidable critic of *colonial* or *settler* racism.

18. *My South African years* (Cape Town, 1975), 182.

19. *CCQ*, 174.

20. *A history of South Africa* (London, 1928), 159.

21. *South Africa 1652-1933* (London, 1933), 59.

22. *The South African melting pot: A vindication of missionary policy, 1799-1836*(London, 1937), 150.

23. *South African Native policy and the liberal spirit* (Cape Town, 1939), 20.

24. 'The British humanitarians and the Cape Eastern Frontier 1834-1836', 37. Pretorius,

it is worth noting, claimed (158) that Andries Stockenstrom (1792-1864), Philip's contemporary — like Philip himself, was also an advocate of *segregation*. 'He strongly advocated segregation between the tribes and the white colonists'. Pretorius, however adds, that Stockenstrom wanted to put a stop 'to the encroachment on native lands'.

See also J. Lewin, who in 1963 stated that Philip was 'one of the earliest advocates of segregation' (*Politics and law in South Africa*, London, 1963, 81 - Legassick seemed to be unaware of this point when he wrote his essay, 'The frontier tradition in South African historiography', 63 and 77). L. Marquard also, in 1966, asserted that Philip 'was a throughgoing segregationist' (*The story of South Africa*, London, 1966, 101).

25. *Researches*, II, 315.

26. E.B. Iwan-Muller, *Lord Milner in South Africa* (London, 1902), 45.

27. Tatz, *Shadow and substance*, 5-6.

28. G.W. Eybers, *Select constitutional documents illustrating South African history, 1795-1910* (London, 1918), 364.

29. S. Trapido (in 'Natal's non-racial franchise, 1856', *African Studies*, 22, 1963, 28) argued that this law was passed as part of a political manoeuvre and was not primarily aimed at the African electorate; he admits however that, 'preventing Africans from qualifying for the voters roll appealed to the interests and the prejudices of the white settlers'.

30. See Mabel Palmer, *The history of the Indians in Natal* (Cape Town, 1957), 54.

31. L.M. Thompson, *The Cape Coloured franchise* (Johannesburg, 1949), 4.

32. Quoted by Chase, *The Cape of Good Hope*, 330.

33. See Macmillan, *Bantu, Boer, and Briton* (1929), 309-10 and (revised ed. 1963), 360 (hereafter cited as *BBB* (1929) and *BBB* (1963).

34. Segregation was, according to P. Rich, 'the political response by a colonial superstructure to a changing economic base, since it sought to reverse any change in the relationship between coloniser and colonised'. See 'The agrarian counter-revolution in the Transvaal and the origins of segregation: 1902-1913', in P.L. Bonner (ed.), *Working papers in Southern African studies*, African Studies Institute, University of Witwatersrand, 1977, 55-6. See also Cell, *The highest stage of white supremacy*, 17.

35. W.K. Hancock and Jean van der Poel (eds.), *Selections from the Smuts Papers*, I, (Cambridge, 1966), 360.

36. See Sir Edgar Walton, *The inner history of the National Convention of South Africa* (London, 1912, repr. Westport, 1970), 121.

37. *Ibid*, 126-7.

38. L.M. Thompson, *The unification of South Africa 1902-1910* (Oxford, 1960), 218.

39. Walton, *The inner history of the National Convention*, 133.

40. J.C. Smuts to W.T. Stead, 4 January 1902, *Selections from the Smuts Papers*, I, 484.

41. Quoted by Tatz, *Shadow and substance*, 62.

42. L. Phillips, *Transvaal problems: Some notes on current policies* (London, 1905), 136.

43. For Shepstone see D. Welsh, *The roots of segregation: Native policy in Natal. 1845-1910* (Cape Town, 1971). For Stuart, see Swanson (note 8 above). For Nicholls, see Shula Marks, 'Natal, the Zulu Royal Family and the ideology of segregation', *Journal of Southern African Studies*, IV, 2 (1978).

44. See Marion Lacey, *Working for boroko: The origins of a coercive labour system in South Africa* (Johannesburg, 1981), 16-17.

45. For Lionel Curtis, M. Legassick, 'British hegemony and the origins of segregation in South Africa, 1901-1914', Institute of Commonwealth Studies (February, 1974, mimeographed), 4.

161

46. Marion Lacey, 16.

47. Tatz, 14.

48. 'General Smut's speech', *Journal of the African society, XVI, No. LXIV, July 1917, 276-8. See also Cell, The highest stage of white supremacy*, 216 and 224-5.

49. Marion Lacey (65) in this regard noted: 'By abolishing the Cape African franchise and putting Africans on a communal roll, the state could create a racially inferior group, politically impotent and economically subordinate'.

50. *Ibid*, 57.

51. *The political future of South Africa* (Pretoria, 1927), 44.

52. Sheila Patterson, *Colour and culture in South Africa*, 31.

53. Macmillan, *CCQ*, 173. The word, *potential* introduces a nuance that did not exist for Philip, for as Ross indicated: 'John Philip's understanding of the one humanity shared equally by all persons of whatever race or ethnic origin was a fundamental part of his evangelical faith' (225). Ross also criticises Macmillan for temporising and shying away from Philip's explicit remarks about *amalgamation* because Macmillan was writing in the 1920s (94).

54. *Researches*, II, 327-8.

55. *CCQ*, 216-7.

56. Quoted by Macmillan, *CCQ*, 217.

57. *CCQ*, 153.

58. See Legassick, 'British hegemony and the origins of segregation', 1.

59. *CCQ*, 172. Ross notes that Bethelsdorp and Kat River were guaranteed separate settlement, but this, as far as Philip was concerned, was a holding measure; he never regarded the settlements as a permanent solution (94).

60. Boyce, *Notes on South African Affairs*, 209.

61. *Aborigines Report*, 635, 626, 627 and 633 respectively. See also J.S. Marais, 'The imposition and nature of European control', in I. Schapera (ed.), *The Bantu-speaking tribes of South Africa* (London, 1937), 336, where he stated that in the fourteen years between 1820 and 1834 'the Bantu were still essentially a frontier problem'.

62. *Researches*, II, 288.

63. Ross points out (*John Philip*, 194) that 'However much colour played a part in the Voortrekker's ideal society with its proper relations between master and servant, the Voortrekkers had no ideology of race - no vision of progress with the *savage* disappearing before the advance of civilisation as part of *the immutable law of nature*'.

64. M. Bowker, *Speeches, letters and selections* (Grahamstown, 1864, repr. Cape Town, 1962), 125. See 116-25 for the entire speech. Ross (189) considers the appeal a literal demand for 'genocide'.

65. *Researches*, II, 288.

66. *Aborigines Report*, 633-4.

67. *Ibid*, 635.

68. See *BBB* (1929), 124 and *BBB* (1963), 146.

69. See Ross (167), where he quotes a part of Philip's letter (25 August 1842) to Napier.

70. See J.C. Beaglehole, 'The case of the needless death', in *The historian as detective* (New York, 1968), 281.

71. Cape liberalism in 1910, R. Davenport points out, 'was not the untarnished creed of a confident, ... minority as it had appeared to be in 1830'. See 'The Cape liberal tradition to 1910' in J. Butler, R. Elphick and D. Welsh (eds.), *Democratic liberalism in South Africa* (Connecticut and Cape Town, 1987), 33.

72. For details see B.K. Murray, *Wits: The early years* (Johannesburg, 1982), 216-21.

73. It seems that he was not alone (that is among white academics and writers) in ig-

noring this important distinction between the two concepts. J.S. Marais also evidently lumped the two categories together in stating (in 'The imposition and nature of European control', 334): that the European advance was 'made ostensibly with the aim of ensuring complete *segregation* or separation between White and Black'.

Marion Lacey in her chapter, 'The origins of segregation: A reassessment' (21-51) also fails to distinguish between *segregation* and *separation*; for she wrote: 'When Africans and whites first met in the Cape in the late eighteenth century, the authorities tried to impose complete *segregation* in the interests of peace. At the time, before either race had developed an economic dependence on the other and while Africans, like whites, still had an independent territorial base, a policy of *separation* might have succeeded' (12, emphasis added).

74. *Report of the Select Committee on the subject of the Union Native Council Bill* (June 1972), 52, quoted by Tatz, *Shadow and substance*, 51. A similar point was made by a Transkeian Councillor, Quamata when (in 1920s) he said: 'The Natives desired to be regarded as one nation with the white people'. Quoted by Monica Wilson, 'The growth of peasant communities', *Oxford history of South Africa*, II, 88.

75. M. Midlane, 'Aspects of the South African Liberal tradition' in C.R. Hill and P. Warwick (eds.), *South African research in progress* (New York, 1974), 86-7.

76. As N. Bromberger and K. Hughes stress, 'South Africa is not merely a capitalist state but, more important, it is a *settler state* created and established by conquest and settlement . . . Power, so the colonizers reason, must be retained in their hands, and so long as it is, it can be used to economic as well as political advantage'. See 'Capitalism and underdevelopment in South Africa' in *Democratic liberalism in South Africa*, 219.

77. Cell, *The highest stage of white supremacy*, 14.

78. See *BBB* (1929), 202 and *BBB* (1963), 233 where he stated that British treaties with African Chiefs 'were at least an attempt to preserve the tribes and to prevent the wholesale *intermixture* of black and white areas which the Boers' successors profess to deplore' (emphasis added).

79. Macmillan-Merriman correspondence, Rhodes House Library, Oxford.

80. A. Ross, *John Philip*, 215.

81. T.R.H. Davenport, *South Africa: A modern history* (London, 1977), 332. This contention was formulated earlier by Legassick, see 'British hegemony and the origins of segregation', 1. See also Rich ('The agrarian counter-revolution', 83), who argued (in referring to the Transvaal, of course) that: 'With the establishment of Responsible Government in the Transvaal, a whole debate was initiated over *native policy* and the correct kind of *solution* to the question of power for whites vis a vis non-whites. Out of this debate there emerged the ideology of segregation which, though tentatively introduced by Smuts in the 1911 Mines and Works Act, found concrete form in the agrarian sector with the 1913 Land Act'.

82. *Aborigines Report*, 549.

83. Boyce (in *Notes on South African Affairs*, 186-95) discusses how these lands could *in the future* be colonised by European farmers.

84. Legassick (in 'British hegemony and the origins of segregation', 4) claimed that as far as he was able to determine, the first appearance of the word 'segregation' in a South African context, is contained in a paper, 'The place of subject peoples in the Empire' (1906-7) by Lionel Curtis.

85. 'Forum', *History Today*, March 1983.

86. See R.G. Collingwood, *An autobiography* (Oxford, 1939), 31 and 39.

87. J. Cappon, *Britain's title in South Africa* (London, 1901), 321.

88. W.H. Dawson, *South Africa* (London, 1925), 425. Even as late as April 1943 Mar-

garet Ballinger was protesting in the House of Assembly: 'I contend that this House has never really made up its mind what it does mean by segregation. There is a great deal of confusion in that matter'. See Phyllis Lewsen (ed.), *Voices of protest: From segregation to apartheid, 1938-1948* (Johannesburg, 1988), 121-2.

89. 'In 1913 Hertzog had called his policy segregation. Smuts, who had very much the same ideas, preferred to speak of separation' (L.E. Neame, *The history of apartheid*, London, 1962, 73).

90. See Ross, *John Philip*, 94-5.

91. From a typed, undated manuscript titled: 'Centenary of the Great Trek', Macmillan Papers, Yew Tree Cottage, Long Wittenham, Abingdon, England.

92. Quoted by Sir John Robinson, *A life time in South Africa* (London, 1900), 295-6 (for the original see, *Natal Gazette Supplements;* G.G. No. 205, 9 November 1852). A point corroborated, perhaps, in this observation by Marion Lacey (280): 'Segregation in NP [Nationalist Party] terms was a legal concept which had long defined the relationship as between master and servant in the former Boer Republics'.

CHAPTER FOUR

1. H.G. Smith to his sister (Mrs J. Sargant), 7 May 1835, in G.M. Theal (ed.), *Documents relating to the Kaffir War of 1835* (London, 1912), 151 (hereafter cited as 'Letter to Mrs Sargant').

2. (1787-1860), later Sir Harry Smith, soldier and Governor of the Cape Colony (1847-1852). D'Urban (1777-1849), Governor of the Cape Colony (1834-1837). (1797-1862), 1820 settler and author of *The journal of Harry Hastings* (Grahamstown, 1963). Ayliff and his family were closely associated with the settler community.

3. T. Shepstone, 'Diary', 29 April, which was kept from 26 March to 13 June 1835. A copy of the 'Diary' was very kindly provided by the Sanlam Library, University of South Africa.

4. Alexander, *Narrative of voyage*, II, 128-9.

5. Colonel Smith to D'Urban, 18 May 1835, reproduced in Theal, *Documents*, 171-80 (hereafter cited as 'The May Letter'). And G.C. Moore (ed.), *Autobiography of Sir Harry Smith*, 2 vols. (London, 1903), II, 40-1 (hereafter cited as *Autobiography*); and Cory, III, 141.

6. The May Letter.

7. *A narrative of the irruption of the Kafir hordes into the Eastern Province of the Cape of Good Hope 1834-35* (Graham's Town, 1836, repr. Cape Town, 1965), 126-71 (J. Goldswain, who served on the expedition, reports Hintsa's death, in his important and unique reminiscences, by verbatim extracts from Godlonton's book. See Una Long (ed.), *The chronicle of Jeremiah Goldswain: Albany settler of 1820*, I (Cape Town, 1946), 108-9): *Compendium of South African history*, 218-20, and *History*, VI, 106-28; Cory, III, 116-59; and *A modern history for South Africans* (Cape Town, 1926), 230, and *A history of South Africa* (London, 1928), 192.

8. Ambrose George Campbell (1799-1884), surgeon and journalist. W.M. Macmillan in *Bantu, Boer, and Briton* (1929) described him as a crank but he was really the gadfly of Grahamstown, and of the Colonial establishment. See *DSAB*, III, 123.

9. See Macmillan, *Bantu, Boer, and Briton* (1929), 111-12 and (1963), 132-3.

10. *British Parliamentary Paper 538 of 1836, Cape of Good Hope: Caffre war and the death of Hintza*, 67.

11. The Colonial Secretary, in a despatch, noted: 'With regard to the case of the Chief

Hinza, I am happy to state, that, the information now transmitted, clears up the doubts, and difficulties, which in my despatch of the 26th December, 1835, I described as connected with that subject. It is, I think, now established, that, if not the fomentor of that invasion, that Chief was at least engaged in a secret conspiracy with the authors, and was availing himself of such advantages as it offered him. On himself, therefore, rests the responsibility for the calamity in which he and his people were involved by the contest'. Quoted by W.B. Boyce, *Notes on South African affairs*, xiv-xv.

12. *BBB* (1929), 111-12 and (1963), 132-3.

13. 'Die moord op Hintsa', 19 and 25 February, and 12 and 19 March 1943.

14. 1965 imp. 185. Walker had used identical words in the first (1928) edition, see *History of South Africa*, 192.

15. See the chapter, 'The frontier and the Kaffir Wars 1792-1836' in *CHBE*, 317. Macmillan's revised edition of *Bantu, Boer, and Briton* (1963), also bore no change, as far as the death of Hintsa was concerned.

16. Pretorius, 'The British humanitarians'; A.L. Harrington, *Sir Harry Smith bungling hero*; and J.B. Peires, *The House of Phalo*. In 1983 J. Milton, professor of law at Natal University, produced an account of Hintsa's death that in some respects (notably in his use of the Court of Inquiry's record) happily anticipates this present essay (see *The edges of war*, Cape Town, 1983, 135-141). The Professor's account is, for all that, less far reaching.

17. Shepstone, 'Diary', 29 April 1835. For a more detailed account see Godlonton, 154; and Pretorius ('Appendix 1'), 361-4.

18. The Colonel (a few months later) would lay down one of the ground rules for dealing with the Xhosa Chiefs: 'A Kafir . . . must have the word crammed down his throat' (Smith to D'Urban, 31 August 1835, Theal, *Documents*, 361.

19. 'Diary'. See also Smith's evidence to the Court: Minutes of the proceedings of the Court of Inquiry . . . on the fate of the Caffer chief Hintza (Cape Town, 1837), 20 (hereafter cited as '*COI*').

20. The copy of *COI* in the British Library (London has the findings of the Court in what seems to be a contemporary handwritten copy of the original. There is therefore no page number - but see Pretorius, 277.

21. 'Field Diary of Caesar Andrews', South African Library, Cape Town; see May (actually April) 1835 entry.

22. Shepstone (in his 'Diary', 9 May) when he took in the sight of the cattle that accompanied the Mfengu, noted: 'I never saw such a number of cattle together in all my life'.

23. Letters to Mrs Smith, 5 May, *Autobiography*, II, 368.

24. Letter to Mrs Sargant, 154.

25. Quoted by Smith in The May Letter.

26. See Uys, 'Die Moord op Hintsa - V: Die Tragedie Loop Ten Einde', *Die Huisgenoot*, 12 March 1943.

27. The May Letter. See also *COI*, 20; and *Autobiography*, II, 40-1. Even Monica Wilson (in *The Oxford history of South Africa*, I, 245) credits this claim by stating: 'The administrative and military officers who negotiated with Xhosa chiefs treated them with formal courtesy and repeatedly invited them to their tables: Governor Janssens invited Ngquika and his mother to dine with him at his table, and *Sir Harry Smith similarly invited Hintsa* (emphasis added).

28. Quoted by J.H. Lehmann, *Remember you are an Englishman: A biography of Sir Harry Smith* (London, 1977), 170.

29. Letter to Mrs Sargant, 154.

30. *Autobiography*, II, 366

31. *A narrative of the interruption of the Kaffir hordes*, 156.

32. Cory, III, 142.

33. 'Reminiscences of the Kafir War 1834-1835', *The Friend of the Free State and Bloem-fontein Gazette*, 27 November 1873, 22 January, 26 February, 2, 23 and 30 April 1874. The fifth of the six articles (23 April) is particularly relevant to Hintsa. All future references to Edgar, unless otherwise indicated, will refer to this article.

34. 'Diary', 2 May. Pretorius (188) cited the accounts of Edgar and Shepstone as if they were referring not to one but to two separate incidents.

35. *Autobiography*, II, 364-5.

36. *Ibid*, 366.

37. *Ibid*.

38. *Ibid*, 367.

39. *Ibid*, 371. Smith also, in a letter to his sister, boasted: 'We mean to enjoy the royal so-ciety until he pays his debts' (Theal, *Documents*, 154).

40. Smith reported the treat to his wife: ' "Hintza . . . if you do not fulfil every tittle of the Articles of Peace, we will carry you, . . . Boku, Vadana [a cousin], and your son Kreili, with us into the Colony and keep you until the good faith we have expected from you be extracted by force". You never saw fellows more astonished' (*Autobiography*, II, 365).

41. Cory, III, 144.

42. *The Friend*, 23 April 1874.

43. H.T. Bowker in his 'War Journal', 7 May, 131-2. See I.M. Barberton (ed.) *Comdt. Holden Bowker* (Cape Town, 1970).

44. 'Diary', 10 May.

45. Letter to Mrs Sargant, 154.

46. *COI*, 141.

47. Letter to Mrs Sargant, Theal, 154; and Letters to Mrs Smith, *Autobiography*, II, 366.

48. G. Southey, 'Diary', Wilmot, 424.

49. W.F.A. Gilfillan, an eye-witness, characterised the Chief's treatment as very much like 'the tickling of a trout' (M. Gilfillan, ed., *The story of one branch of the Gilfillan family in South Africa*, Johannesburg, 1970, 37 — hereafter cited as *The story of the Gilfillan family*); while the historian, Harrington (*Sir Harry Smith*, 40), thought, Smith sometimes treated the Chief like a child and sometimes like a dangerous pet.

50. Quoted by Lehmann, 170. See also *Autobiography*, II, 367 where Smith (in referring to himself quipped: 'What a conceited old rascal you are, Mr Enrique!'

51. *Autobiography*, II, 40.

52. *The story of the Gilfillan family*, 39.

53. *Autobiography*, II, 39; Godlonton, 164; Theal, IV, 115; Cory, III, 148; and Lehmann, 174.

54. Theal, *Documents*, 171.

55. *Autobiography*, II, 372-3. Shepstone in his 'Diary' entry for the 10 May; Gilfillan in his entry for the same day; and Caesar Andrews in his 'Field Diary' also for the same day - all indicate that the idea for the expedition was not Hintsa's but Smith's.

56. *COI*, 135.

57. The May Letter.

58. Anonymous, 'Full true and particular account of the death of Hintza', Government Archives, Cape Town, ZP 1/1/88 (microfilm of the Colonial Office, London), CO/48/165.

The anonymous author claims that Smith gave Southey, Shaw and himself a horse each, and that Smith also promised to make him an officer. This reference could be to none

166

other than Bisset. Hereafter cited as 'Bisset, Full true and particular account'.

59. Southey, 'Diary', Wilmot, 428.

60. The May Letter.

61. *Autobiography*, II, 43-4 and 46.

62. *The Friend*. It is difficult to come to a final conclusion on this matter. Pretorius (197) claimed that Edgar was a reliable and dependable witness because 'he had little love for either Hintsa or the Xhosa and was an ardent admirer of Harry Smith', and that he 'was not prompted by ulterior motives to write as he did'. Perhaps but he wrote some forty years after the event, and there is a certain sensational streak running through each of his six newspaper contributions. Whatever the case, Hintsa was allowed (just before that fateful half an hour) to ride his own horse: 'a handsome brown gelding' (Gilfillan, *The story of the Gilfillan family*, 40).

63. See *COI*, 129; and Southey, 'Diary', Wilmot, 429.

64. *COI*, 145.

65. *Sport and war in South Africa*, 28.

66. Pretorius, 276.

67. *COI*, 129; and Moodie, I, 358.

68. A number of historians (Uys, Harrington and Peires) have speculated on the possibility of the Chief's horse having bolted. This, however, seems unlikely, for Hintsa was an experienced rider; and he was riding — certainly at that crucial moment — his own horse.

69. Bisset, 'Full true and particular account'; H.J. Halse, Journal, 43.

70. Caeser Andrews, Moodie, I, 359.

71. The May Letter.

72. Bisset, *Sport and war in South Africa*, 24; Edgar, *The Friend*.

73. Uys, *Die Huisgenoot*, 19 March 1943. Allen F. Gardiner (of Natal fame) while travelling through the Cape district near King William's Town, met the Chief 'Tchatchou [Probably Tzatzoe, father of Jan Tshatshu]; and referred (at one moment) to the Chief and his followers in these terms: 'we drew up in front, *the chief holding a single assegai in his hand*, while his people, . . . [held each . . . an ample bundle of these destructive missiles'. See *Narrative of a journey to the Zoolu country in South Africa* (London, 1836, repr. Cape Town, 1966), 5 (emphasis added).

74. Robert Daniels, one of the Corps of Guides, told the Court (*COI*, 171) that he recovered, near the spot Hintsa fell, a single assegai, which he later gave to Colonel Smith.

75. The Corps of Guides was made up entirely of British settlers, whose homes had been destroyed by the Rharhabe in December 1834. They were filled with a keen loathing for their Xhosa neighbours and were goaded with a sharp inspiration to even accounts with them (see Lehmann, 159). George Southey admitted that the War had left him destitute (*COI*, 187).

76. Bisset, 'Full true and particular account'. The traditional version claims that Smith called out: 'Fire, fire at him' (*Autobiography*, II, 47).

77. *COI*, 130.

78. *Ibid* (emphasis added).

79. *Ibid*, 186.

80. Pretorius, 210.

81. *COI*, 170.

82. George Southey in his 'Diary' (Wilmot, 429) said the shot entered the right side. Pretorius (211) relied on the assistant-surgeon, W.M. Ford's account, but Ford in recalling what he had found seemed unsure about the details of this particular injury. Shepstone, who was not on the spot, heard (five days later) and recorded (from those

that had been present) that the second ball went through Hintsa's wrist ('Diary', 17 May).

83. See page 82 above.

84. *COI*, 148.

85. *Ibid*, 163.

86. The daring and enterprise of the Khoi soldiers and scouts accompanying the expedition is evident in the testimonies of Smith and Gilfillan. Smith noted (on 1 May): 'There never were such game fellows as these Hottentots. The other night in the Kei, after a terrific march, when we got up to the enemy, I hallooed them on like a pack of hounds, and upon my word, they flew past me through the bush like buffaloes, making everything crack before them' (Letters to Mrs Smith, *Autobiography*, II, 363); while Gilfillan, more significantly, observed — minutes before Hintsa was found and killed — 'We let our boys loose, who immediately scattered about, beating up every bush which could serve as a cover. They might well be compared to set of bloodhounds, ranging for the scent of their prey' (*The story of the Gilfillan family*, 40).

87. The words, according to Pretorius (218) were probably: 'Taruni, maphakathi'. *Taruni* meaning have or show mercy; while *maphakathi* signifies councillor. They were, in brief, words of plea and courtesy.

88. 'True full and particular account'.

89. South African Library, Cape Town (emphasis added).

90. *COI*, 178.

91. *Ibid*, 14.

92. *Ibid*, 7 and 11.

93. *The story of the Gilfillan family*, 40.

94. There is evidence that Smith stage-managed much of the proceedings of the Court. He told D'Urban (in a letter, 12 March 1836): 'I have been very quiet in searching for evidence as I do not wish to make it appear I am active in the business' (Government Archives, Cape Town, Acc. 519, vol. 4 262-5). Moreover, he took on the role of defence advocate and personally questioned and cross examined witnesses during the actual inquiry.

95. The capital importance of Shepstone's words (Professor Uys chanced upon the 'Diary' almost a century after Hintsa was killed) is emphasized by Pretorius (280) when he stressed: 'In all probability Southey's and Smith's lies would have remained undetected forever, and Hintsa's crying for mercy would have been regarded as only another one of the figments of the fertile imagination of the humanitarians, but for the discovery of Theophilus Shepstone's diary'.

96. Smith observed on 3 May that Sarhili was 'a very nice modest youth' (Letters to Mrs Smith, *Autobiography*, II, 366); while on 7 May he noted that the missionary John Ayliff spoke *very highly of the heir apparent*, Sarhili (Letter to Mrs Sargant, Theal, 153).

97. 'War Journal', 131.

98. D'Urban, in a letter (18 May 1835) to Colonel John Bell (Theal, *Documents*, 171), anticipated that the death of Hintsa 'may serve as a handle of mischief to a certain party at home'.

99. (1799-1878), missionary of the Glasgow Missionary Society and Xhosa linguist. Although he suffered personal property losses during the Frontiers Wars, he retained an understanding and a sympathy for the Xhosa. For further details see *DSAB*, I, 681-3.

100. Quoted by Pretorius, 276.

101. The force of this version is manifest when as late as 1986 and, what is more, in an enlightened and generally anti-traditional study, Ross (in *John Philip*, 136) is able to report that Hintsa agreed with the peace terms and that he was killed while trying to es-- cape.

102. Quoted by Pretorius, 216.

CHAPTER FIVE

1. *The Covenant*, 596.
2. *The Voortrekker Museum, Pretoria: Official guide* (Pretoria, 1955), 43 and 49; and E.W. Smith, *The life and times of Daniel Lindley* (New York, 1952), 135.
3. *Voyage dans l'Afrique centrale . . . durant les années 1838-1844*, 2 vols. (Paris, 1847), II, 82-143.
4. *Three lectures on the emigration of the Dutch Farmers from the Colony of the Cape of Good Hope* (Pietersmaritzburg, 1852).
5. *Five lectures on the emigration of the Dutch Farmers from the Colony of the Cape of Good Hope, and their settlement in the districts of Natal, until the formal submission to her majesty's authority in the year 1843* (Cape Town, 1856).
6. *History of the Great Boer Trek and the origin of the South African Republics* (London, 1899), 109-10.
7. *Voyage*, II, 136; Cloete, *History of the Great Boer Trek*, 110.
8. *History of the Great Boer Trek*, 110.
9. *History of the Colony of Natal* (London, 1855), 94; *The Kaffirs of Natal and the Zulu country* (London, 1857), 329; *South Africa as it is* (King Williams Town, 1871), 44; *L'Expansion des Boers au XIX scièle* (Paris, 1905), 242; *The story of the Zulus* (London, 1911), 71-2; *Piet Retief* (Cape Town, 1920), 252; *The cradle days of Natal 1497-1847* (London, 1930), 245; *The Great Trek* (London, 1938), 188; *The Zulu aftermath* (London, 1960), 45; *Histoire de L'Afrique du Sud* (Paris, 1965), 121; *The washing of the spears* (London, 1966), 150; 'Co-operation and conflict: The Zulu Kingdom and Natal' in *The Oxford history of South Africa*, I, 362, and 'Dingane: A reappraisal' in the *Journal of African history*, X, 2 (1969), 239; *The Great Trek* (Newton Abbot, 1973), 157; 'The period of the Great Trek' in *500 Years*, 166-7; and *Andries Pretorius in Natal* (Pretoria, 1977), 41.
10. 'Retief-Dingane Treaty', *The Cape Times*, 12 July 1923.
11. The area so designated covered virtually the present province of Natal and included the Port of Natal territory.
12. The facsimile of the treaty can be found in W.J. Leyds, *De eerste annexatie van de Transvaal* (Amsterdam, 1906), opp. 53; J. Ploeger and Anna H. Smith *Pictorial atlas of the history of the Union of South Africa* (Pretoria, 1949), 80; and *Die Huisgenoot* (centenary edition), December 1938.
13. The Reverend Francis Owen (1802-1854), representative of the Church Missionary Society. Arrived in South Africa in March 1837 and stayed at Dingane's capital between October 1837 and February 1838. G.E. Cory (ed.), *The diary of the Rev Francis Owen* (Cape Town, 1926), 108.
14. It must be borne in mind that the principle of acquiring territory belonging to the African tribesmen by simple conquest was morally nullified after the Sixth Frontier War.

A further necessity which would have spurred on the invention of the treaty was Pretorius' intelligence that on 4 December — twelve days before his engagement with the Zulu — a British force of 100 soldiers had landed at Port Natal. Charl (or Sarel) Celliers, for instance, noted on 2 January 1939: 'We . . . went back to our encampments, where we were greatly excited by a proclamation which the British Government sent us, in which we were threatened that, if we ventured to enter Dingaan's territory with our

169

forces, they would help Dingaan against us. But we thanked God that the war had then already been waged' (J. Bird, *The annals of Natal 1495-1843*, 2 vols. (Pietermaritzburg, 1888, repr. Cape Town, 1965), I, 249). See also Thompson, *The political mythology of apartheid*, 156-58.

15. J. Barzun and H.F. Graff (*The modern researcher*, New York, 3rd ed. 1977, 85) distinguish between 'genuine' and 'authentic', noting that the two terms 'may seem synonymous but they are not; that is genuine which is not forged, and that is authentic which truthfully reports on its ostensible subject. Thus an art critic might write an account of an exhibition he had never visited; his manuscript would be genuine but not authentic. Conversely, an authentic report of an event by X might be copied by a forger and passed off as the original. It would then be authentic but not genuine.'

16. 'Cory bewerings ontsenuw', *Die Volkstem*, 12 July 1923. According to Leonard Thompson (*The political mythology of apartheid*, 36) Preller was 'preeminent in the moulding of Afrikaner mythology in the first half of the twentieth century'.

17. 'A note on the Retief-Dingaan Treaty', *South African Quarterly* (June-August 1923), 3.

18. *Ibid*, 4.

19. 'Het raadsel van het Retief traktaat', *Het Zoeklicht*, August 1923.

20. The contributions were assembled and published, with an introduction by S.F.N. Gie, *Annals of the University of Stellenbosch*, IIB1, 5 May 1924). This will, hereafter, be referred to as *Ooreenkoms*. The Stellenbosch University Library very kindly provided the author with a complimentary copy of the *Annals*. Preller's account, with additional notes, was published in a book of essays, *Sketse en opstelle* (Pretoria, 1928), 166-219, and will, hereafter, be referred to as *Sketse*.

21. *South Africa as it is* (King William's Town, 1871), 41.

22. Du Plessis (in 'Het raadsel van het Retief traktaat', 237) claimed that he had evidence, before and independent of Cory, that Owen had not been the author of the treaty: his claim, unfortunately, was made public only after Cory's declaration.

23. Dehérain, *L'Expansion des Boers au XIX siecle*, 228.

24. E. Walker observed that Owen's diary was 'far and away the best authority among the tiny handful of European survivors who were on the spot or near it during the fatal week'. 'A Zulu account of the Retief massacre', *The Critic* (January 1935), 70.

25. *Ooreenkoms*, 18-19 and 77; *Sketse*, 173-75.

26. D.C.F. Moodie, *The history of the battles and adventures of the British, the Boers, and the Zulus in Southern Africa*, 2 vols. (Cape Town, 1888), I, 425; Preller, *Ooreenkoms*, 18; and *Sketse*, 173-75.

27. Blommaert, *Ooreenkoms*, 71.

28. Preller, *Ooreenkoms*, 18; and *Sketse*, 174.

29. *Ooreenkoms*, 3.

30. *Ooreenkoms*, 78.

31. A.R. Booth (ed.), *Journal of the Rev. George Champion* (Cape Town, 1967), 109. See also C. de B. Webb and J.B. Wright (eds.), *The James Stuart Archive* (Pietermaritzburg, 1976), I, 329-30, where this point is made with greater emphasis and more detail.

32. Capt A. Gardiner, *A narrative of a journey to the Zoolah country*, 34 and 68; and Owen, *Diary*, 42, 52 and 55. See also *The James Stuart Archive*, I, 329-30.

33. *Ooreenkoms*, 11.

34. Gibson, *The story of the Zulus*, 64.

35. *Ibid*. Gibson in a later study (*The evolution of South African Native policy*, Pietermaritzburg, 1919) referred to the Retief-Dingane agreement as 'a supposed treaty' (17).

36. Preller, *Ooreenkoms*, 37; and *Sketse*, 198.

37. 'Behalwe Dingaan, was daar van die indoenas aanwesig Tambooes, en Oemhlela, Maoro, Joelawoesa, en Manonda' (*Piet Retief*, 254).

38. G.S. Preller (ed.), *Voortrekkermense*, 6 vols. (Cape Town, 1918-1938), I, 289.

39. H. Stander, 'Die verhouding tussen die Boere en die Zoeloe tot die dood van Mpande in 1872', *Archives Year Book for South African history*, 27, II, 1964, 223; Gardiner, *Narrative of a journey*, 68.

40. See Owen, *Diary*, 117.

41. See *The James Stuart Archive*, I, 329.

42. 'We, the undersigned, A.W. Pretorius and Carel Landman, hereby certify and declare, that the foregoing is a literal copy from the original, found among other papers, on the 21st December last, at the residence of Dingaan, in a leathern bag, laying by the bones of the late Retief. We, the joint Subscribers, Hercules Pretorius and P. du Preez, do likewise certify and declare, that we found the document above mentioned by the bones of the late Retief, and which we knew by pieces of his clothes, the document being among other papers in a leathern shooting bag, and which we delivered to the chief Commandant - Evert Potgieter being also present when we found it. We are ready to verify this, our certificate, if required, on oath'. See J.C. Chase, *The Natal papers 1498-1843* (Graham's Town, 1843, repr. Cape Town, 1968), part 2, 72.

43. 'I hereby certify that the above Document is a true Copy of the Original Grant made by Dingaan to the Emigrant Farmers and found on the murdered body of the late Pieter Retief, in my presence by Evert Potgieter on or about the 23rd day of December 1838'. See G.W. Eybers (ed.), *Select constitutional documents illustrating South Africa history, 1795-1910*, 149.

44. Bird, *Annals*, I, 247-48.

45. Chase, *The Natal papers*, part 2, 67; W. Holden, *The past and future of the Kaffir Races* (London, 1866), 71.

46. In February 1835 Gardiner witnessed the execution of two Zulu servants on Kwamatiwane. Visiting the spot the next afternoon he found only skeletons - the hyenas and vultures had done their work of stripping the dead of flesh and blood in less than twenty-four hours. Gardiner, *Narrative*, 44-45.

47. Chase, *The Natal papers*, part 2, 71.

48. It should be pointed out that he referred to a previous letter but emphasised that the 31 December letter bore the same contents. H.F. Schoon (ed.), *The diary of Erasmus Smit* (Cape Town, 1972), 154 (hereafter cited as 'Smit, *Diary*').

49. Smit, *Diary*, 156 (emphasis added).

50. *Ibid*, 159-60.

51. *Ibid*, 161.

52. There is also an account by D.P. Bezuidenhout, to which reference will be made later on. See Bird, *Annals*, I, 370.

53. Bird, *Annals*, I, 234.

54. *Ibid*, 235.

55. R.B. Hulley, *Zululand under Dingaan: Account of the Rev. Mr. Owen's visit to Zululand in the year 1837, as related by Mr. R.B. Hulley (n.p., [1880]), 12.

56. See note 46 above.

57. Owen, *Diary*, 11 and 121.

58. Gardiner, *Narrative*, 87; Andrew Smith and Natal, 9) said between September and April; Bird, *Annals*, I, 236.

59. Owen, *Diary*, 120; P. Becker, *Rule of fear: The life and times of Dingane, King of the Zulu* (Harmondsworth, 1979), 261; Smit, *Diary*, 104, 137, 145 and 152.

60. Cloete, *History of the Great Boer Trek*, 110; Voigt, *Fifty years*, II, 46; Theal, *History of the Boers*, 119; Walker, *The Great Trek*, 188; and Liebenberg, *Andries Pretorius*, 41.

61. 'Die stuk buitendien nog geberg in 'n afsonderlike sakkie van leer, namelik binne in die tas of bladsak' (*Ooreenkoms*, 33; and *Sketse*, 193). Du Plessis (in 'Het raadsel van het Retief traktaat', 243) argued, earlier, that Retief might have wrapped the document in 'waterdicht papier' (waterproof paper) before depositing it in his leather bag. These hypotheses have the merit of imagination but their authors overlook the council of Barzun and Graff: 'When the researcher finds himself multiplying hypotheses in order to cling to a belief, he had better heed the signal and drop the belief' (*The modern researcher*, 88).

62. 'Het raadsel van het Retief traktaat', 237.

63. *Voyage*, II, 135.

64. Chase, *The Natal papers*, part 2, 67.

65. See William Wood's testimony (in Bird, *Annals*, I, 381).

66. Smit, *Diary*, 77.

67. (1865-1930), journalist, editor, founder of *The Pretoria News* and personal friend of Paul Kruger.

68. *The Pretoria News*, 29 August 1923. Also quoted by Preller, *Ooreenkoms*, 48; and *Sketse*, 212.

69. *Ooreenkoms*, 47; and *Sketse*, 211. The hallowed, mystical aspect of Pretorius' campaign against Dingane is analysed and exposed by Thompson in his *The political mythology of apartheid*, 152-65.

70. *Ooreenkoms*, 52; and *Sketse*, 216-17.

71. *The Voortrekker Monument*, 49 (emphasis added).

72. A confident and sincere, Mrs C.W. Coppejans, claimed (letter to the author, 31 October 1984) that 'the wallet' was in the Voortrekkermuseum, Pietermaritzburg; and that Dr I. Pols, the curator there, would provide all the relevant details. Unfortunately Dr Pols, after much unexplained delay — three letters, including one that was registered, had to be sent before a response was forthcoming — replied negatively: 'I am sorry to have to disappoint you and Mrs Coppejans with the true facts. The 'wallet' which you refer to, which contained the *treaty* was never in the possession of this museum; this applies for the original treaty as well. As far as we know it was lost during the Anglo-Boer War. I will inform Mrs Coppejans of this regrettable fact.' (Letter to the author, 14 March 1985.)

73. *Ooreenkoms*, 32-5; *Sketse*, 192-6. Du Plessis (in 'Het raadsel van het Retief traktaat', 242) also thought that the treaty bore the handwriting of Thomas Halstead.

74. *Ooreenkoms*, 81.

75. The Soutter Collection ref. A 3, packet No. 4 (2), 168; and A 3, packet No. 4 (2 A), 170.

76. See 'Controversy of the treaty' by Preller in the *Rand Daily Mail*, 11 February 1926.

77. 'More light on the Retief-Dingaan treaty', *The Star*, 17 February 1926.

78. *Ibid.*

79. See Soutter to Goldman, 13 April 1926, Transvaal Archives Depot, 44 T. A 136/23.

80. See 'Treaty of tragedy - Dingaan and Retief - Writer found', *Rand Daily Mail*, 6 February 1926.

81. Sketse, 192; 'Wie het die Traktaat geskryf?', *Ons Vaderland*, 9 February 1926 and 'Wat 'n dogter van Jan Bantjes vertel', *Ons Vaderland*, 16 February 1926.

82. *Diary*, 15; see also Thompson, *The political mythology of apartheid*, 271.

83. *DSAB*, I, 51.

84. *Rand Daily Mail*, 6 and 11 February 1926; and *Ons Vaderland* 9 and 26 February 1926; *Hoe ons aan Dingaansdag kom: Jan Bantjes se dagverhaal van die winkommando* (Bloemfontein, 1928); and *Sketse*, 192.

85. D.J.J. de Villiers, *Die Jongspan*, 1 July 1938.

Ransford (in *The Great Trek*, Newton Abbot, 1973, 124 — though a popular account nevertheless makes a few points that more serious works have failed to note) observed (in a footnote entry): 'It is rather curious that the document was drawn up in English; the handwriting suggests that it was written by Jan Gerrit Bantjes.'

C.J. Uys (in *DSAB*, I, 50) did refer to Preller's belief that Bantjes (without mentioning that he was a Coloured) was the author of the Dingane-Retief treaty.

86. *Pictorial atlas of the history of the Union of South Africa*, 80.

87. *DSAB*, I, 50.

88. *Voyage*, II, 118.

89. Smit, *Diary*, 79-83.

90. *Ooreenkoms*, 7.

91. *Ibid*, 6-8.

92. *Ibid*, 5.

93. *Ooreenkoms*, 40; and *Sketse*, 202.

94. *Ooreenkoms*, 40; and *Sketse*, 202-3.

95. Quoted by Cory, *Ooreenkoms*, 6.

96. Andrew Smith, see *Andrew Smith and Natal*, 43.

97. Owen, *Diary*, 47 and 50.

98. *Ibid*, 117.

99. Becker, *Rule of fear*, 229.

100. 48, 55, 59 and 60.

'He is beginning to see', George Champion noted of the Chief, 'that paper messengers tell no lies'. *Journal*, 17 May 1837, 96.

101. *DSAB*, II, 148.

102. 'Si, Dingan avait attaché une importance quelconque au document qu'il avait signé, il se serait empressé de le faire rechercher et détruire après le massacre' (*L'Expansion des Boers*, 229).

103. In February 1926 Lyal Soutter claimed that he was present with Weinthal. See 'More light on the Retief-Dingaan treaty', *The Star*, 17 February 1926.

104. See *Ooreenkoms*, 48; and *Sketse*, 211.

105. An inquiry, to the Natal Archives Depot, Pietermaritzburg, requesting information on this letter, elicited the following reply from the Chief archivist: 'I have found several published copies of this letter, but not the original. One source comments that copies of the original letter were sent to the newspaper *De Zuid-Afrikaan*, which published it on the 15 February 1839 . . . If this is the case and if the letter still exists it will be very difficult to trace (letter to the author, 1 July 1985).

A further inquiry, which included the information of the Natal Archives, was addressed to the Cape Archives Dept; and this produced the following: 'Via the computer terminal the manuscript holdings of the various repositories participating in the National Register of Manuscripts programme were consulted, but the whereabout of said letter could not be traced.

It seems probable from various published sources dealing with Voortrekker documents that the letter in question has not remained preserved' (Letter to the author, 27 August 1985).

106. W.J. Leyds in a letter to Du Plessis in the 1920s (a portion of which is reproduced in 'Het raadsel van het Retief traktaat', 238-9) claimed that, on the eve of the British

occupation of Pretoria in 1900, six cases of state documents, one of which contained the treaty, were addressed to him in the Netherlands. Four of the six cases reached him, two fell into the hands of the invading force - into the hands, probably, of Alfred Milner. The original treaty was therefore with the British.

A letter to the Transvaal Archives Depot, Pretoria, inquiring if anything new has since been learnt of the whereabouts of the treaty, produced the following reply: 'The treaty is still not in the custody of the . . . Depot and the situation surrounding the treaty is the same as it was in 1923' (Letter to the author, 27 August 1985).

107. In September 1923, Cory, in his Stellenbosch contribution, observed: 'Mr Weinthal makes the statement that he made the tracing of the original treaty . . . great credit is due to Mr Weinthal for the care he must have taken in reproducing writing so like that of Retief and the three Boer signatories. Mr Weinthal speaks further of the original having been on parchment. I wonder whether his memory is not playing him false in this respect. *Ooreenkoms*, 11-12.

108. J.M. Berning, librarian at the Cory Library for Historical Research - who was extremely helpful as far as this particular chapter was concerned - advanced the following: 'It seems possible, but I offer this very tentatively, that Cory's retraction was in part a diplomatic move made because of the storm raised by his original view' (Letter to the author, 2 June 1984). Cory in the 1920s wrote an autobiography, *Recollections of the Past*. Perhaps he dealt less enigmatically with the reasons for his change of view but the republished *Recollections* is quite infortunately 'closed to investigations'. (See *A Guide to the South African Manuscript Collections in the South African Library*, Cape Town, 1977, 130, item no. 216.)

109. *Ooreenkoms*, 1.

110. Cory, IV, 78.

CHAPTER SIX

1. *The adventures of Hans Sterk: The South African hunter and pioneer* (London, 1869), 87.

2. E.H. Brookes and C. de B. Webb, *A history of Natal* (Pietermaritzburg, 1965), 30. Sheila Patterson (in *The last trek*, London, 1957), 22) refers to Retief as the *Boers' Moses*; while, W. Smith (Daniel Lindley, 131) refers to Retief as 'one of the most honourable men' in the Cape Colony.

3. See E.A. Walker, *The Great Trek*, 119; and O. Ransford, *The Great Trek*, 127 and 110-11. In a recent piece of historical fiction (J.A. Michener, *The Covenant*, 387) Dingane is portrayed as a 'Nero, a tyrannical despot caring more for entertainment and intrigue than solid governance'.

4. MacCrone, *Race attitudes in South Africa*, 267-8. About 100 Trekkers, including thirty Khoi (or Coloureds) were killed.

5. H. Cloete, *The history of the Great Boer Trek*, 95. One writer, to cite another example, describes conditions in Zululand among its sparse and peripheral European residents (there were thirty-eight in all) and then, without further ado announced: 'This was then the condition of affairs when Pieter Retief visited Natal' (Theal, *History of the Boers in South Africa*, London, 1887, repr. Cape Town, 1973, 101); while another noted: 'It was in the midst of this confusion that Retief and his companions rode' (Walker, *The Great Trek*, 151). Even Thompson's reference to Retief's entry into Zulu territory is conventional: 'In November 1837 Piet Retief, whom most of the emigrants accepted as their leader, led a party of horsemen to Dingane's Zulu headquarters, seeking his ap-

proval for them to settle in the region' (*The political mythology of apartheid*, 150). For other similarly complacent though slightly different versions, see: Muller, 'The period of the Great Trek, 1834-1854', in *500 Years*, 162-3; and Brookes and Webb, *A history of Natal*, 30.

6. Cloete, *The history of the Great Boer Trek*, 95.

7. J.A.I. Agar-Hamilton, *The Native policy of the Voortrekkers* (Cape Town, 1928), 25.

8. It was 'the usual practice' when visiting the Chief to offer him a gift. See J. Stuart and D.M. Malcolm (eds.), *The diary of Henry Francis Fynn* (Pietermaritzburg, 1949), 176.

9. R.U. Kenney, *Piet Retief, the dubious hero* (Cape Town, 1976), 153. This, like Ransford's *The Great Trek*, is a popular account but it, too, makes a number of points that are absent in those that are more academic. See also Smith, *Daniel Lindley*, 136, where he stated: 'That Dingane should so easily surrender so vast a tract of land for so small a consideration - the recovery of a few stolen cattle - a tract which he had already granted to others, was in itself strange'.

10. *Marie* (London, 1912, repr. 1925).

11. 'The Zulu land-system was communal. There were no privately owned estates, no land-titles, no land-sharks, no fences, no rents . . . The whole country belonged to the clan, and no individual thereof, be he commoner or king, was justified in usurping any portion of the common inheritance as his own personal property for all time'. A.T. Bryant, *The Zulu people* (Pietermaritzburg, 1949), 464.

12. A point that Julius Caeser noted: 'They consider it a tribute to their strength when neighbouring tribes are forced to retire from their lands and when none dares enter there. Also, they hold that such makes them more secure as it removes the fear of sudden attack or invasion'. P.L. Hughes and R.F. Fries (eds.), *Readings in Western Civilization* (New Jersey, 1960), 4.

13. *Diary*, 63. See also Bird, *Annals*, I, 361-2; and Chase, *The Natal papers*, part 1, 131-2.

14. *500 Years*, 163.

15. As A. Nevins, the American historian (in 'The case of the cheating documents: False authority and the problem of surmise', in *The historian as detective*, 210), stressed: 'Translations may be of all degrees of goodness or badness . . . But it is important to remember that a translation no matter how excellent is always a change.'

16. This refers to Dingane's signing of a 'treaty' on 6 May 1835 with Captain Allen Gardiner (1794-1851), of the Church Mission Society.

17. Owen, *Diary*, 64.

18. Owen, *Diary*, 65. The Missionary noted that Dingane 'knows full well what part of the country they [the Trekkers] *wish* to posses and he has been giving them to understand that the whole country, called Victoria, is still *his*. (Of this I was informed by Mr Retief), but he has not expressly promised to transfer any part of it to them'.

19. 'Dingaan and the Retief Treaty: Was it Genuine', *Natal Witness*, 2 August 1923.

20. See Owen, *Diary*, 3 November 1837, 59-60; and 9 November 1837, 65. This view is endorsed by Smith (in *Daniel Lindley*, 132) when he stresses: 'What Dingane meant to do was to transfer to the Boers the country lately occupied by Mzilikazi beyond the Vaal.'

21. Smit, *Diary*, 183.

22. See J. Backhouse, *A narrative of a visit to the Mauritius and South Africa* (London, 1844), 402-5.

23. Bird, *Annals*, I, 369. A different version of this irregular capture appears in Owen, *Diary*, 3 February 1838, 105, where the claim is made that deceit was practised not by Bezuiden-hout but by Retief himself.

24. Kenney, *Piet Retief*, 158.

25. Ransford, a recent commentator, believed that there was 'something rather distasteful about the manner in which Retief dealt with Sekonyela' (*The Great Trek*, 120). Most other reports of the event are bland: 'Mr Retief . . . sent for Sikonyela, and when that chief appeared informed him that he would be detained as a prisoner until the cattle stolen from the Zulus were given up' (Theal, *History of the Boers*, 103); for similar complacent accounts see: Dehérain, *L'Expansion des Boers*, 226; Preller, *Piet Retief*, 218; Walker, *The Great Trek*, 160; A.J.H. van der Walt and others (eds.), *Geskiedenis van Suid-Africa*, 2 vols. (Cape Town, 1951), II, 297; H. Stander, 'Die verhouding tussen die Boere en Zoeloe', 221; and Morris, *The washing of the spears*, 140.

26. Backhouse, *A narrative of a visit to Mauritius and South Africa*, 404.

27. A.J. du Plessis, 'Die Republiek Natalia', *Archives year book of South African history*, 1942, II, 123-4. See also Chase, *The Natal papers*, part 1, 126, where Retief, in a letter dated 23 October 1837, also refers to the *theft*.

28. 57.

29. Smit, *Diary*, 92.

30. Gibson, *The Story of the Zulus*, 62. See also Kenney (*Piet Retief*, 158), who observed that 'Retief's role in the Sikonyela affair . . . conflicted with the accepted norms governing relations between societies and states'.

31. See, for instance, Theal, *History*, VI, 358; Becker, *Rule of fear*, 242; and Walker, *The Great Trek*, 161.

32. See Du Plessis, 'Die Republiek Natalia', 125, where he stressed that Retief wanted to go to Umgungundhlovu with 200 men.

33. Owen, *Diary*, 3 February 1838, 104.

34. *The Great Trek*, 163.

35. See Owen's diary entry on 14 December 1837, 84-5.

36. Ransford, for instance, after having stated that Dingane finally resolved to annihilate all the Trekkers on his territory, noted: 'He requested that the chief of the Boers would send to all his people and order them to come up to the capital with him, but . . . without their horses' (*The Great Trek*, 123). Ransford obviously obtained this information from Owen, for on 2 February Dingane sent for the Missionary and asked him to address a letter to Retief, where (as Owen noted, *Diary*, 104): 'He requested that the chief of the Boers would send to all his people and order them to come up to the capital with him, *But without their horses*: he promised to gather together all his army to sing and dance in the presence of the Dutch, who he desired would also dance'.

37. Retief (in a letter to the *Graham's Town Journal*, 18 November 1837) reported that Umgungundhlovu had '1 700 huts, each capable of accommodating twenty warriors'. See Chase, *The Natal papers*, part 2, 129.

38. *Diary*, 85.

39. *Diary*, 2 February 1838, 104.

40. *Journal of the Rev George Champion*, 118; and Owen, *Diary*, 21 December 1837, 87.

41. *Journal of the Rev George Champion*, xiii.

42. Owen, *Diary*, 21 December 1837, 88-9.

43. *Ibid*. 104.

44. Ransford, *The Great Trek*, 128.

45. See the letter of J. Boshoff to the *Graham's Town Journal*, 9 August 1838, in Bird, *Annals*, I, 406-8.

46. 'The fortunes of the Trekkers were now at their lowest ebb' (Walker, *A history of South Africa*, 216); 'The Great Trek reached its nadir in the difficult winter of 1838' (Muller, *500 Years*, 165). Ransford (in *The Great Trek*, 122-34) has a chapter dealing

with these losses, titled: 'The great murder'.

47. See Smith, *Daniel Lindley*, 141; and Kotzé, *Letters of the American missionaries*, 222 (the letter is incongruously dated *27 January 1838)*).

48. Ransford, *The Great Trek*, 135.

49. *Ibid.* 128 and 134.

50. See page 116 above.

51. Owen, *Diary*, 23 January 1838, 100.

52. On the day of Retief's first meeting with Dingane in October 1837, Owen (*Diary*, 64) pleaded with Retief not for him and his men to serve as the Chief's *emissaries in making war*.

53. *A narrative of a visit to the Mauritius and South Africa*, 403.

54. *Diary*, 23 January 1838, 100.

55. *Ibid.* 101.

56. Owen, (*Diary*, 29 November 1837, 72) noted: 'The white people [Dingane complained] were not *one with him*. They granted him some things, but other things they withheld (alluding to . . . gunpowder): yet he was ready to do all the white people asked him'.

57. See note 20 above.

58. 'Bantu law knew nothing of an out-and-out alienation of the land on which the life of the tribe depended, but merely the grant of hunting, grazing and such other privileges as might cover the use of whatever its being on that land'. Walker, *The Great Trek*, 149.

59. As Theal (in *History*, VI, 359) observed: 'Grants similar to this [the one supposedly made to Retief], and covering the same ground, or portions of it, had been previously made by Tshaka and Dingane himself to Messrs Farewell, Fynn, King, Isaacs, and Gardiner; and under no circumstances would such a cession in the minds of the bantu mean more than permission to occupy the ground during the lifetime of the chief who made it, whose supremacy would be assumed'.

60. The 'supremacy' of the Chief over the territory concerned, like 'a feudal lord', would have been assumed. See Theal, *Compendium of the history and geography of South Africa*, (3rd ed. London, 1878), 90-1.

61. Owen, *Diary*, 8 February 1838, 112; and the 'General letter [by the American missionaries] to Anderson', 2 April 1838, in Kotzé, *Letters of the American missionaries*, 238.

62. Kotzé, *Letters of the American missionaries*, 237.

63. *Ibid.*

64. *Diary*, 7 February 1838, 111. Walker observed (in *The Great Trek*, 164) that, 'Retief's force was a formidable one, of much the same strength as the Mosega commando and three-fourths of that which had routed the Matabele on the Marico'.

65. *Diary*, 10 February 1838, 114 (emphasis added).

66. *Ibid.* 116. Cetewayo, the son of Dingane's half-brother, Mpande, who at the time was just over ten years old, stated (in 1886) that, the Trekkers 'made a demand on Dingaan to give up a lot of the cattle that he had taken from Umzilikazi, saying they had been stolen by that chief from them'. See C. de Webb and J.B. Wright (eds.), *A Zulu speaks: A statement made by Cetshwayo ka Mpande on the history and customs of his people* (Durban, 1978), 11.

67. A Zulu named Lunguza provided this information to James Stuart on 14 March 1909. See *James Stuart archive*, I, 318.

68. Dingane, on that fateful Tuesday morning when Retief and his men were seized but not yet executed — and more than twenty-four hours after the meeting, sent a messenger to Owen calling on the Missionary not to be afraid, and informing him that he was going

to kill the Trekkers, for 'he had *now* learned all their plans' (Owen, *Diary*, 106-7).

69. 4 February 1838, 105.

70. See B. Gardner, *Mafeking: A Victorian legend* (London, 1966, 1968), 63, 97 and 133.

71. See Owen (*Diary*, 60) Saturday, 4 November 1837, where the diary entry reads: 'On my observing that I thought the Dutch would be here the day after tomorrow, he [Dingane] asked if the obstacle to their coming tomorrow was Sunday'.

72. *A narrative of a journey to the Zoolah country*, 209.

73. If the treaty was forged by Bantjes, there must have been a good reason why he chose to date it the 4th: was Retief's intention premeditated long in advance? Did he — while he was still in the Trekker camp — make known his intention of meeting Dingane on that particular Sunday?

74. See his 'Manifesto of the Emigrant Farmers', in Chase, *The Natal papers*, part 1, 83.

75. Retief's action against Sekonyela was supposed to have infuriated Allison: when Retief asked him to hold a service for the Trekkers before they left his station, the Missionary took as his text the words: 'He who sows wickedness, reaps wickedness' (Ransford, *The Great Trek*, 120).

76. *Diary*, 97.

77. Retief to Dingane, 19 October 1837, Bird, *Annals*, I, 360.

78. Retief to Dingane, 8 November 1837, Bird, I, 362. In sending this letter to Dingane, Retief had (Walker observed in *The Great Trek*, 155) 'countersigned his own death warrant'.

79. Theal, *History*, VI, 356.

80. 'The expansion of the Boers and the superiority of European technology, symbolised in the gun, determined when and where a pastoral economy could continue'. Duly, 'A revisit with the Cape's Hottentot Ordinance of 1828', 27.

CHAPTER SEVEN

1. C.P. Lucas, *The history of South Africa to the Jameson Raid*, 91.

2. Theal, *History*, VII, 415-20. For a fictionalised account of the standard version, see S. Cloete, *The mask* (London, 1958, paperback ed. 1960).

3. J.M. Orpen, *Reminiscences of life in South Africa* (Cape Town, 1964), 254-56.

4. Walker, *History of Southern Africa*, 280-1, and *History of South Africa*, 290; J.A.I. Agar-Hamilton, *The Native policy of the Voortrekkers, 1836-1858*, 163-64; L.M. Thompson, 'Co-operation and conflict: the High Veld' in the *Oxford history of South Africa*, I, 400. Thompson calls him 'Makapane'.

5. P. Kruger, *The memoirs of Paul Kruger*, 2 vols. (London, 1902, 2 vols.), I, 46-53.

6. *Dictionary of South African biography*, II, 436-37 and 478-79. Jackson is the author of 'The history and political structure of the Mapela Chiefdom of the Potgietersrus District', which was submitted for a D. Phil. degree, University of the Witwatersrand, 1969.

7. *Ibid*, ii, 436. Orpen (in *Reminiscences*, 251) noted as early as 1909 that 'the names of the two chiefs are often jumbled up and variously spelled'.

8. Theal, *History*, VII, 415.

9. G.W. Stow (ed. G.M. Theal), *The Native races of South Africa* (London, 1905), 499.

10. Jackson, *DSAB*, II, 478.

11. Theal, VII, 416.

12. Walker, *History of Southern Africa*, 281, and *History of South Africa*, 290.

13. Theal, VII, 416.

14. See I. Schapera (ed.), *Livingstone's missionary correspondence, 1841-1856* (London, 1961), 97-98 and 11-12; Orpen, *Reminiscences*, 250-51; and J.J. de Waal, 'Die verhouding tussen die Blankes, en die Hoofmanne Mokopane en Mankopane in die omgewing van Potgietersrus (1836-1869)', M.A. dissertation, University of South Africa, 1978, 84-89.

15. Quoted in J.P.R. Wallis (ed.), *The Matabele journals of Robert Moffat, 1829-1860* (London, 1945), 377-87.

16. Transvaal Archives Depot, Pretoria, S.S.6, R633/54, declaration of H.J. van Staden and others, 14 May 1854 (actually, 1853).

17. Presumably it was this double standard of justice which made chief Khosilintse complain to Robert Moffat in this vein: 'Are we only to obey the word of God because we are black? Are white people not to obey the word of God because they are white? . . . You tell us that God may yet punish us and the Bakhatla more than he had done, for having rejected the Gospel. Did those tribes which the Boers have destroyed and made their slaves, reject the Gospel?' (*The Matabele journals of Robert Moffat*, 377-798).

18. Theal, *History*, VII, 417.

19. See T. Gerdener, 'Die grootte wat mense geëet het', *Die Brandwag*, 18 July 1952.

20. The inscription plate on the monument outside the city hall of Potgietersrus claims that the victims were: 'Willem Prinsloo, Nellie Prinsloo en 3 kinders. Lourens Bronkhorst. Jan Breedt, Maria Breedt en 3 kinders. Philluppus du Preez'. See Nancy C. Acutt, 'Makapaan se gruweldade', *Die Huisgenoot*, 6 May 1938.

21. Transvaal Archives Depot, S.S.7, 733/54 (hereafter cited as 'Pretorius' Report'). C. Pinnaar (in *De Volkstem*, 6 January 1890), who claimed to have visited Moorddrif or Mahalakwena fourteen days after the killings, declared, in 1890 - forty-six years after the event, that the heads of the children were smashed against the wagon wheels, and that the men and women were cut to pieces. This is also the version of Acutt, *Die Huisgenoot*, 6 May 1938. D. Nel, 'Die drama van die Makapansgrot' (Soos deur die Naturelle vertel), *Die Huisgenoot*, 24 March 1933, who obtained his information from Africans living in the area of the killings (in the 1930s), claimed that some parts of the victims were removed for medicinal purposes. The African witness (in Orpen, *Reminiscences*, 225) claimed that some of the slain were scalped.

22. Pretorius' Report.

23. Before accepting this account literally, perhaps one should consult, e.g., A. Ponsonby, *Falsehood in war-time* (London, 1928), 13-14 and 67-70.

24. Nel, in his version of the killings ('Drama'), differs slightly from that of the African witness' (in Orpen *Reminiscences*).

25. See De Waal, 'Verhouding', 3-8.

26. *Ibid*, vii.

27. The Wesleyan missionary, W.B. Boyce (no enemy of the settlers) in reference to the Cape noted: 'The real cause of the Kaffer, as well as of other wars, between colonists and aborigines, may be traced to the unjust system of European colonization . . . or territorial aggression' (*Notes on South African affairs* 26 and 28). The observation was just as relevant and just as pertinent for the Transvaal.

28. De Waal, 'Verhouding', 27-28.

29. 'The Boers, well knowing that they had very little chance of success in dealing with the Meetibele returned homewards: but unwilling to face their wives without some proof of their prowess, actually fell upon a tribe which had furnished its quota of men for the expedition. The chief secured most of his cattle but a large seizure was made of goats

and children, and the latter were separated from their mothers in the same way calves are taken from their dams in the country. The name of the chief is Mankopane, and there was not even the shadow of a pretext for attacking him. Some of these children were sold ... almost in sight of the colony'. *Livingstone's missionary correpsondence*, 11-12.

30. P. Delius claims that one of the factors of 'critical importance' inducing the Northern Transvaal tribes to become migrant labourers was a 'desire to accumulate guns'. He also has a passage reading: 'One of the most detailed descriptions of a returning group is of the Transvaal Ndebele, subjects of Mapela [Mankopane]: There were 130 men. They all carried guns over their shoulders' and had besides 'fifteen horses'. 'Migrant labour and the Pedi, 1840-80', in *Economy and society in pre-industrial South Africa*, 297.

31. *Livingstone's missionary correspondence*, 97.

32. Transvaal Archives Depot, S.S.5, 562e/53, H.J. Potgieter to P.J. Potgieter, 8 September 1853.

33. J.H. Breytenbach (ed.), *Notule van die Volksraad van die Suid-Afrikaanse Republiek, 1844-1868*, numbers 1-6 (Cape Town, 1949-56), part 2, 153.

34. De Waal, 'Verhouding', 27.

35. G.S. Preller, 'Baanbrekers' in *Oorlogsoormag en ander sketse en verhale* (Cape Town, 1923), 153-54.

36. De Waal, 'Verhouding', 105.

37. *Ibid*, 109.

38. How news reached the other settlers, and how the commandos were formed are succinctly covered by H. Potgieter, 'Moord in Makapansvalle', *Die Brandwag*, 3 September 1954, and in detail in De Waal, 'Verhouding', 100-03.

39. De Waal, 'Verhouding', 106.

40. The article, 'Makapansgat' in *The standard encyclopaedia of South Africa* (Cape Town, 1970-1976, 12 vols.), VII, 124-27, contains a good description of the Cave.

41. T. Baines, *The gold regions of South East Africa* (London, 1877), 68.

42. R. Dart, *Adventures with the missing link* (London, 1959), 44.

43. De Waal, 'Verhouding', 112.

44. *Ibid*.

45. Transvaal Archives Depot, S.S.7, R719/54, M.W. Pretorius to S. Schoeman, 12 November 1854.

46. Theal, *History*, VII, 410.

47. Pretorius' Report.

48. De Waal, 'Verhouding', 115.

49. *Ibid*, 121; Gerdener, *Die Brandwag*, 18 July 1952.

50. Theal, *History*, VII, 419.

51. Dart, *Adventrues*, 94.

52. Kruger stated that 'a small portion of them escaped through underground passages into the mountains'; while Dart claimed that 'numbers [of the Kekana] escaped at night by scaling down the clift from the western entrance on the darkest nights and eluding the guards'. Kruger, *Memoirs*, I, 52; Dart, *Adventures*, 94-95.

53. The skeletons in the Cave were gradually 'dispersed into the homes of sightseers from all over the country'. Six skulls turned up at the Royal College of Surgeons, London; while local African doctors, for medicinal purposes, used the Cave as a bone store. See Dart, *Adventures*, 97. The Cave was also exploited by mining companies in search of lime. These mining activities might also have destroyed or removed the remaining traces of the siege. See 'Into the cave of death', *The New Nation*, 1 October 1987

54. Theal, *History*, VII, 419.

55. Kruger (*Memoirs*, I, 52) stated that 'the chief had disappeared', whereas the African witness (Orpen, *Reminiscences*, 256) claimed that Mokopane 'lived for many years' after the cave siege. Nel ('Drama') claimed that within days after he had survived the siege with some of his followers, 'Sejwamadie' [Mokopane] committed suicide by drinking poison. Dart (*Adventures*, 92) agrees with the African witness.

56. *Memoirs*, I, 53. Maraba was supposed to have been a friendly chief, but the attack - even to some contemporaries - appeared sordid and gratuitous, so much so that S.J. Schoeman, a commander, was forced to write the following letter to *The Friend of the Free State and the Bloemfontein Gazette* (28 April 1855): 'The Kaffir Captain Maraba - during the whole campaign . . . against Makapaan, and the other hordes - furnished shelter to the bloodthirsty people of Makapaan and Mapele, . . . the said Maraba, who wears the mask of friendship, is guilty of the blood of women and children; and that by his people the defenceless children were delivered over to those evils incarnate to be most shockingly butchered, boiled in pots, and their flesh devoured by them, and that Maraba makes constant reports to our declared enemies, regarding the situation and proceedings of the commando; by all which I was led to look upon him as one of the chief murderers. All this, and much more, compelled us to march against these blood thirsty cannibals, and to drive them out of the bush, before they should have perpetrated a second deed of horror. And after effecting this, we found several articles belonging to the murdered women and children, in their town; many of them stained with blood, and full of assegai stabs: and what I have done I will make known to the world.

Let any who will, speak openly against it, and like an honest man, give his name. I am, &c'.

57. De Waal, 'Verhouding', 118.

58. *Ibid*, 126-27. In 1857 landdrost A. du Toit complained to Pretorius that there were no volunteers coming for an expedition against Mankopane. Some of the Farmers even went so far as to blame Mankopane's 'rebelliousness' on Pretorius. De Waal, 'Verhouding', 133.

59. *With the Boers in the Transvaal and Orange Free State in 1880* (London, 1882), 59. The author, in fact, is merely echoing the views of Duncan Moodie, who (in *The history of the battles and adventures of the British, the Boers, and the Zulus, in Southern Africa*, 2 vols., Cape Town, 1879, II, 579-81) regretted that the British did not, like the settlers of the Transvaal Republic, 'hunt savages after a savage fashion' (580).

60. *History of South Africa*, 290. Theal (*History*, VII, 420), more circumspect, observed: it was hoped that the punishment inflicted on Mokopane would deter his confederate 'from committing any acts of violence against Europeans for a long time to come'.

61. De Waal, 'Verhouding', 191.

62. Kruger, *Memoirs*, II, 48. Nel, 'Drama', claimed that everyone definitely recognised that Potgieter's skin was entirely removed.

H.C. Bosman in his ficitonalised account, 'Makapan's caves', has Potgieter's skin iconoclastically transformed into a dagga pouch (see *Mafeking road*, South Africa, 1947, 47-8).

63. 'In die verhouding tussen Mankopane en die blankes kan 'n mens nie anders as om groot agting vir Mankopane as persoon te hê nie' (In the relations between Mankopane and the whites one cannot but have great respect for Mankopane as an individual). De Waal, 'Verhouding', 191.

CHAPTER EIGHT

1. *Gandhi in South Africa: British imperialism and the Indian question*, (Ithaca and London, 1971), 177.

2. *Collected works of Mahatma Gandhi*, I-XII (New Delhi, 1858-1964), (hereafter referred to as *CW*), 'Statement of the Transvaal Indian case', 16 July 1906, IX, 296. He also said, 'We certainly appreciate the sentiment that the country being suitable for European settlement, it should be kept for them so far as it is consistent with the well-being of the Empire as a whole'. 'With what measure', *Indian Opinion*, 11 June 1903, *CW*, III, 337.

3. 'The labour question in the Transvaal', *Indian Opinion*, 24 September 1903, *CW*, III, 453.

4. 'Letter to Dr Porter', *Indian Opinion*, 9 April 1904, *CW*, IV, 130-1.

5. 'My experience in gaol[-1]', *Indian Opinion*, 7 March 1908, *CW*, VIII, 135.

6. 'The Coloured People's petition', *Indian Opinion*, 24 March 1906, *CW*, V, 241-2.

7. 'Letter to Minister of Education', 5 September 1905, *Indian Opinion*, *CW*, V, 58-9.

8. M.K. Gandhi, *An autobiography or my experiments with truth*, (Ahmedabad 1927, reprint ed. 1972), 235.

9. 'The Natal rebellion' *Indian Opinion*, 14 April 1906, *CW*, V, 282.

10. Letter to W.T. Stead, 16 November 1906, *CW*, VI, 168.

11. 'My second experience in goal[-III]', *CW*, IX, 149; see also 'The foot-path bye-law', *Indian Opinion*, IV, 105 and 'Letter to W.T. Stead', VI, 168.

12. 'My experience in gaol[-1]', *Indian Opinion*, 7 March 1908, *CW*, VIII, 135.

13. Maureen Swan, *Gandhi: The South African experience* (Johannesburg, 1985), 137-8.

14. Maureen Swan, *Gandhi*, chapter one, 'Merchants and migrants: social stratification and politics', 1-37. But the author (in 'Ideology in organised Indian politics, 1891-1948' in, *The politics of race, class and Nationalism in twentieth century South Africa*, 182-204) modifies some of these categories and introduces further distinctions when she refers to 'lower middle classes', 'emerging elite', 'big traders', 'petty traders' and 'the white-collar/petty-trader elite' - these, it seems, reveal the extreme fluidity and challenge, not to say the inconsistencies, of such sociological classifications or definitions.

15. See H. Tinker, *A new system of slavery* (London, 1974).

16. See Maureen Swan, *Gandhi*, 17. Later, when the Transvaal Government deported some of these ex-indentured Indians because of their passive resistance, Gandhi would ask their wives and children if they wanted to join their husbands and fathers in India. Their indignant reply was: 'How can we? We were brought to this country as children, and we do not know anybody in India. We would rather perish here than go to India, which is a foreign land to us.' 'Letter to G.K. Gokhale', *CW*, X, 232.

17. 'To Satyagrahis and other Indians', 13 October 1908, *Indian Opinion*, 17 October 1908, *CW*, IX, 97.

18. M.K. Gandhi, *Satyagraha in South Africa*, (Ahmedabad, 1928, reprint ed. 1972), 93 and 22.

19. 'The Indian franchise', 16 December 1895, *CW*, I, 273-4; see also 'Lord Milner on the Asiatic question', *Indian Opinion*, 11 June 1903, *CW*, III, 336.

20. 'Interview to *The Transvaal Leader*', 21, 21 August 1908, *Indian Opinion*, 22 August 1908, *CW*, VIII, 468.

21. 'A mare's nest', *Indian Opinion*, 26 January 1907, *CW*, VI, 290-1.

22. 'The Transvaal struggle', *Indian Opinion*, 2 February 1909, *CW*, IX, 184.

23. 'The Indian offer' 19 October 1899, *CW*, III, 113-4.

24. Gandhi, *Satyagraha in South Africa*, 65.

25. 'Petition to Chamberlain', 31 December 1898, *CW*, III, 27.

26. 'In 1865 a thousand muskets were ordered from England to be stored ready for issue to Coolies in an emergency.' L.M. Thompson, 'Indian immigration into Natal, 1860-1872', *Archives year book of South African history* (Cape Town, 1952), II, 35.

27. 'There was hardly any traders in the Corps.' Gandhi, *Satyagraha in South Africa*, 70.

28. See 'The Indian ambulance corps in Natal', 14 March 1900, *CW*, III, 137.

29. *Ibid*, 140.

30. *Ibid*, 141.

31. *Satyagraha in South Africa*, 95; G. Bolton, *The tragedy of Gandhi*, (London, 1934), 115; Huttenback, *Gandhi in South Africa*, 166; B. Pillay, *British Indians in the Transvaal* (London, 1976), 213; and L. Fischer, *The life of Gandhi* (New York, 1950), 73-6.

32. Maureen Swan, *Gandhi*, 120-1.

33. *Satyagraha in South Africa*, 95.

34. Maureen Tayal, 'Indian passive resistance in the Transvaal 1906-08', in B. Bozzoli (ed.), *Town and countryside in the Transvaal* (Johannesburg, 1983), 243.

35. 'Johannesburg letter', *Indian Opinion*, 22 September 1906, *CW*, V, 442.

36. As early as 1904, according to Maureen Swan, *Gandhi*, 117.

37. Fischer, *The life of Gandhi*, 86.

38. *Ibid*, 79; and Huttenback, *Gandhi in South Africa*, 204.

39. B. Pachai, 'The history of the "Indian Opinion", 1903-1914', *The archives year book of South African history* (Cape Town, 1961), 49-50.

40. Maureen Swan, *Gandhi*, 170-1.

41. 'Letter to L.W. Ritch', 8 April 1911, *CW*, XI, 16.

42. See Maureen Tayal, 'Indian passive resistance in the Transvaal', 250.

43. Maureen Swan, *Gandhi*, 161.

44. 'Johannesburg letter', *Indian Opinion*, 2 February 1907, *CW*, VII, 328.

45. 'Message to Tamil brethren', 25 February 1909, *Indian Opinion*, 6 March 1909, *CW*, IX, 199.

46. 'Letter to Transvaal Indians', 21 June 1909, *Indian Opinion*, 26 June 1909, *CW*, IX, 259-60.

47. Maureen Tayal observes (in 'Indian passive resistance in the Transvaal', 261) that Habib's 'lightening switch from conciliation to resister had secured him a nomination as delegate'. Gandhi's comment on Habib's 'switch' is generous as well as telling: 'it was a matter of regret for many Indians that Mr Hajee Habib, who had served the community over many years, had shown himself weak. Now that he is in full form again, the community feels happy'. 'Deputation', *Indian Opinion*, 19 June 1909, *CW*, IX, 257.

48. *Satyagraha in South Africa*, 209 (emphasis added).

49. *Ibid*, 210.

50. *Ibid*, 211.

51. *Ibid*, 207.

52. 'Sarvodaya[-VIII]', *Indian Opinion*, 4 July 1908, *CW*, VIII, 337-39.

53. Maureen Swan, *Gandhi*, 178 and 108.

54. *Ibid*, 114.

55. 'Speech at Calcutta meeting', 19 January 1902, *CW*, III, 217.

56. See *CW*, I, 360; and *Autobiography*, 114.

57. See Frene Ginwala, 'Class, consciousness and control: Indian South Africans 1860-1946', Ph.D. thesis, Oxford, 1974, 153-4.

58. Huttenback, *Gandhi in South Africa*, 300.

59. *Satyagraha in South Africa*, 246. It is suggested that Gandhi suddenly in 1911; that is, before the coming of Gokhale, became conscious of the £3 Tax being 'the most pressing of South African Indians' problems' (Maureen Swan, *Gandhi*, 215), but the evidence for this contention is - if not misplaced - rather tenuous.

60. 'The indenture tax', *Indian Opinion*, 7 April 1906, *CW*, V, 267-9. *CW*, X, 238.

61. *Satyagraha in South Africa*, 246.

62. 'Indentured Indians', *Indian Opinion*, 22 April 1905, *CW*, IV, 417.

63. 'Reply to welcome address at Verulam', 29 January 1906, *Indian Opinion*, 5 January 1907, *CW*, VI, 261.

64. 'An Asiatic policy', *Indian Opinion*, 19 May 1906, *CW*, V, 318. This was a reply to a series of articles in the *Rand Daily Mail* by L.E. Neame, which was later expanded and published as *The Asiatic danger in the colonies* (London, 1907).

65. 'The last satyagraha campaign: my experience', *Golden number, Indian Opinion*, 1914, *CW*, XII, 512-13.

66. 'Lord Ampthill', *Indian Opinion*, 29 June 1907, *CW*, VII, 62-3.

67. 'The Proclamation of 1858', *Indian Opinion*, 9 July 1903, *CW*, III, 358. It should be noted that this adherence to the British Empire principle was not unique to Gandhi. Without imprudence it would be fair to state that every nationalist in every British colony adhered to the same principle with the same degree of conviction. See, for example, the case of the Kimberley African elite (contemporaries of Gandhi) in B. Willan,'An African in Kimberley: Sol T. Plaatje, 1894-1898' in Shula Marks and R. Rathbone (eds.), *Industrialisation and social change in South Africa* (London, 1982), 241-42.

68. *Autobiography*, 128; and Huttenback, *Gandhi in South Africa*, 82.

69. 'Speech at mass meeting', 23 August 1908, *Indian Opinion*, 29 August and 12 September 1908, *CW*, VIII, 475.

70. Fischer, *The life of Mahatma Gandhi*, 41.

71. 'The Empire has been built up as it is on a foundation of justice and equity. It has earned a world-wide reputation for its anxiety and ability to protect the weak against the strong. It is the acts of peace and mercy, rather than those of war, that have made it what it is'. 'The anti-Asiatic convention and the British Indian meeting', *Indian Opinion*, 26 November 1904, *CW*, IV, 302.

It must also be borne in mind that at the turn of the century two Indians: Dadabhai Naoroji and Sir Mancherjee Bhownaggree, were able to win, and occupy seats in the British Parliament. See Huttenback, *Gandhi in South Africa*, VIII.

72. 'True imperialism', *Indian Opinion*, 2 July 1903, *CW*, III, 355. See also 'India and Natal', 'The Voice of India', 31 May 1902, *CW*, III, 252, where he states: 'There can be no true imperialism unless we have oneness, harmony and toleration among all classes of British subjects'.

73. 'Tribute to Queen Victoria', *The Natal Advertiser*, 2 February 1901, *CW*, III, 175.

74. See the illustration opposite 184, in *CW*, III.

75. Quoted in 'The memorial to Mr Chamberlain', 6 April 1897, *CW*, II, 282.

76. 'The Indian franchise', *CW*, I, 280.

77. 'The second reading', *Indian Opinion*, 17 May 1913, *CW*, XII, 72. Plaatje in South Africa, in 1917, referred to the 'wonderful sense of British justice'. See B. William, *Sol Plaatje: South African nationalist 1876-1932*, 213.

78. 'Letter to J.C. Gibson', 6 January 1910, *Indian Opinion*, 10 December 1910, *CW*, X, 119.

79. 'Gokhale's speech in Bombay', 14 December 1912, *Indian Opinion*, 25 January and 1 February 1913, *CW*, XI, 586.

80. Letter to Gandhi, 11 September 1909, *CW*, IX, 588.

81. Gandhi, in referring to Schreiner's offer, noted that though the Cape Politician was honest in his opinions, he nevertheless was unable to realise - because he was convinced that the Indians were an inferior people - that it was insulting to allow six Indians to enter as *a matter of favour*. 'Deputation notes[-VIII]', *Indian Opinion*, 18 September 1909, *CW*, IX, 365.

82. Maureen Swan, *Gandhi*, 109.

83. P. Duncan, 'The Asiatic question in the Transvaal', *The State*, vol. 2, February 1909, 171-2 (emphasis added).

84. Speech at farewell banquet, 14 July 1914, *CW*, XII; see also 'Duncan's, views', *Indian Opinion*, 13 February 1909, *CW*, IX, 189-90.

85. 'The second reading', *CW*, XII, 72.

86. See Frene Ginwala, 'Class, consciousness and control', 146.

87. 'Deputation notes[-X]', *Indian Opinion*, 2 October 1909, *CW*, IX, 385.

88. Speech at Y.M.C.A., 18 May 1908, *Indian Opinion*, 6 June 1908, *CW*, VIII, 246.

89. The details of the period and the events mentioned are ably provided by Pyarelal, *Mahatma Gandhi*, I, (Ahmedabad, 1965), 111-170; and by A.R. Desai, *Social background of Indian nationalism* (Bombay, 1948, reprint ed. 1966), 307-380.

90. See *CW*, X, 6-68. His other articles (before and after *Hind Swaraj*) demonstrating his concern for what was happening in India are too frequent and too many to enumerate here but the following are representative: 'Indian National Congress and Russian Zemstovs a comparison', *Indian Opinion*, 14 January 1905, *CW*, IV, 336-38; 'The heroic song of Bengal', *Indian Opinion*, 2 December 1905, *CW*, V, 156; 'India for Indians', *Indian Opinion*, 18 August 1906, *CW*, V, 396-7; 'Unrest in India', *Indian Opinion*, 1 June 1907, *CW*, VII, 6-7; 'Turmoil in India', *Indian Opinion*, 9 May 1908; *CW*, VIII, 223-4; 'Preface to *Indian Home Rule*', *Indian Opinion*, 2 April 1910, *CW*, X, 382; and 'Hind Swaraj', *Indian Opinion*, 29 April 1914, *CW*, XII, 411-12.

91. Speech at Johannesburg mass meeting, 5 December 1909, *Indian Opinion*, 11 December 1909, *CW*, X, 91. See also B.S. Cohn, 'Representing authority in Victorian India', in E. Hobsbawm and T. Ranger (eds.), *The invention of tradition* (London, 1983), 209; where he notes: 'The British idiom was effective in that it set the terms of discourse of the nationalist movement in its beginning phases. In effect, the early nationalists were claiming that they were more loyal to the true goals of the Indian Empire than were their English rulers'.

92. Letter to the Indian press, 12 November 1909, *CW*, IX, 538-9. Perhaps the clearest expression of this idea by Gandhi is to be found in the speech he made in London on 12 November 1909. 'He must pause and ask himself what was the meaning of the British Constitution. Did it not confer equality upon the different members of the Empire comprised in the British Constitution? He could understand that. He could consent to remain a subject of an Empire based upon this principle, but, in the light of his experience, he must declare it was utterly impossible for him to give his allegiance to an Empire in which he was not to be treated, even in theory, as an equal of any other member of that Empire. If he was to be treated as an inferior, then he would never aspire to a position of equality. He might be content to be a member of an Empire in which he participated to the extent even of one per cent share, but if he was to be merely a slave, then the Empire had absolutely no meaning for him. The term *British subject* then became meaningless to him, and it was this effect of that legislation that he would like to impress upon the meeting, and which they had been feeling for the last three years. This legislation of the Colony of the Transvaal was cutting at the root of the British Empire, and in resisting the doctrine implied by such legislation, they had been rendering a service not only to British India but to the British Empire'. 'Speech at farewell meeting',

Indian Opinion, 11 December 1909, *CW*, IX, 542.

But Gokhale had also pronounced similarly in 1894 when he said, in relation to a piece of discriminatory legislation passed by the British in India: 'The pledges of equal treatment which England had given supplied us with a high and worthy ideal for our nation, and if these pledges are repudiated, one of the strongest claims of British rule to our attachment will disappear'. Quoted by Pyarelal, *Mahatma Gandhi*, I, 115.

93. Speech at farewell banquet, 14 July 1914, *CW*, XII, 476.
94. 'My second experience in gaol[-V]', *Indian Opinion*, 30 January 1909, *CW*, IX, 179.
95. 'Triumph of truth', *Indian Opinion*, 8 February 1908, *CW*, VIII, 61.

BIBLIOGRAPHY

Archives and Manuscript Collections

Government Archvies, Cape Town:
Andrews, C, 'Reminiscences of the Kafir War of 1834-1835', Acc. 983.

Smith, H., Letter to Governor D'Urban, 12 March 1836, Acc. 519, vol. 4, 262-5.

Anonymous (J. Bisset), 'The full true and particular account of the death of Hintza, ZP 1/1/88 (microfilm of the Colonial Office, London), CO/48/165.

Smith, H., Letter to Governor D'Urban, 12 March 1836, Acc. 519, vol. 4, 262-5.

Sanlam Library, University of South Africa:
Shepstone, T., Copy of unpublished diary, 26 March-13 June 1835.

South African Library, Cape Town:
'Field Diary of Caeser Andrews'.

Transvaal Archives Depot, Pretoria:
The Soutter Collection ref. (Copies of the Dingaan-Retief treaty written by Bantjes in English and in Dutch): A 3, packet No. 4 (2), 168; and A 3, packet No. 4 (2 A), 170.

Letter of L. Soutter to Goldman, 13 April 1926, 44 T.A. 136/23.

Declaration of H.J. van Staden and others, 14 May 1854 (actually, 1853). S.S.6, R633/54.

Report of M.W. Pretorius, 6 December 1854, S.S.7, 733/54.

H.J. Potgieter to P.J. Potgieter, 8 September 1853, S.S.5, 562e/53.

M.W. Pretorius to S. Schoeman, 12 November 1854, S.S.7, R719/54.

Rhodes House Library, Oxford:
Macmillan-Merriman correspondence.

Yew Tree Cottage, Long Wittenham, Abingdon, England:
Macmillan Papers.

Unpublished Theses and Dissertations

De Waal, J.J., 'Die verhouding tussen die Blankes, en die Hoofmanne Mokopane en Mankopane in die omgewing van Potgietersrus (1836-1869)', M.A. dissertation, University of South Africa, 1978.

Donaldson, Margaret, 'The Council of Advice at the Cape of Good Hope, 1825-1834', Ph. D. dissertation, Rhodes University, 1974.

Ginwala, Frene, 'Class, consciousness and control: Indian South Africans 1860-1946', Ph.D. thesis, University of Oxford, 1974.

Kapp, P.H., 'Dr John Philip se opvattinge en sy werksaamhede in Suid-Afrika, D. Phil. thesis, University of Stellenbosch, 1974.

Pretorius, J.G., 'The British humanitarians and the Cape Eastern frontier, 1834-1836', Ph.D. thesis, University of the Witwatersrand, 1971.

Newspapers

Gerdener, T., 'Die grootte wat mense geëet het', *Die Brandwag*, 18 July 1952.

Potgieter, H., 'Moord in Makapansvalle', *Die Brandwag*, 3 September 1954.

'Retief-Dingane Treaty', *The Cape Times*, 12 July 1923.

Schoeman, S.J., letter to *The Friend of the Free State and the Bloemfontein Gazette*, 28 April 1855.

Edgar, 'Reminiscences of the Kafir War 1834-1835', *The Friend of the Free State and Bloemfontein Gazette*, 27 November 1873, 22 January, 26 February, 2, 23 and 30 April 1874.

Nel, D., 'Die drama van die Makapansgrot (Soos deur die Naturelle vertel), *Die Huisgenoot*, 24 March 1933.

Acutt, Nancy C., 'Makapaan se gruweldade', *Die Huisgenoot*, 6 May 1938.

Die Huisgenoot (centenary edition), December 1938.

Uys, C.J., 'Die moord op Hintsa', *Die Huisgenoot* 19 and 25 February, and 12 and 19 March 1943.

De Villiers, D.J.J., *Die Jongspan*, 1 July 1938.

Gibson, J.Y., 'Dingaan and the Retief Treaty: Was it Genuine', *Natal Witness*, 2 August 1923.

'Into the cave of death', *The New Nation*, 1 October 1987.

(L. Weinthal's statement on the treaty), *The Pretoria News*, 29 August 1923.

'Treaty of tragedy — Dingaan and Retief — Writer found', *Rand Daily Mail*, 6 February 1926.

Preller, G.S., 'Controversy of the treaty', *Rand Daily Mail*, 11 February 1926.

'More light on the Retief-Dingaan treaty', *The Star*, 17 February 1926.

'Wie het die Traktaat geskryf?', *Ons Vaderland*, 9 February 1926.

'Wat 'n dogter van Jan Bantjes vertel', *Ons Vaderland*, 16 February 1926.

Pinnaar, C., *De Volkstem*, 6 January 1890.

'Cory bewerings ontsenuw', *Die Volkstem*, 12 July 1923.

Books, Pamphlets and Journal Articles

Agar-Hamilton, J.A.I., *The Native policy of the Voortrekkers* (Cape Town, 1928).

Auerbach, F.E., *The power of prejudice in South African education* (Cape Town, 1965).

Backhouse, J., *A narrative of a visit to the Mauritius and South Africa (London, 1844)*.

Baines, T., *The gold regions of South East Africa* (London, 1877).

Baldwin, J., *The fire next time* (Harmondsworth, 1964).

Barberton, I.M. (ed.), *Comdt. Holden Bowker* (Cape Town, 1970).

Barzun, J. and Graff, H.F., *The modern researcher* (New York, 3rd ed. 1977).

Beaglehole, J.C., 'The case of the needless death', in *The historian as detective* (New York, 1968).

Becker, P., *Rule of fear: The life and times of Dingane, King of the Zulu* (Harmondsworth, 1979).

Bell, F.W., *The South African problem: A suggested solution* (n.p., 1909).

Beyers, C.J. (ed.), *Dictionary of South African Biography*, vol. IV (Cape Town, 1987).

Bhana, S. and Pachai, B. (eds.), *A documentary history of Indian South Africans* (Cape Town, 1984).

Bird, J., *The annals of Natal 1495-1843*, 2 vols. (Pietermaritzburg, 1888, repr. Cape Town, 1965).

Bisset, Lieut-General Sir John, *Sport and war, or recollections of fighting and hunting in South Africa from the years 1834 to 1867* (London, 1875).

Bolton, G., *The tragedy of Gandhi*, (London, 1934).

Booth, A.R. (ed.), *Journal of the Rev. George Champion* (Cape Town, 1967).

Bosman, H.C., *Mafeking Road* (South Africa, 1947).

Bowker, J.M., *Speeches, letters and selections* (Grahamstown, 1864, repr. Cape Town, 1962).

Boxer, C.R., *The Dutch seaborne empire* 1600-1800 (London, 1965, 4th imp. 1977).

Breytenbach, J.H. (ed.), *Notule van die Volksraad van die Suid-Afrikaanse Republiek, 1844-1868*, numbers 1-6 (Cape Town, 1949-56).

Brookes, E.H., *The political future of South Africa* (Pretoria, 1927).

Brookes, E.H. and Webb, C. de B., *A history of Natal* (Pietermaritzburg, 1965).

Brown, D., *Bury my heart at Wounded Knee: An Indian history of the American West* (London, 1972).

Bryant, A.T., *The Zulu people* (Pietermaritzburg, 1949).

Butler, J., Elphick, R. and Welsh, D. (eds.), *Democratic liberalism in South Africa* (Connecticut and Cape Town, 1987).

Caesar, *The Conquest of Gaul*, trans. by S.A. Handford, revised by Jane F. Gardner (Harmondsworth, 1951 and 1982).

Cappon, J., *Britain's title in South Africa* (London, 1901).

Cell, J.W., *The highest stage of white supremacy: The origins of segregation in South Africa and the American South* (Cambridge, 1982).

Chase, J.C., *The Cape of Good Hope and the Eastern Province of Algoa Bay* (London, 1843, repr. Cape Town, 1967).

Chase, J.C., *The Natal papers 1498-1843* (Graham's Town, 1843, repr. Cape Town, 1968).

Clinton, D.K., *The South African melting pot: A vindication of missionary policy, 1799-1836* (London, 1937).

Collingwood, R.G., *An autobiography* (Oxford, 1939).

Cloete, H., *Five lectures on the emigration of the Dutch Farmers from the Colony of the Cape of Good Hope, and their settlement in the districts of Natal, until the formal submission to her majesty's authority in the year 1843* (Cape Town, 1856).

Cloete, H., *History of the Great Boer Trek and the origin of the South African Republics* (London, 1899).

Cloete, S., *The mask* (London, 1958, paperback ed. 1960).

Cohn, B.S., 'Representing authority in Victorian India', in E. Hobsbawm and T. Ranger (eds.), *The invention of tradition* (London, 1983).

Cornevin, Marianne, *L'apartheid: Pouvoir et falsification historique* (Paris, 1979).

Cory, G.E., *The rise of South Africa* (London, 1910-1930, repr. Cape Town, 1965), 5 vols.

Cory, G.E. (ed.), *The diary of the Rev. Francis Owen* (Cape Town, 1926).

(Court of Inquiry) *Minutes of the proceedings of the Court of Inquiry . . . on the fate of the Caffer chief Hintza* (Cape Town, 1837).

Dart, R., *Adventures with the missing link* (London, 1959).

Davenport, T.R.H., *South Africa: A modern history* (London, 1977).

Dawson, W.H., *South Africa* (London, 1925).

Dehérain, H., *L'Expansion des Boers au XIX sièle* (Paris, 1905).

Dehérain, H., *Le Cap de Bonne-Espérance au XVII sièle* (Paris, 1909).

De Kock, W.J. (ed.), *Dictionary of South African biography*, vol. I (Cape Town, 1968).

De Kock, W.J. and Krüger, D.W. (eds.), *Dictionary of South African biography*, vol. II (Cape Town, 1972).

Delegorgue, A., *Voyage dans l'Afrique centrale, notamment dans le territoire de Natal, dans celui des Cafres Amazoulous et Makatisses, et jusqu' au tropique du Capricorne, exécuté durant les années 1838, 1839, 1840, 1841, 1842, 1843, et 1844*, 2 vols. (Paris, 1847).

Desai, A.R., *Social background of Indian nationalism* (Bombay, 1948, reprint ed 1966).

De Webb, C. and Wright, J.B. (eds.), *The James Stuart archive*, vol. 1 (Pietermaritzburg, 1976).

De Webb, C. and Wright, J.B. (eds.), *A Zulu speaks: A statement made by Cetshwayo ka Mpande on the history and customs of his people* (Durban, 1978).

Drayson, Major-Gen. A.W., *The adventures of Hans Sterk: The South African hunter and pioneer* (London, 1869).

Duly, L.C., 'A revisit with the Cape's Hottentot Ordinance of 1828' in Kooy, M. (ed.), *Studies in economics and economic history* (London, 1972).

Duncan, Pl, 'The Asiatic question in the Transvaal', *The State*, vol. 2, February 1909.

Du Plessis, A.J., 'Die Republiek Natalia', *Archives year book of South African history*, II, 1942.

Du Plessis, J., 'Het raadsel van het Retief traktaat', *Het Zoeklicht*, August 1923.

Dvorin, E.P., *Racial separation in South Africa* (Chicago, 1952).

Elphick, R., *Kraal and castle: Khoikhoi and the founding of White South Africa* (New Haven, 1977).

Elphick, R. and Giliomee, H., (eds.), *The shaping of South African society, 1652-1820) (Cape Town, 1979)*.

Encyclopaedia. The standard encyclopaedia of South Africa, vol. VII, 12 vols. (Cape Town, 1970-1976).

Eybers, G.W. (ed.), *Select constitutional documents illustrating South African history, 1795-1910* (London, 1918).

Fischer, L., *The life of Gandhi* (New York, 1950).

Forman, L., *Black and white in S.A. history* (n.p., n.d.).

Gailey, H.A., 'John Philip's role in Hottentot emancipation', *Journal of African history*, III, 3(1962).

Gandhi, M.K., *Collected works of Mahatma Gandhi*, I-XII (New Delhi, 1958-1964).

Gandhi, M.K., *An autobiography or my experiments with truth*, (Ahmedabad 1927, reprint ed. 1972).

Gandhi, M.K., *Satyagraha in South Africa*, (Ahmedabad, 1928, reprint ed. 1972).

Gardner, B., *Mafeking: A Victorian legend* (London, 1966, 1968).

Gardiner, A.F., *Narrative of a journey to the Zoolu country in South Africa* (London, 1836, repr. Cape Town, 1966).

Gibson, J.Y., *The story of the Zulus* (London, 1911).

Gibson, J.Y., *The evolution of South African Native policy* (Pietermaritzburg, 1919).

Gie, S.F.N., *Annals of the University of Stellenbosch*, IIB1, 5 May 1924.

Gilfillan, M. (ed.), *The story of one branch of the Gilfillan family in South Africa* (Johannesburg, 1970).

Godée-Molsbergen, E.C., *De stichter van Hollands Zuid-Afrika: Jan van Ribeeck, 1618-1677* (Amsterdam, 1912).

Godée-Molsbergen, E.C., *Jan van Riebeeck en zijn tijd* (Amsterdam, 1937).

Godée-Molsbergen, E.C., *Jan van Riebeeck en sy tyd* (Pretoria, 1968).

Godlonton, R., *A narrative of the irruption of the Kafir hordes into the Eastern Pro-*

vince of the Cape of Good Hope 1834-35 (Graham's Town, 1836, repr. Cape Town, 1965).

Goodwin, A.J.H., 'Jan van Riebeeck and the Hottentots, 1652-1662', *South African Archaeological Bulletin*, VII(25), March 1952.

Great Britain Parliamentary papers, 538 of 1836, Report of the Select Committee on Aborigines (British Settlements).

Great Britain Parliamentary papers, 279 of 1836, Cape of Good Hope: Caffre War and the death of Hintza.

Haggard, H. Rider, *Marie* (London, 1912, repr. 1925).

Hancock, W.K. and Van der Poel, Jean (eds.), *Selections from the Smuts Papers*, vol. I, (Cambridge, 1966).

Hancock, W.K., *Smuts: The fields of force 1919-1950* (Cambridge, 1968).

Harrington, A.L., *Sir Harry Smith bungling hero* (Cape Town, 1980).

Hattersley, A.F., *South Africa 1652-1933* (London, 1933).

Hill, C., 'Forum', *History Today*, March 1983.

Hoernlé, R.F.A., *South African Native policy and the liberal spirit* (Cape Town, 1939).

Holden, W.C., *History of the Colony of Natal* (London, 1855, repr. Cape Town, 1963).

Holden, W., *The past and future of the Kaffir Races* (London, 1866).

Hulley, R.B., *Zululand under Dingaan: Account of the Rev. Mr. Owen's visit to Zululand in the year 1837, as related by Mr. R.B. Hulley* (n.p., [1880]).

Huttenback, R.A., *Gandhi in South Africa: British imperialism and the Indian question*, (Ithaca and London, 1971).

Iwan-Muller, E.B., *Lord Milner in South Africa* (London, 1902).

Jabavu, D.D.T., *The Black problem* (Lovedale, 1920).

Joos, L.C.D., *Histoire de L'Afrique du Sud* (Paris, 1965).

Kenney, R.U., *Piet Retief, the dubious hero* (Cape Town, 1976).

Kirby, P.R., (ed.), *Sir Andrew Smith 1795-1850* (Cape Town, 1965).

Kirk, T., 'Progress and decline in the Kat River Settlement, 1829-1854', *Journal of African history*, 14, 3 (1973).

Kotzé, D.J. (ed.), *Letters of the American missionaries 1835-1838* (Cape Town, 1950).

Krüger, D.W. and Beyers, C.J. (eds.), *Dictionary of South African biography*, vol. III (Cape Town, 1977).

Kruger, P., *The memoirs of Paul Kruger*, 2 vols. (London, 1902).

Kruuse, J., *Madness at Oradour* (London, 1969).

Lacey, Marion, *Working for boroko: The origins of a coercive labour system in South Africa* (Johannesburg, 1981).

Lamar, H. and Thompson, L. (eds.), *The frontier in history* (New Haven, 1981).

Legassick, M., 'British hegemony and the origins of segregation in South Africa, 1901-1914', Institute of Commonwealth Studies (February, 1974, mimeographed).

Leipoldt, C.L., *Jan van Riebeeck: A biographical study* (London, 1936).

Lehmann, J.H., *Remember you are an Englishman: A biography of Sir Harry Smith* (London, 1977).

Leibbrandt, H.C.V., Précis of the archives of the Cape of Good Hope: Letters and documents received, 1649-1662, 2 vols. (Cape Town, 1898-9).

Leibbrandt, H.C.V., *Précis of the archives of the Cape of Good Hope: Letters despatched from the Cape, 1652-1662*, 2 vols. (Cape Town, 1900).

Liebenberg, B.J., *Andries Pretorius in Natal* (Pretoria, 1977).

Lewin, J., *Politics and law in South Africa* (London, 1963).

Lewsen, Phyllis (ed.), *Voices of protest: From segregation to apartheid, 1938-1948 (Johannesburg, 1988)*.

Leyds, W.J., *De eerste annexatie van de Transvaal* (Amsterdam, 1906).

Long, Una (ed.), *The chronicle of Jeremiah Goldswain: Albany settler of 1820, 2 vols. (Cape Town, 1946 and 1949)*.

Lucas, C.P., *The history of South Africa to the Jameson Raid* (Oxford, 1899).

MacCrone, I.D., *Race attitudes in South Africa* (London, 1937).

Mackeurtan, G., *The cradle days of Natal 1497-1847* (London, 1930).

Mackness, R., *Oradour: Massacre and aftermath* (London, 1988).

Macmillan, W.M., *Bantu, Boer, and Briton* (London, 1929), revised edition (Oxford, 1963).

Macmillan, W.M., *The Cape colour question* (London 1927).

Macmillan, W.M., *My South African years* (Cape Town, 1975).

Majeke, N. (Dora Taylor), *The role of the missionaries in conquest* (Johannesburg, 1952).

Marais, J.S., 'The imposition and nature of European control', in I. Schapera (ed.), *The Bantu-speaking tribes of South Africa* (London, 1937).

Marais, J.S., *The Cape Coloured people 1652-1937* (London, 1939).

Marks, Shula, 'Khoisan resistance to the Dutch in the seventeenth and eighteenth centuries', *Journal of African history*, IV, 2(1978).

Marquard, L., *The story of South Africa* (London, 1966).

Michener, J.A., *The Covenant* (London, 1980, paperback ed., 1983).

Midlane, M., 'Aspects of the South African Liberal tradition' in C.R. Hill and P. Warwick (eds.), *South African research in progress* (New York, 1974).

Millin, Sarah Gertrude, *General Smuts*, 2 vols. (London, 1936).

Molema, S.M., *Bantu past and present* (Edinburgh, 1920, repr. Cape Town, 1963).

Moodie, D., *The history of the battles and adventures of the British, the Boers, and the Zulus, in Southern Africa*, 2 vols. (Cape Town, 1879).

Moore, G.C. (ed.), *Autobiography of Sir Harry Smith, 2 vols. (London, 1903)*.

Morris, D.R., *The washing of the spears* (London, 1966).

Moyer, R.A., 'The Mfengu, self-defence and the Cape frontier wars', in C. Saunders and R. Derricourt (eds.), *Beyond the Cape frontier* (London, 1974).

Muller, C.F.J. (ed.), Five Hundred Years: A History of South Africa (2nd rev. ed., Pretoria, 1975).
Muller, B.K., *Wits: The early years* (Johannesburg, 1982).

Neame, L.E., *The history of apartheid* (London, 1962).

Okaye, F.N.C., 'Dingane: A reappraisal', *Journal of African history*, X, 2 (1969).

Omer-Cooper, J.D., *The Zulu aftermath* (London, 1960).

Orpen, J.M., *Reminiscences of life in South Africa* (Cape Town, 1964).

Pachai, B., 'The history of the *Indian Opinion*, 1903-1914', *The archives year book of South African history* (Cape Town, 1961).

Palmer, Mabel, *The history of the Indians in Natal* (Cape Town, 1957).

Patterson, Sheila, *Colour and culture in South Africa: A study of the Cape Coloured people within the social structure of the Union of South Africa* (London, 1953).

Patterson, Sheila, *The last trek* (London, 1957).

Peires, J., *The House of Phalo* (Johannesburg, 1981).

Philip, J., *Researches in South Africa*, 2 vols. (London, 1828, repr. New York, 1969).

Phillips, L., *Transvaal problems: Some notes on current policies (London, 1905)*.

Pillay, B., *British Indians in the Transvaal* (London, 1976).

Ploeger, J. and Smith, Anna H., *Pictorial atlas of the history of the Union of South Africa* (Pretoria, 1949).

Preller, G.S., *Piet Retief* (Cape Town, 1920).

Preller, G.S., *Sketse en opstelle* (Pretoria, 1928).

Preller, G.S., (ed.), *Voortrekkersmense*, 6 vols. (Cape Town, 1918-1938).

Preller, G.S. (ed.), *Hoe ons aan Dingaansdag kom: Jan Bantjes se dagverhaal van die win-kommando* (Bloemfontein, 1928).

Preller, G.S., 'Baanbrekers' in *Oorlogsoormag en ander sketse en verhale (Cape Town, 1923)*.

Pringle, T., *Narrative of a residence in South Africa* (Cape Town, 1966).

Ponsonby, A., *Falsehood in war-time* (London, 1928).

Pyarelal, *Mahatma Gandhi*, I, (Ahmedabad, 1965).

Ransford, O., *The Great Trek* (Newton Abbot, 1973).

Read, J. (Junior), *The Kat River Settlement in 1851* (Cape Town, 1852).

Rich, P.B., 'The agrarian counter-revolution in the Transvaal and the origin of segregation: 1902-1913', in P.L. Bonner (ed.), *Working papers in Southern African studies*, African Studies Institute, University of Witwatersrand, 1977.

Robertson, H.M., 'Jan van Riebeeck and his settlement', *South African Journal of economics*, 20(4), December 1952.

Robinson, Sir John, *A life time in South Africa* (London, 1900).

Rosenthal, E., *Encyclopaedia of Southern Africa* (London, 1961).

Ross, A., *John Philip (1775-1851): Missionaries, race and politics in South Africa* (Aberdeen, 1986).

Sales, Jane, *Missions stations and the Coloured communities of the Eastern Cape 1800-1852* (Cape Town, 1975).

Saunders, C., *The making of the South African past* (Cape Town, 1988).

Schapera, I. (ed.), *Livingstone's missionary correspondence, 1841-1856* (London, 1961).

Schapera, I. (ed.), *David Livingstone South African papers 1849-1853* (Cape Town, 1974).

Schoon, H.F. (ed.), *The diary of Erasmus Smit* (Cape Town, 1972).

Schutte, G.E.F., 'Dr John Philip's observation regarding the Hottentots of South Africa', *Archives year book of South African history*, part 1, 1940.

Shooter, J., *The Kaffirs of Natal and the Zulu country* (London, 1857).

Smith, E.W., *The life and times of Daniel Lindley* (New York, 1952).

Smuts, J.C., 'Problems in South Africa', *Journal of the African Society*, XVI, No. LXIV, July 1917.

(Smuts, J.C.), 'General Smut's speech', *Journal of the African society*, XVI, No. LXIV, July 1917.

Spilhaus, Margaret, W., *South Africa in the making, 1652-1806* (Cape Town, 1966).

Stander, H., 'Die verhouding tussen die Boere en die Zoeloe tot die dood van Mpande in 1872', *Archives Year Book for South African history*, 27, II, 1964.

Stow, G.W. (ed. by G.M. Theal), *The Native races of South Africa* (London, 1905).

Stuart, J. and Malcolm, D.M. (eds.), *The diary of Henry Francis Fynn* (Pietermaritzburg, 1949).

Swan, Maureen, *Gandhi: The South African experience* (Johannesburg, 1985).

Swanson, M.W., 'The Durban system: Roots of urban apartheid in Colonial Natal', *African Studies*, 35, 3-4, 1976.

Tatz, C., *Shadow and substance in South Africa: A study in land and franchise policies affecting Africans 1910-1960* (Pietermaritzburg, 1962).

Tayal, Maureen, 'Indian passive resistance in the Transvaal 1906-08', in B. Bozzoli (ed.), *Town and countryside in the Transvaal* (Johannesburg, 1983).

Taylor, A.J.P., *Essays in English history* (Harmondsworth, 1976).

Theal, G.M., *South Africa as it is* (King Williams Town, 1871).

Theal, G.M., *Compendium of the history and geography of South Africa* (Lovedale, 3rd rev. ed. 1878).

Theal, G.M. (ed.), *Documents relating to the Kaffir War of 1835* (London, 1912).

Theal, G.M., *History of South Africa*, 11 vols. (London, 1888-1919, repr. Cape Town, 1973).

Thom, H.B. (ed.), *The journal of Jan van Riebeeck*, 3 vols. (Cape Town and Amsterdam, 1952).

Thompson, L.M., *The Cape Coloured franchise* (Johannesburg, 1949).

Thompson, L., *Politics in the Republic of South Africa* (Boston, 1966).

Thompson, L., *The political mythology of apartheid* (New Haven and London, 1985).

Tinker, H., *A new system of slavery* (London, 1974).

Trapido, S., 'Natal's non-racial franchise, 1856', *African Studies*, 22, 1963.

Van de Berghe, P., *South Africa: A study in conflict* (Berkeley, 1967).

Van der Horst, Sheila, T., *Native labour in South Africa* (London, 1942).

Van der Walt, A.J.H. and others (eds.), *Geskiedenis van Suid-Africa*, 2 vols. (Cape Town, 1951).

Varley, D.H. and Matthew, H.M. (eds.), *The Cape journals of Archdeacon N.J. Merriman, 1848-1855* (Cape Town, 1957).

Voigt, J.C., *Fifty years of the history of the Republic in South Africa, 1795-1845*, 2 vols. (London, 1899, repr. Cape Town, 1969).

The Voortrekker Museum, Pretoria: Official guide (Pretoria, 1955).

Walker, E.A., *A history of South Africa* (London, 1928).

Walker, E.A., 'A Zulu account of the Retief massacre', *The Critic*, January 1935.

Walker, E.A., *The Great Trek* (London, 1938).

Walker, E.A. (ed.), *Cambridge history of the British Empire*, vol. VIII, South Africa (2nd ed. Cambridge, 1963).

Walker, E., *History of Southern Africa* (London, 1957, 1965 imp.).

Wallis, J.P.R. (ed.), *The Matabele journals of Robert Moffat, 1829-1860* (London, 1945).

Walton, Sir Edgar, *The inner history of the National Convention of South Africa* (London, 1912, repr. Westport, 1970).

Watermeyer, E.B., *Three lectures on the Cape of Good Hope under the government of the Dutch East India Company* (Cape Town, 1857).

Watermeyer, E.B., *Selections from the writings of the late E.B. Watermeyer with a brief sketch of his life* (Cape Town, 1877).

Willan, B., *Sol Plaatje South African Nationalist 1876-1932* (London, 1984).

Wilmot, A and Chase, J.C., *History of the Colony of the Cape of Good Hope* (Cape Town, 1869).

Wilmot, A., *The life and times of Sir Richard Southey* (Cape Town, 1904).

Wilson, Monica and Thompson, L. (eds.), *The Oxford history of South Africa*, 2 vols. (Oxford, 1969 and 1971).

Wood, W.S., 'A note on the Retief-Dingaan Treaty', *South African Quarterly*, June-August 1923.

INDEX

Abdulla, Dada, 149
Abalonga, 127
Act 2 of 1907, 158
Afrikanerdom, 92
Agar-Hamilton, J.A.I., 131
Alexander, J., 45, 71
Allison, James, 117, 118, 126
Ambulance Corps, 148
Ampthill, Lord, 151, 152
Andrews, Caesar, 74, 80, 83, 84
Anglo-Boer War, 57, 144, 148
Apartheid, 53
Apprenticeship law (of 1812), 37
Asiatic Act, 155
Asiatic question, 147
Ayliff, John, 70

Backhouse, James, 122
Balasundaram, 153
Baldwin, James, 12
Balfour, Lieutenant, 80, 82, 83, 84
Bantjes, J.G., 98, 99, 102, 103, 106, 107, 109, 111
Bambatta, 144
Bande Mataram - the Indian *Marseillaise*, 160
Bantu and land, 123
Bashee River, 79
Batavia, 31, 33, 35
Batlokoa Chief, 115, 117, 118
Beaufort District, 41
Bechuana, 45
Bell, F.W., 53
Bengal in revolt, 160
Bengalis, 146
Bethelsdorp, 40, 45, 49
Bezuidenhout, D.P., 102, 111, 117
Bhuru (Boku), 74, 77
Biddulph, T.J., 50
Boeseken, Dr Anna, 20-22, 28, 29
Blommaert, W., 93, 94-96, 105, 108
Blood (Ncome) River, battle of, 93, 99
Boshoff, J., 99, 111
Botha, General Louis, 151, 152
Botha, Jonas, 42
Bowker, J.M., 43, 62
Bowker, H.T., 49, 50
Bowker, T.H., quoted, 86

Boyce, W.B., 42
Britain, 157
The British Empire: and Gandhi, 144, 148, 156-162
British Indian Association, 149
British Indians, 144, 145
Brookes, E.H., 59, 60
Brownlee, Charles, 124, 125
Burgers, J.J., 104, 108
Buxton, T.F., 61, 87

Cachalia, Ahmed Mohammed, 150
Campbell, Dr Ambrose, 14, 71, 72
The Cape colour question, 55
The Cape of Good Hope Government Gazette, 39
Cape Mounted Rifles, 84
Cape Town, 19, 20, 56
Cartwright, A., 157
Celliers, (Sarel) Charl, 98, 99, 102
Champion, George, 96, 120
Chariguriqua, 33, 36
Chase, J.C., 49
Chorachouqua, 33
Christian, 129
Christie, George, 50, 51
Ciskei, 70
Class, 143, 146, 147, 148, 151
Clinton, D.K., 55
Cloete, H., 89, 94, 102, 103
Cole, Sir Galbraith Lowry, 49
Colenso, 121, 152
Colonial-born, 146, 147, 153, 157
Commissioners, see Cunaeus, and Van Goens
Coolie, 144
Cory, G.E. (1862-1935), 11, 15, 71, 89, 91-94, 97, 98, 106-109, 111-113
Councillors, 117, 125
Cowie, A., 110
Crazy Horse, 13
Cunaeus, Joan, 33
Custer, General, 13
Curtis, Lionel, 59

Daniels, Robert, 83
Dawson, W.H., 68
Delf Chamber (Directors of), 24
Deherain, H., 89, 94, 110
De Kiewiet, W., 9

Delegorgue, L.A., 88, 89, 102, 103, 107
Dingane (Dingaan, Dingarn), 1, 8, 14-16, 88, 90, 91, 96, 97, 99, 110, 114-121, 124-128
Doke, J.J., 157
Draft Asiatic Law Amendment Ordinance, 155
Drayson, Capt. A.W., 114
Driver, Edward, 77, 83
Duly, L.C., 12
Duncan, Patrick, 159
Du Plessis, J., 93, 102
Du Preez, P.D., 97
Durban, 144, 157
D'Urban, Sir Benjamin, 15, 70, 72, 75, 77, 86, 87
Durban Women's Patriotic League, 149
Dyzel's Kraal, 42

Eight Frontier War, 48, 51
Elliot, William, 49
Elphick, R., 21, 22
Encyclpaedia of Southern Africa, 17
Engelbrecht, J.J., 136
England, 151, 155,, 157, 158
Englishmen, 160
Empire Theatre, 149, 151
Europe, 56

Fieldcornet, 133, 160
Firearms, 73, 81
First World War, 160
Ford, John, 9
Ford, W.A., 84
Fordsburg, 149
Fothane, 134
Franchise, 36, 57-60, 144
Fourie, Cobus, 44
Fynn, H.F., 110

Gandhi, Mohandas Karamchand (1869-1948), 17, 18, 143-150, 152-162
Gardiner, A.F., 96, 97, 110, 126
Gcaleka (ama), 70, 74-76, 79
Gcalekaland, 70, 74
Geyl, Pieter, 9
Gibson, J.Y., 96, 117,
Gilfillan, W.F.A., 76, 85
Glenelg, Lord, 72, 85
Godee-Molsbergen, 13, 21, 26

Godlonton, R., 49, 71
Gokhale, G.K., 154, 155, 158, 160
Goodwin, A.J.H., 21, 26
Gorachouqua, 22, 34, 36
Goringhaicona, 22, 30, 31-34, 36
Goringhaiqua, 22, 25-27, 29-31, 33-36
Gqunukhwebe, 70
Graham's Town Journal, 70
Green, B, 110
Greijling, A.C., 90, 95
Griqua, 13, 63
Grocott's Mail, 112
Grondwet (of 1858), 56
Gujarat, 146
Gujarati, 146, 149, 152
Guns, 115, 118, 119, 122, 130, 132, 137, 139, 141

Habib, Hajee (Sheth Haji Habib), 149, 151, 152
Haggard, H, Rider, 117
Halstead, Thomas, 106, 124, 125
Hamidia Islamic Society, 149
Hancock, W.K., 53
Harlow, V.T., 19
Harrington, A.L., 14
Hattersley, A.F., 55
Herrman, Dr Louis, 15
Herry (Autshumao), 28-30, 32-35
Hertzog, J.B.M., 53, 54, 57, 58, 66, 68
Hill, C.H., 67
Hindi, 149
Hind Swaraj, 161
Hindus, 146
Hinduism, 160
Hintsa, 9, 14, 15, 70, 71-87
History of South Africa, 73
History of Southern Africa, 73
Hoernle, R.F.A., 55
Holden, W., 89
Hoole, Abel, 83
Die Huisgenoot, 73
Hulley, R.B., 101, 116
Huttenback, R.A., 143

Immigration Restriction Act of 1907, 143, 156
Indentured labourers, 146, 147, 155
India, 23, 27, 143, 146, 157, 158, 160, 162
The Indian Franchise: An appeal to every

Briton in South Africa, 158
Indian independence, 161
Indian Press Act, 161
Indian National Congress (of India), 160
Indian Opinion, 154
Indian Sepoy Revolt (Indian Mutiny), 156
Inliwanio: treaty witness, 90, 95
Innes, James Rose, 49, 59
International law, and Retief's entry into
    Zulu territory, 16
Isuquabana (Sigwebana), 120

Jabavu, D.D.T., 9
Jackson, A.O., 131
Jagger, J.W., 57
Johannesburg, medical health officer of,
    143
Joos, L.C.D., 89
Journal of Jan van Riebeeck, 26
Julie, Windfogel, 84

Kacholhoffr, 105
Kaffir, term used by Gandhi, 144
Kat River Loyal Burgher Association, 51
Kat River Settlement, 44, 46, 49-51
Kei River, 70, 77, 78
Keiskamma, 50
Kekana, 132, 133, 136-141
Khangela, 120
Khosilintse, 132, 133
Kitchin, H., 157
Kitchingman, J., 40
Kok, 63
Kotze, C.F., 54
Kretzen, J., 53
Kruger, Paul, 131, 141
Kwamatiwane, 100-103
KwaZulu, 102

Landman, C.P., 98
Langa (Bamapela), 130-133
Legislation: and social malpractices, 12
Leibbrandt, H.C.V., 26
Leipoldt, C.F.L., 21
Lewin, Julius, 66
Liebenberg, B.J., 90, 95, 102
Limoen, 103
Lindley, Daniel, 105, 121
Little Big Horn, 13
Livingstone, David, 10, 11, 19-21

London Missionary Society, 38, 48, 50,
    72, 92
Lucas, C.P., 129

MacCrone, I.D., 21
Mackeurtan, G., 89
Macmillan, W.M., 9, 11, 12-14, 38, 39, 42,
    54, 64-67, 69, 73
Madras, 146
Madrasis, 146
Magaliesberg, 133, 134
Mahalakwena, 133, 134, 136
Majeke, Nosipho (Dora Taylor), 12, 38
Makapan Cave (Makapansgat), 129,
    136-142
Makapan Cave Massacre, 9, 16, 17
Malan, F.S., 57
Manger, M., 92
Mankopane (Mangkopane, Mangopane,
    Mapela, Makapan, Makapaan), 129-
    134, 141-143
Manondo, 90, 95
Mapita, ka Soyiyisa, 97
Maqoma, mentioned by Philip, 54, 70
Maraba, 141
Marais, J.S., 9, 38
Maritz, Gert, 105, 119
Marks, Shula, 11, 13
Marquand, L., 66
Masipula, Dingane's head servant, 97
Massacres: of My Lai, Oradour-sur-
    Glane, Wounded Knee, and Maka-
    pan's Cave, 16, 17, 129-142
Masters and servants Ordinance (of 1841),
    42
Mauritius, 146
Melmoth, 88
Memons, 150
The memoirs of Paul Kruger, 133
Menzies, Judge William, 42, 49
Merriman, J.X., 66
Mfengu, 45, 46, 74-76
Michener, James A., 37, 88
Middle Ages European beliefs, 53
Migrant workers, 45, 46
Millin, Sarah Gertrude, 17
Moerdyk, G.L.P., 104
Moffat, Robert, 132
Moguls, 160
Mokopane (Setswamadi, Setsumadi),

132-136, 140, 141
Molema, S.M., 14
Moodie, Donald, 20, 21, 26
Mooimeisjiesfontein, 112
Moordrif, see Mahalakwena
Moordplaas, 88
Morley-Minto Reforms, 160
Morris, D.R., 89
Mosheshwe, 14, 63
Mpande, 97, 126
Mphrane, 117
Mtini (Hintsa's principal councillor), 76, 77
Muller, C.F.J., 89
Muslims (Mohomedans), 146, 149
Mzilikazi (Moselekatse), 14, 125, 127, 132, 135
Mzimvubu (Umzimvubu, Umsimvubu, Omsoboebo) River, 90, 91, 116, 123, 124

Napier, Sir George, 49
Natal, 56, 57, 59, 88, 102-104, 106, 107, 116, 117, 134, 143-150, 153, 154
Natal Indian Congress, 147, 153
Natal Law No. 11 (of 1856), 56
The Natal Mercury, 157
Nationalism, 160, 162
National struggle, 162
The National Convention, 57
Native Question, 57
Ndebele, 117, 124, 134
Ndhlele (Umthlella), 96, 97, 126
Netherlands, 30, 34, 36
Newcastle, 155
Newton-King, Susan, 12, 38, 52
Nicholls, Heathen, and the idea of segregation, 59
Nguabara River, 79, 80
Nguni: chief, 119, 123
Noena: treaty witness, 90, 96, 97
Nongoma, 88
Norris-Newman, C.L., 141, 142
Nyl River, 133
Nzobo (Dambuza), 96, 97, 126

Okaye, F.C.N., 89
Olifantsrivier, 135
Oosthuijse, M., 90, 95
Oradour-sur-Glane, 16, 17

Orange Free State, 56, 57, 67, 69
Orange River Colony, 144
Ordinance 49 (of 1828), 44, 47
Ordinance 50 (of 1828), 12, 37-42, 45, 47, 52
Ordinance 2 (of 1827), 40
Ordinance 3 (of 1848), 46
Orphan law (of 1819), 37, 38
Owen, Francis, 89, 90, 91, 94, 110, 115, 120, 122, 127, 129

Panjabis, 146
Parker, Ward E.D., 97, 98
Parsis, 146, 147
Passive Resistance Campaign, 147, 150, 151
Pecaltsdorp, 41
Peddie, 45
Pedi, 132
Peires, J., 14
Peninsulars: the Goringhaicona, the Goringhaiqua and Gorachouqua Khoi tribes, 22
Phato (Chief), 70
Philip, John (1775-1851), 12, 13, 39, 40, 42, 45, 47, 48, 51, 53-55, 60-69, 87
Philip's Papers, 64, 66
Phillips, Lionel, 58, 59
Pietermaritzburg, 89, 109
Polak, H.S.L., 157
Political differentiation, and segregation, 60
Port Elizabeth, 46
Potgieter, E.F., 91, 92, 94, 108, 109
Potgieter, Evert T., 98
Potgieter, Hermanus, 129-134, 136, 142
Potgieter, P.G., 130, 135
Potgietersrus, 133, 134
Pottinger, Henry, 48
Precis of the Archives of the Cape of Good Hope, 26
Preller, G.S. (1875-1943), 11, 89, 92-97, 102, 105-107, 109, 111, 112
Pretorius, Andries, W.J., 98, 99
Pretorius, Hercules, 98
Pretorius, J.G., 14, 55
Pretorius, M.W., 130, 134, 138, 140, 141
Pretorius, William Jurgens, 100, 101
Province of Queen Adelaide, 77
Pruissen, 134

Quathlamba Mountains, 121
Queen Victoria, 156, 157

Race, 143, 162
Ramaglabootla, 133
Rand Daily Mail, 106
Ransford, O., 89
The Record, 20, 26
Read, James Jr., 51
Read, John, 12
Researches in South Africa, 12
Retief-Dingaan ooreenkoms, 93
Retief-Dingane treaty, 15, 88, 90-92, 95,
    105, 108, 109, 111, 113
Retief's leather bag, 89, 99 101-104, 111
Retief, Piet (1780-1838), 9, 15, 16, 88-91,
    98-100, 102-107, 110-119, 122, 124-
    128
Rhodes, Cecil John, 59, 147
Rharhabe (ama), 70, 74, 78
Riebeeck East, 112
The rise of South Africa, 113
Robben Island, 34, 77
Robertson, H.M., 21
The role of the missionaries in conquest,
    12

Saldaniers (Saldanhaman), 27, 28
San children, 37, 38
Sarhili (Kreili), 74, 76, 77, 86
Satyagraha, 161
Satyagraha in South Africa, 154
Sauer, J.W., and the franchise question, 57
Scheepers, F.C., 69
Schmidt, A., 102
Schoeman, S., 138
Schoemansdal, 133, 136
Schools, 47, 48
Schreiner, W.P., and Gandhi's plea, 158,
    159
Schutte, G.E.G., on Philip, 54
Seditious Meeting Act, 160
Sekonyela (SinKoyella), 90, 106, 115,
    118-120, 124
Separation, and segregation, 64-66
Seventeen (the Council of), 23, 24, 29-36
Seventh Frontier War, 50
Shaka, 123
Shaw, William, 81, 82
Sheep, 23, 25, 26, 29, 32, 34, 36

Shepstone, Theophilus, 59, 85
Shooter, J., 89
Slagtersnek, 10
Smartt, T.W., 57
Smit, Erasmus, 100, 106, 107, 118
Smit, Mrs Erasmus, 104
Smith, Sir Harry, 15, 48, 70, 71, 74-82, 86,
    87
Smuts, General Jan, 17, 53, 57-59, 68, 69,
    151, 159
Somerset, Colonel, 79
Sooilaer, 99
*The South African Commercial Adver-
    tiser*, 71, 72
Spionkop, 148
Southey, George, 72, 73, 79, 81, 82, 84, 85
Southey, S., 49
Soutpansberg, 133
Soutter, J. Lyall, 92, 105, 106
Spilhaus, Margaret, 21
Stanford (Colonel), 57
The Star, 105
Stuart, James, 59
Suid-Holland, 134
Surti, 150
Swadeshi movement, 160
Swellendam, 53

Tamils, 146, 151, 154
Theal, G.M., 11, 21, 38, 52, 54, 71, 89, 94,
    102, 129-132, 134, 139
Theopolis, 45, 46
Thompson, Leonard, 9, 10, 89, 131
Thomson, W.R., 51
Thunkela (Tugela, Tugala, Doogela), 90,
    116, 123
Tilak, 160
Transvaal, 56, 57, 59, 69, 104
Treaty states, 63
Tregardt, Louis, 134
Tyhali, 70

Uitenhage, 46
Uithaalder, 51
Umhlatusi, 124
Umgungundhlovu (Umkongloof, Um-
    kunginsloave, Unkunkinglove), 89,
    90, 91, 103, 114, 119, 123-125
Union Buildings State Archives, 105
University of Stellenbosch, 93, 112

204

Uys, C.J., 73
Uys, Dick, 97, 107

Vaalkranz, 148
Van der Kemp, Dr J.T., 12, 53
Van Goens, Rijklof, 31-34
Van Riebeeck, Jan, 10, 11, 19-29, 31-33, 35, 36
Van Riebeeck principle, 19-22, 26, 27, 29-34
Van Staden, H.J., 133
Venter, M.A., 134
Verulam, 155
Verwoerd, H.F., 54
Victoria District, 50
Victoria East, 45
Vier-en-Twintig Riviere, 134
VOC (Vereenigde Oostindische Compagnie - Dutch East India Company), 22, 24, 25
Voigt, J.C., 102
Die Volkstem, 102
Voortrekker Monument Museum, 88, 104

Walker, E.A., 9, 14, 55, 71, 73, 89, 103, 121, 132, 142
Walton, E.H., 57
Waterberg, 129
Waterboer, 63
Watermeyer, E.E., 21
Wayne, John, 10
Weinthal, Leo, 104, 112, 113
Wesleyan: missionary, 70, 117
West, A., 157
Williams, Jane, 95
Willow Grange, 121
Witwatersrand, University of, 64
Wood, W.S., 93
Wylde, Sir John, 49
Wyllie, Curzon, 160

Xhosa, 13, 45, 46, 49, 51, 62, 63, 70, 80

Zoutpansberg, 129
Zulu (Zulus, Zoolas), 90, 95, 100, 101, 102, 113, 115, 117, 119, 121-123, 125-128, 144, 145, 148
Zululand, 101, 115, 124

Sarah Gertrude Millin

GOD'S STEPCHILDREN

First published in 1924, *God's Stepchildren* is no less relevant today. Miscegenation had long been a preoccupation of Sarah Gertrude Millin, and in this novel, the poignant story of segregation and people of mixed heritage, it is the dominant theme. The book begins in 1821 when Andrew Flood becomes a missionary in a remote section of the Cape Colony and, after failing to establish any spiritual contact with his Hottentot charges, marries one of them as a gesture of brotherhood. The marriage is a failure in all respects, and Sarah Gertrude Millin traces the lives of the next four generations, concentrating on one person in each, and emphasising their problems. These people question 'But is God himself not white?' and come to the final conclusion, 'Perhaps we brown people are his stepchildren.'

320 pages, a paperbook

Olive Schreiner

THE STORY OF AN AFRICAN FARM

The Story of an African Farm was first published in 1883, under the pseudonym Ralph Iron. Only later did it transpire that the author was actually a woman — Olive Schreiner. When the book first appeared it was received with mixed feelings by its Victorian readers, some of whom were shocked by the 'morality' of the author, and felt that it would have been better if the book had never been published. Schreiner's perseverance paid off, and today the novel, set on a farm in the Karoo, is considered important for South African literature, as the beginning of a national literary tradition. This new paperbook edition is introduced by Cherry Clayton.

281 pages, a paperbook